THE FAERIE QUEENE
A Companion for Readers

THE FAERIE QUEENE

A Companion for
Readers

ROSEMARY FREEMAN

UNIVERSITY OF CALIFORNIA PRESS

BERKELEY AND LOS ANGELES · 1970

UNIVERSITY OF CALIFORNIA PRESS
Berkeley and Los Angeles, California

ISBN 0 520 01732 3

Library of Congress Catalog Card Number: 70 116114

Printed in Great Britain

FOR GUY

FOR GUY

CONTENTS

FOREWORD

THIS book is divided into two parts. The first deals with three general topics, the second discusses each section Book by Book. Repetitions between the two parts have proved inevitable. The only defence I can offer is from respect to my author. 'Surely,' we say in the process of reading, 'he has said this before.' He has, but as a prodigiously imaginative writer he has made something different out of it. No comparison between critic and author is suggested, but some analogy in method ultimately arises. In pursuing the points which come up in each chapter I am horribly conscious that I too have said this before. This is probably a testament to the Spenserian manner. What mattered to him mattered profoundly enough to drive him to discover yet another way of expressing it, a way that was no doubt intellectually the same but imaginatively different. This is the reason for one's instinctive desire to select an example which is identical with the one cited in a previous and fuller context, for instance, in Scudamour's view of the blacksmith's forge or in the ferryman's skill at rowing to the Bower of Bliss. Each is important to a mind questing into *The Faerie Queene* for the genius of its creator, each had to be measured in a dissimilar critical setting. No other illustration carries quite the same weight for a reader in the process of exploring Spenser's habit of mind. Process is the word that has to be emphasised, for exploration is always what Spenser's enigmatic outlook requires. The impression is never the same each time, but neither will it be contradictory. Hence the importance of recognising the value of process in the establishment of conclusions. This may be an indication of the failure of sound critical reading, but it may equally well be an evidence of the demands made by the text of *The Faerie Queene*.

I realised the necessity of qualifying each point I was making as I read the words I had written. Changes and reservations sprang up, but they would have made the book out of keeping with the subject I was tackling. 'Read the poem again,' one thinks. 'And again.' Remembering the opinion that it is a difficult work and that it becomes more difficult as the number of Books multiply I can only say in defence 'Read it again'. This book may be repetitive, but so was my author. It may change in style, but so does its subject. And so to write on *The Faerie Queene* one has to be free to follow the mysterious lead it gives one and to say 'I have been faithful to thee, Cynara! in my fashion'.

To search for a design that will prove satisfactory is to lose the essential character of the poem as it exists. One important element lies in the Allegory, yet it seems better to evade its tyranny. Spenser was doing very well without it; his art was filled in the beauty and delight he found to give it. He wrote excellently when the didactic Palmer and the learned Natalis Comes and Caesar Ripa were out of the scheme. Can we not act rightly apart from that haunting undesired presence of the dark conceit which Spenser insisted had rights of access? It has pushed itself in and has transformed its readers into partisans of 'the allegory'. And there it is, inescapable and 'significant'.

I have had to devote a chapter to it and I have attempted to include another on the general art which brings its own authenticity, and a third upon the narrative and structure. The purpose in these three preliminary sections has been to elucidate the necessity of thinking of the poem as a whole: we can better estimate the significance of Orgoglio if we connect him with other giants, the cave of Mammon gains by all the links with hell that are made in other parts.

The next stage was to investigate the poem Book by Book. This method reveals the great differences in theme, structure and total impression. Very few single episodes can be wrenched from one Book and be put into another, not so much because they are logically or causally essential to its argument (though this may probably be so of Book I), but because their tone and interest fits them into one particular Book. Each Book has been explored separately under titles which appeared appropriate to its substance and individuality. If the consequence of this is to produce what Ruskin describes as the disastrous activities of system-makers, I can only maintain that the first system of the allegory-supporters would have been just as disastrous.

> Much time is wasted by human beings, in general, on establishment of systems; and it often takes more labour to master the intricacies of an artificial connection, than to remember the separate facts which are so carefully connected. I suspect that system-makers, in general, are not of much more use, each in his own domain, than, in that of Pomona, the old women who tie cherries upon sticks, for the more convenient portableness of the same. To cultivate well, and choose well, your cherries, is of some importance; but if they can be had in their own wild way of clustering about their crabbed stalk, it is a better connection for them than any other; and, if they cannot, then, so that they be not bruised, it makes to a boy of a practical disposition not much difference whether he gets them by handfuls, or in beaded symmetry on the exalting stick.
>
> *Modern Painters* Part IV. i.

So we gladly end just as we began, with a handful collected from the rich tree of that great poem.

I began this study with an award from Girton College of the Ottilie Hancock Research Fellowship, and it is appropriate that the work should be concluded in the College's Centenary Year. In her book on Girton, Professor Muriel Bradbrook, its Mistress, advises us that we should 'never trust the image, trust the live encounter'. As one who has experienced the live encounter, I can gladly endorse the truth and wisdom of this advice.

A list of friends from whom generous assistance came during the writing of this study would be tedious to those recorded. I shall therefore name only Robin Hammond and Rosemary Beresford; and Eleanor Robertson, the ex-Registrar of Birkbeck College, who patiently endured a continually changing manuscript and transformed it into a legible typescript.

The text upon which the quotations are based is the *Oxford English Texts* edition, edited by J. C. Smith (2 vols., Clarendon Press, 1909).

R. F.

PART ONE

PART ONE

Chapter I

THE SEARCH FOR A STARTING POINT

'I am reading the Fairy Queen—with delight . . . I can't think out
what I mean about conception: the idea behind F.Q. How to express
a kind of natural transition from state to state. And the air of natural
beauty.'

Virginia Woolf. *Diary*, p. 238

VIRGINIA WOOLF was not the only reader who wished to
explain the effect of *The Faerie Queene* upon the mind. Lamb,
too, had met the same difficulty on reading the account of the
cave of Mammon:

'the transitions in this episode are every whit as violent as in the
most extravagant dream, and yet our waking judgment ratifies
them.'

This effect was for him the evidence of the sanity of true genius.
For each here sensed the impact of great imaginative poetry, an
impact which did not lie simply in the melody of rhythm nor in
the beauty of imagery but seemed to be lurking in the substance
of the poem itself, particularly in the mysteriousness of its
transitions.

Is it possible to track this 'conception', this 'idea', this
dream-like quality to its foundation? Spenser, we are told, was
'of all poets the most poetical', yet this phrase takes us little
further: it suggests a category too vague to define the nature of
his appeal although it appears to point in the right direction.
The Faerie Queene undoubtedly possesses an outstanding 'poetical'
quality, and it is not necessarily to literary critics we need to
turn for an account of the impression created by poetry upon
readers who were naturally unlikely to respond to it. John
Stuart Mill, for example, a philosopher little acquainted with
its power until he read Wordsworth, pointed out to his friend
Roebuck what poetry could offer to unpoetical natures. He was
convinced that 'the imaginative emotion which an idea, when
vividly conceived, excites in us, is not an illusion but a fact, as

15

real as any of the other qualities of objects: and far from imply-
ing anything erroneous and delusive in our mental apprehension
of the object, is quite consistent with the most accurate knowledge and most perfect practical recognition of all its physical
and intellectual laws and relations'. Scientific knowledge was
not a contradiction to the knowledge given by poetry, and he
goes on to develop his point by arguing that 'the intensest feeling
of the beauty of a cloud lighted by the setting sun, is no
hindrance to my knowing that the cloud is a vapour of water,
subject to all the laws of vapours in a state of suspension; and I
am just as likely to allow for, and act on, these physical laws
whenever there is occasion to do so, as if I had been incapable of
perceiving any distinction between beauty and ugliness'.[1] In all
this Mill was edging towards the belief that poetry is just as
much a strenuous labour of knowledge as is the acquisition of
physical science. The two do not get into each other's way but
are complementary, both relying upon a conviction of the
validity of human reason. He sees that reality could be discovered as much in poetic thought as in scientific. The word
'illusion' was applicable to neither. It was false and misleading
to draw such a distinction as Roebuck had drawn between the
two ways of interpreting the world; and Mill, though never a
poet, set up a standard of literary judgment which has remained
acceptable for many critics to whom poetry is a wholly convincing kind of learning.[2]

To return to *The Faerie Queene*, it must be agreed that there
are few poets in later generations who do not owe their sense
of rhythmical beauty to what they first heard from Spenser. On
the other hand it would be a mistake if we regarded 'illusion',
so apparently pre-eminent in that poem, as the principal character of his poetry. Its dangerous enticement, closely entwined
with his poetic art, is never carried to any degree of falsehood.
Only a thorough exploration of the material of *The Faerie
Queene* will enable us to see how well Spenser was aware of the
appearance of illusion his narrative was creating and how skil-

[1] John Stuart Mill, *Autobiography*, 1873, pp. 151-2.
[2] See D. G. James in *The Dream of Learning* in which a place is made for
the right of the poetic imagination to be recognised as a part of the life of
reason, and its discoveries to be as much a contribution to knowledge as
those of the scientist.

fully he outweighed its deception. The topic of Book I is focussed upon the nature of illusion, and each of the subsequent Books examines the difference between the apparent and the real nature of the Virtue they are treating. Good and evil are, in effect, concealed within the varying shades of beauty and ugliness, and the progress of the narrative makes plain enough in the techniques of the allegory where Spenser's moral sympathy lies.

Part of the appeal of *The Faerie Queene* seems to have depended upon recognition of moral sympathy. We may remember Charles I reading it in captivity at Carisbrooke, Pitt, whose sister Ann said (absurdly) that '*The Faerie Queene* was the only thing he knew thoroughly', and Gibbon composing *The Decline and Fall* with a copy of Spenser open upon his desk. All were men occupied with the problems of statesmanship and the ordering of public affairs. Spenser might perhaps be called for them an escape, but that is a superficial version of his attraction. Mill gives a better reason in ascribing an inward joy to a poet's work, and Lamb does so, too, in attributing the exaltation of rapturous poetry to what must be ratified by man's waking judgment.

The truth is even wider. 'There is something in the work of Spenser that pleases one as strongly as in one's old age it did in one's youth,' Pope told Spence with his customary acumen. Spenser's resilience, his power of survival in the face of all changes of human circumstance, is conspicuous. The appeal poets make to the young is not necessarily of the kind to last always. Yet Spenser's apparently was. Recollections of childhood experiences often revive among those who read *The Faerie Queene* later in life. Admittedly many were poets themselves, and for them what Mill called 'the idea vividly conceived' proved an exciting experience. Cowley became absorbed in it as he read in his mother's parlour, Pope himself met it at the age of 12, and Scott found the adventurousness, the surprises, the compulsion to read on that boys look for, all that he then needed in it. 'Spenser I could have read for ever,' he said. As poets to be, they naturally enjoyed like Cowley the 'Chimes of Verse . . . the tinckling of the Rhyme and the Dance of the Numbers', but also the society of knights and ladies, giants and dragons, which swept them up. Later they

could return, grown-up, suffering men of the world, to that
absorbing book in which, regardless of their doom, they had
once been absorbed. It was not quite the same book, but it still
had a quality which fortified rather than denied the earlier
impression and gave it depth in the eyes of the experienced.

What that quality was can scarcely be expressed in a few
sentences. It might be described as a power of the poet, an
exhaustless faculty of invention and formulation, so that time
and again a new magical phrase springs out, or a new character
or episode. Or it may be another image or picture. It was this
which the old lady to whom Pope read parts of *The Faerie
Queene* noticed. He had, she said, shewn her a gallery of pictures.
There was an enchantment which evoked a response on the
simplest as well as on the more complex levels, a magic which
could fascinate the old and the young.

Fascination depends not only on the action, or the character,
or the gallery of pictures, nor even upon the magic phrase, but
a combination of all together. Spenser can achieve subtlety of
movement, firmness of effect, repetition which is deliberate but
never dull, surprise which brings delight without inconsistency.
In him, beauty and art join as distinctive qualities. The fineness
of his perceptions, the sudden, extraordinary impact of a
moment of human feeling, the inescapable insistence of
imaginative realisation create the quality which is peculiarly
Spenserian. Its prime source lies within the specially invented
stanza form which gives the poem its framework within which
Spenser could build every changing kind of effect. The technique of verse structure requires critical appraisal and it is to
Coleridge that it is right to turn for its expression.

. . . the Stanza of Spenser (that wonder-work of metrical Skill and
Genius! that nearest approach to a perfect Whole, as bringing the
greatest possible variety into compleat Unity by never interrupted
inter-dependence of the parts! — that 'immortal Verse', that
'winding bout
    of linked sweetness long drawn out
    Untwisting all the chains that tie
    The hidden soul of Harmony').[1]

[1] Coleridge, 'The Improvement in taste since Johnson's Day'. MS
quoted in *Inquiring Spirit*, edited by Kathleen Coburn, 1951, p. 158.

Coleridge heard the sound of the verse but it was to another
equally melodious poet, profound in his knowledge of music, he
went for words to define it—John Milton. For Coleridge the
subtlety of the stanza form reflected its variety of thought and
feeling. The variety possessed a unified element, interdepend-
ence of the parts. The stanza is held together by the alexandrine
and the rhyme at the unexpectedly important fifth line.
Coleridge does not mention the fifth line but that surely is an
essential factor. Through it the stanza slides along undivided to
its concluding alexandrine. Here, for instance, is an occasion
where an inconspicuous division achieved by a simile preserves
the composition of a unit: it is the familiar description of Morpheus:

> And more, to lulle him in his slumber soft,
> A trickling streame from high rocke tumbling downe
> And ever-drizling raine upon the loft,
> Mixt with a murmuring winde, much like the sowne
> Of swarming Bees, did cast him in a swowne:
> No other noyse, nor peoples troublous cryes,
> As still are wont t'annoy the walled towne,
> Might there be heard: but careless Quiet lyes,
> Wrapt in eternall silence farre from enemyes.

> I. i. 41

The long slow-moving words, the participles which create a
cadence through each of the first five lines, the absence of any
syntactical breaks, collectively build up the stanza by metrical
skill. This example is not unique, but it illustrates Spenser's
power to draw upon diction and rhythmical movement to
devise a particular effect. Stanzas where the tempo is precisely the opposite still rely upon the art of the alexandrine and
the fifth line. Britomart here faces the flames outside Busyrane's
House:

> Therewith resolv'd to prove her utmost might,
> Her ample shield she threw before her face,
> And her swords point directing forward right,
> Assayld the flame, the which eftsoones gave place,
> And did itselfe divide with equall space,
> That through she passed; as a thunder bolt
> Perceth the yielding ayre, and doth displace

The soring clouds into sad showres ymolt;
So to her yold the flames, and did their force revolt.

III. xi. 25

Spenser is describing an important episode in the redemption of
Amoret. The vocabulary is straightforward but elaborated by a
simile to define the nature of the flames, and Britomart's movement through them is expressed in short rapid verbs. There is
no lingering, and the purpose is to emphasise by repetition the
flames through which the heroine successfully passed. Coleridge
points out Spenser's choice of a form which suits him exactly.
One would expect such perceptiveness from a poet of Coleridge's literary range but other readers were equally quick in
identifying the special genius of the style of *The Faerie Queene*.
The framework of the whole poem depends upon the art with
which the stanza form is used, because all the narratives,
characterisation, descriptions and incantations are contained by
it. The first person who observed the importance of the alexandrine was the maligned Gabriel Harvey. In Gascoigne's
Certain Notes of Instruction, Harvey having read it carefully and
taken in the order that you should 'keep the verse form with
which you begun', made a critical manuscript note 'the difference of the last verse from the rest in everie Stanza, a grace in the
Faerie Queen'. A grace, and indeed an art it was, for the structure of the verse not only holds a single stanza together but also
holds several sections in a block, directing them towards a unity
of not only one but of many stanzas; ultimately of a whole Book,
and finally of the poem itself.

Other poets have turned the nine-line verse Spenser invented
to their own purposes. Thomson in *The Castle of Indolence* and
Byron in *Childe Harold* have demonstrated what can be done
with it without trying to come near the first example. Which is
as it should be. Readers of *The Faerie Queene* discover no serious
competition from them but can merely see what other types of
richness exist in the form. Both poems are admirable in their
own way, but they do not pretend to offer the enchantment of
that original version which first enthralled us. So we return to
the attraction that lies within it and begin to investigate the
other qualities which are so distinctive there.

Beyond the allurement of the stanza form there stands out

constantly Spenser's visual imagination, the appeal to the eye
as well as to the ear. Through the whole composition there is
the continual recrudescence of elements of sight. Pictorial
representation often makes a strong impression; consequently
there is recalled the very minute when the Red Crosse Knight,
Una and the Dwarf enter into our vision. A whole population of
personified characters, indoor and external, sail into our perception, mythological, abstract, and even surprisingly human
figures, creatures belonging to the earth, the sea, underground.
These portrayals are what Spenser's contemporaries must
always have recognised as at once literal and fictional, for however much credit they attached to the allegory, these were always
visible. Milton, recalling the Bower of Bliss insists that Spenser
has described it so that Guyon might *see* and know and yet
abstain; and he was to remember eventually the struggle
between the Red Crosse Knight and the Dragon when he described Satan making his journey to earth 'half-flying and
half-footing in his haste', just as the Dragon in Book I had
lumbered itself towards its enemy. Spenser was always possessed
of a very strong visual faculty and he draws upon it to record
the external scenes which constitute the substance of his poem.

Naturally, it is necessary to delve into physical elements
which underlie the visual apprehensions. There is evidently an
intensification of Spenser's emotions on certain topics, a
heightening in emotion with regard particularly to the sea.
It was, after all, the great divider between Ireland and his own
English past so that strong feelings are always present when it
enters into *The Faerie Queene*. In Guyon's voyage, the vigour,
the urgency, the vitality of detail and the enrichment of the
vocabulary, emphasise the significance of much that is felt.
Marinell's *Rich Strond* bears out this experience in containing
'the spoyle of all the world'; Cymoent's journey over the ocean
becalmed by the care of Neptune and her grief created by the
sound of the beautiful classical names of the water-nymphs in
her train; Florimell, imprisoned in the depths of Proteus's
dwelling lamenting 'know Marinell that all this is for thee', all
embody the eloquence of the sea in Spenser's outlook. Even in
minor sections such as those in Book V where Artegall is seen
arguing the law of property on the cliff's edge with a giant or

applying clear principles of Justice to the problem of two brothers' right to an island, the sea possesses an important function even though its emotional force is deliberately ignored. It remains an element in the external world which promoted Spenser's imaginative activity just as did the forests in Books I and VI.

In *The Faerie Queene* there are other kinds of visual experience which Spenser's fineness of response takes into account. Light occupied a particularly high place in his consciousness. Light against shadow, against darkness, in movement over the water, imaged in the human face was noticed by him. Observed by his own natural instinct, each was recognised as a means of artistic adornment. His awareness of their existence was often very subtle. Starlight to him was brighter when it was reflected in the water than when it was seen in the sky, cloud only half concealed the light of the moon and so the impression created by cloud and moon produced its own peculiar result:

> Vew of cheerful day
> Did never in that house it selfe display,
> But a faint shadow of uncertain light;
> Such as a lamp, whose life does fade away:
> Or as the Moone cloathed with clowdy night
> Does shewe to him, that wakes in feare and sad affright.
>
> II. vii. 29

Similarly the moon on a foggy winter's night:

> Doth seeme to be herselfe, though darkned be her light.

Starlight is equally obscure in spasms of mist, and the sun in clouds created a mysterious illumination when its rays were held back until at last it made itself seen in 'azure streams'. Light in motion was always evident on armour when shields flashed against each other; just as it often is, when air and atmosphere are related to character by imagery or by straightforward presentation. Pastorella, for instance, imprisoned in darkness by the brigands, gave signs of survival by permitting her eyes to shine through the twinkling of her eyelids.

Spenser's originality was not of course confined to this particular interest and many other elements became a pretext for imaginative realisation. His poetry is allegedly memorable for its sense of colour, although this is comparatively simple and

conventional. It is largely confined to bright colours, suitable
for heraldic, enamelled objects, in shields and chivalric
pageants. Occasionally colours are decorative in their own

tles fringd with silver
eneral they are rarely
fore. What gives them
ey embody: Malecasta
ped in a cloak of scarlet
rasting with 'the blacke
sonified illustration of
essed in a quilted jacket
pitchy night', while the
, or upon green grass,
ss victims share similar
rily out of the symboli-
xts, but they are not of
ch. To it Spenser was
had no direct training
that one needs to go for
erist painting; his inter-
nce of art which he had
ith Languet. In *Arcadia*
d in the description of
l of the heroines' faces
ournaments,
is his sense of texture in
Accuracy of detail de-
material to its wearer:
am as a typical forester,
with silver lace, abstract
mer unlined silk, and
a robe made not of silk
mblem of his flightiness.

Texture is even more fully exploited in the strangely ornate suit
of armour in which Radigund decks herself for her combat with
Artegall. It is cut high enough for her to move as an Amazon.

> All in a Camis light of purple silke
> Woven uppon with silver, subtly wrought,

> And quilted uppon sattin white as milke,
> Trayled with ribbands diversly distraught . . .
>
> V. v. 2

Yet the truly original descriptions are attached to figures which are set beyond the physical world entirely. Thus the enchantment of the Medway belongs to the remote bridal procession of rivers and water-nymphs. Mercilla is both the personification of the idea of royalty and a literal embodiment of Queen Elizabeth. The importance of her role is signified in the cloth of state under which she is seated. Spenser here adopts his characteristic technique of description by rejection. The material made neither of rich tissue nor of cloth of gold, but possessing both, was like a cloud.

> That her brode spreading wings did wyde unfold.

Its splendour is enlarged by the presence of angels who creep through the brightness of the throne and bring with them reminiscences of divine hymnody. Beauty, hierarchy, and heavenly music combine in this majestic portrait. Indeed, Queen Elizabeth had the poet she deserved, the poet who could recognise her greatness and was also capable of giving humanity to the woman who could speak to the sailors before the Armada in words they understood. Spenser was a writer who could raise his poetry to the level of grandeur and at the same time keep it on the ground of simplicity.

Visual faculties and the command of a subtle stanza form are not the only constituents of Spenser's imaginative genius. There is everywhere his sense of language. Its range can best be formulated when it is set beside the mistaken attempt of Ralph Knevett to continue the unfinished poem along the same lines. What is wrong here exposes what is always right in Spenser. Knevett had nothing new to bring: the three additional Virtues, Albanio for Prudence, Callimachus for Fortitude, Belcoeur for Liberality offer adventures which are mere extensions of those which had previously occurred in Books I to VI.[1] Some are

---

[1] 'A supplement to Spenser's Fairy Queene', Cambridge University Library. MS Ee 3.53. The author has been identified by C. Bowie Millican, *Review of English Studies* XIV, 1938, pp. 44-52, as Ralph Knevett of Norfolk who is known to be connected with the Paston family. v. C. B. Millican, *Spenser and the Table Round*, preface to edition of 1967.

brought into contact with figures in earlier narratives, una-
shamed plagiarism occurs with the entry of Feare, afraid of his
own shadow, and Despair, complete with halter and rusty
knife. Worse still is Knevett's effort at image making. The
'dragon huge'

> whose sparkling eyes
> Like comets blazed . . .
> Came bustling from his denne with hideous cryes.

His gift for the unsuitable word is startling. The 'elder Tityrus'
is introduced:

> Who shall the warbling Swannes of Po constraine
> To listen to his various melodyes.

'Warble' is scarcely the *mot juste* for the note of a swan. Knevett's
desire to be Spenserian teaches the negative lesson of failure; the
total loss of the freedom and unique style of his model.

Spenser's style finds its expression in *The Faerie Queene* in
generous expansiveness. First there are marvellous seminal
phrases that constitute the character of its idiom. These are not
confined simply to the style that is by definition 'poetic', the
beautiful, decorative, and freely adorned. Every page offers
some phrases that are memorable, immediately quotable; words
which arouse an aesthetic response and create an instant
desire to hear a repetition. When Phaedria's boat ferries Guyon
to her island the movement is so easily defined and the image so
lovely in its identification with the movement that it cannot be
forgotten and we continue to read the whole stanza to complete
the delight first enjoyed.

> Eftsoones her shallow ship away did slide,
> More swift, then swallow sheres the liquid skie,

And thus we go on to follow the swallow-like glide and see how
it proceeds:

> Withouten oare or Pilot it to guide,
> Or winged canvas with the wind to flie,
> Only she turn'd a pin, and by and by
> It cut away upon the yielding wave,
> Ne cared she her course for to apply:
> For it was taught the way, which she would have,
> And both from rocks and flats it selfe could wisely save.

> II. vi. 5

The journey is light, unhampered by obstacles, and the rhythm, vocabulary, and sound effects extend in words and epithets. This is indeed a voyage that is swift, carefree, the embodiment of idleness and pleasure.

For many, this is the characteristic Spenser, the writer nearest to the romantic conception of his craft, the man whom Wordsworth thought of as

> Sweet Spenser moving through the clouded heaven
> With the moon's beauty and the moon's soft pace.

And there is no doubt that a first glimpse of a Canto in *The Faerie Queene* will be attended by illustrations which support this interpretation. Yet other passages will produce effects that are surprisingly different. At certain rare moments, the tenor of scene stands out as that of direct realism. The Irish girl's walk with her jug seen by Una, or the blacksmith's cottage with its squalid pool where Scudamour spent the night, are examples of other kinds of poetry:

> Under a steepe hilles side it placed was
> There where the mouldred earth had cave'd the banke;
> And fast beside the little brooke did pas
> Of muddie waters, that like puddle stanke,
> By which few crooked sallows grew in rank.
>
> IV. v. 33

Such an example adds a further conception of Spenserian imaginative power for it is penetratingly factual in another fashion than that of descriptive realism. It provides a literal setting but concentrates upon mental experience: with it enters the device of allegory since Scudamour's sleepless despair is surveyed in terms of the activity of the smithy. (The blacksmith was named Care and his bellows were sighs moved by Pensifeness.) Spenser's imagination includes an ability to draw his characters' state of mind and to bring, unexpectedly, vitality to his representation of personality.

These are only some aspects of what Spenser's sense of language contributed to the quality of his great poem. It was to him that Johnson went in search of the source of the language of poetry and fiction, just as he went to Shakespeare for the language of common life. Yet *The Faerie Queene* builds up its art in other fields: in its substance through the variety of its figures, the range of its narratives, and finally through its philosophical thought.

The figures originate in the extraordinary extent of Spenser's grasp of the language of poetry and of fiction. They are sometimes recognisably creatures of this world but more often of other worlds, denizens of the underworld, embodiments of ideas of darkness or formlessness. They may be mythical figures deriving from classical tradition, they may be personifications, they may be giants or monsters. It is not difficult to trace their origins but the purpose to which Spenser puts them is frequently more subtle than any method of source-hunting could propose. To categorise them is less profitable than to recognise that they represent what is true of what we know, or have learnt since from psychologists about the facts of the mind. So often they amount to more than what Natalis Comes or Caesar Ripa tells us about their moral or aesthetic significance, or more than what Homer or Virgil report on the role of Proteus or Night. And the unisolatable quality in each is to a considerable extent due to the positive settings in which they occur.

All the figures live in a fairy world, and the poem relies upon the construction of a setting in which they can act. Forests, the sea, the world beneath the sea, the underearth, bring distinctive images to the context of *The Faerie Queene*. The general landscape is spacious and continuous, but also vague and unlocalised, so neutral that it suits a fairy context. It is not a background, nor a mere setting, but a medium closely combined with the life conducted by the figures who make up the plots. To borrow a phrase from sociologists, the people 'make use of their environment', or rather Spenser makes use of it for them, regarding it as a three-dimensional place for them to move about in, not simply as a flat back-cloth.

Two suggestions can be made about the connection between figure and scene. Beginning with a neutral medium, only 'the world's wide wilderness', the poem acquires a series of specific locations which create, through repetition, memories of each other. Forests are particularly significant in the first Book and in Books IV and VI. There, after the wanderings in the Wood of Error Una teaches the satyrs, from it the churl brought

squirrels and wildings to Florimell, there is the home of the
Salvage Man, there Timias retreats in his shame, and there in
Book VI the good live and are happy in an uncomplicated
fashion. But it would be misleading to maintain that the forest
represents only scenes of virtue. Satyrs may be innocent and
capable of conversion in Una's company but they are also evil
and corruptible when Hellenore comes to them. In the forest
live Lust and the cannibals. The Blatant Beast also finds protection there. Forests, in fact, give Spenser his fullest scope as a
moral and aesthetic poet and we shall find the richest and most
specific kinds of poetic effect in the scenes which are based on
them for a landscape. In the later Books the scenery is diversi-
fied by lakes and shores, which reflect the impact of Ireland
upon Spenser's mind.

Forest, lake, river and sea all share one common feature. The
landscape of *The Faerie Queene* is never a noiseless landscape. The
faculty of hearing is as noticeably and constantly appealed to as
is the faculty of sight. Indeed, silence becomes just as prominent
as darkness when one of these two faculties is abandoned. Thus
the mystery of atmosphere is felt when the Red Crosse Knight
and Duessa arrive beside the enchanted trees, and the cry of
Fradubio when a branch is torn from his trunk owes its startling
effect to the silence surrounding him. No bird sang there (as
Keats noticed) and the shepherd would not play his pipe beside
them. Even in the Wood of Error, Una and the Red Crosse
were allured by the 'birds sweet harmony' as well as by the
diversity of the trees that made it up. It is difficult to find any
occasion when sound is not emphasised, for to Spenser poetry
was so often an imitation of the music created in the world by
fountains, birds, or the human voice.

The second suggestion involves the relation between the
landscape and the figures who are part of it. What we see in the
appropriateness of the various localities to single Books and the
art Spenser uses in presenting them can also hold good for the
connection between place and character. In Book V Artegall's
principles of Justice are strict and visibly supported by the
activity of Talus. There is no complication in the ideas he sets
forth. On the other hand, the Fradubio scene with its folk-lore
associations, or the Marinell-Britomart episode with its mytho-

logical and legendary material, or the journey of Guyon and the Palmer to Acrasia's Circe-like island depend for their interpretation upon response to the poetic character of the environment within which they take place. There is no difficulty for us with Artegall and the problems he has to solve; but the tragedy of Fradubio, recounted in the presence of the woman who caused it, creates an effect of double illusion and should amount to a warning to the Knight of the danger in which he has set himself. Yet the conduct of Duessa, or Fidessa as she calls herself, towards Fradubio and his Fraelissa is never seen in relation towards himself and Una. It will be long before the knight realises the real identity of Duessa in spite of all that he has heard from Fradubio.

In the other two cases, Marinell and Britomart, and Acrasia, there is less deception. The destruction of the Bower of Bliss is demanded by the conviction that for all its beauty Acrasia's world expresses the wickedness of her life. It must be done, Spenser insists, because evil has made its mark wholly in the scene surrounding it and she cannot be seen apart from it. The wounding of Marinell is also necessary, for the *Rich Strond* upon which he lives expresses, if not wickedness, at least a limitation, a scale of values which promotes suffering in Florimell. Britomart stands for a virtue far beyond Marinell's self-contained outlook and her fight with him is governed not so much by hostility as by contrast. The *Rich Strond* is very beautiful, as also is Cymoent's lament for her son. Yet Spenser has necessarily to draw the distinction between the qualities represented by Marinell and Britomart in terms of a battle.

So far the imaginative force of *The Faerie Queene* is best seen in its language and in its scenic nature. But there are two other essential features which occupy the centre of the poem. First there are what makes the core of the epic, its narrative. Again, as with the various types of figures, it is open to all sorts of classification. In *The Faerie Queene* Spenser is introducing much material that belonged to the medieval literary past he inherited, and to Italian contemporary epic forms. Thus among all that makes up the stories, the courts of love allegories are developed at length for the purpose of underlining ideas which are truly significant; for instance, the climax of Book II and the central episode of Book IV where Scudamour describes how he obtained his Amoret are matters of profound meaning within the structure of the poem, and several minor events can be included within that group, for instance the Mirabella story in Book VI. Myths are also central for the more significant parts of Books III and IV. On a slighter level, Spenser is glad to seize occasions for recounting *fabliaux* where wittier, more realistic tales can be subjected to the day-to-day tone of certain scenes, as for example in the Squire of Dames' Chaucerian story of his search for a chaste woman. This does not jar with the framework where it occurs since the Squire has only to recount accurately things which have happened to him *as* they happened, and these carry on the level of conversation which has gone on ever since the knights met each other on their way to the tournament. It is unnecessary to enlarge on Spenser's debt to Chaucer, but it is notable that the two Books of *The Faerie Queene* where the connection is most evident are III and IV, those in which the narrative is focussed upon Love. Differences of source and tone do not prevent even a minor joking anecdote by the Squire of Dames from being consistent with the two Books. In fact, it helps to give a rounded concept of the idea with which Spenser is so deeply concerned.

Narrative in *The Faerie Queene* cannot be treated as a single aspect of Spenser's pursuit of his design. Each story is inevitably a reflection of experience within the mind of the recipient, as the mind responds to things outside and things within together. Hence the nature of the various categories which can be identified. Narratives demand considerable art and control, and with these Spenser was plentifully supplied. But they remain resolutions of inner meanings discovered through personification or mythology or folk-lore or romantic conventions, in fact all the fictional material available to the poet for his purposes. Yet they, too, however firmly classified, cannot be wrenched from the whole. Like the art of language and the art of characterisation they belong to one finished unity.

There is a final element which cannot be neglected any more than the others, and which is equally a shining quality in Spenser's poetic vision. This is what may crudely be called the 'thought'. It can sometimes be labelled philosophy, expressions of abstract ideas in verse, and sometimes may be called 'themes', governing principles implicit in the external objects, the narratives and figures, which are built up and at times emerge plainly as ideas. They exist memorably in brief phrases flowering out of the longer expositions of thought as in:

> It is the mynd, that maketh good or ill,
> That maketh wretch or happie, rich or poore:
>
> VI. x. 30

or

> Knights ought be true, and truth is one in all.
>
> V. xi. 56

They may also be introduced into parts of Books as a central philosophical discourse as on the occasion when the Red Crosse Knight has to counter the arguments of Despair or Guyon those of Mammon. More often, however, they are felt rather than expressed directly, because Spenser is elaborating his poetry out of them as half-conscious assumptions, and they become for him, as for us, deductions out of the poetry. What is entirely credible about all Spenser's thinking, however it is formulated, is its consistency. Small matters of detail may give us pause and yet the conviction remains that nowhere do radical contradictions occur. For this reason the imaginative power of Spenser's writing continues to exist; it is not the power of magic, or of fiction, but ultimately of truth. The strength of the first two are, of course, overwhelming and the delight of a continual exploration is always present, but beyond them there remains the balance of true judgment. If it did not, we should lose eventually the uninterrupted glow of assent.

These various impressions spring out of every reading of the poem. The imaginative qualities press upon each other without pause. It is only when reflection comes into play and the reader, so far absorbed in the moving images of the poem, begins to think as a critic that the difficulties appear. The situation was early defined by Hughes:

> The Author seems to be possessed of a kind of poetical magick; the figures he calls to our view rise so thick upon us, that we are at once pleased and distracted by the exhaustless variety of them, so that his faults may, in a manner, be imputed to his excellencies:

his abundance betrays him into excess, and his judgement is overborne by the torrent of his imagination.

Hughes, like other critics of his period, was led by his sense of
form to deplore Spenser's lack of it. All recognised weakness in
the structure of *The Faerie Queene* as it stood and attributed the
failure to mistakes in the planning. And this unfavourable
estimate of the design of the poem has continued, leading with
Hazlitt to the making of a bogy of the allegory and with Miss
Spens and Mrs Bennett to the finding of solutions in changes of
plan in the process of composition.

Each critical account of the poem's failure to hold together
consistently has considerable plausibility, and appears to take
cognisance in greater or lesser degree of the substance of the
poem. Most readers will find themselves agreeing with the
arguments put forward, and yet return to the poem conscious
that the imaginative excitement experienced in the reading was
a surer way to its understanding than the explanations they
have been following. The torrent of Spenser's imagination may
perhaps not have overborne his judgment but directed it.
Lamb's comment offers a most perceptive opinion of Spenser's
treatment of his material when he said: 'He is not possessed by
his subject but has dominion over it'. Each reader begins to
explore again.

The result of reading *The Faerie Queene* more than once (and
as Mr C. S. Lewis notes, no one ever says that he '*used to* like
The Faerie Queene', so one may conclude the experience is com-
moner than is generally supposed) is the discovery that, critic
or no critic, the imaginative excitement weathers all. It operates,
of course, most powerfully where Spenser's emotional commitment to his poetic world is most deeply engaged, but not only
there. It accompanies the poem through its duller tracts of
country, unexpectedly sparking up in a phrase or a moment of
action. No one would maintain that the poem preserves the
same degree of interest throughout; that is one of the penalties
(or virtues) of writing a long poem. But what *The Faerie Queene*
does possess is that early recognised and astonishing resilience.
It is a common experience that every reading of the poem makes
a slightly different impact: things not much appreciated before

may perhaps be brought into prominence, things once vividly admired may be diminished. Moreover, the poem must be read in fairly long sessions. A single passage makes a feebler impression than was originally made. And yet, as Kipling's painter in *The Light that Failed* urged 'continuez, mes enfants, toujours continuez', the poem comes back to the reader as he sinks himself into it, the poetic genius of the greater moments spreads to the less, and the flat passages give strength and depth to the more brilliant. That is why we are justified in talking about Spenser's 'poetic universe'; the experience of the process of reading convinces us that there is such a thing and that it exists in poetry, as a vision held together by its own inner compulsion. It is a way of seeing things and it is also a thing seen.

In such a discovery arising out of the realisation that repeated readings produce patterns not the same yet not contradictory either, lies a clue to an approach to the poem. Its life is grounded in the imagination, it makes its appeal to the imagination, instantly on a single occasion, and by degrees through longer acquaintance. There is a coherence about it so that it is impossible for any part of it to be thrown aside however obscure the links between each may be. The impression is that of a kaleidoscope: another reading, another shake, the pattern changes, there is a new emphasis, and still the poem preserves its coherence. That coherence is not based on a consistent acceptance of any fixed set of principles in design or direction, not even those outlined for it in Spenser's prefatory Letter to Raleigh. It exists, mysteriously, in the face of all the variations in plotting, contradictions in characterisation, changes in allegorical techniques, and it defeats all attempts at systematisation. *The Faerie Queene* takes the right of self-determination to its furthest limit; and justifies its freedom by making it the means by which a vision of the poetic mind can come into being.

The form Spenser has found has laid him open to the charge of being out of contact with the world in which he lived, or in which any man lives. Giants and fairies, mythology and enchantment, legendary knights and ladies supply the matter; archaic words and obsolete syntax the language. It all appears too remote. Yet this, like the failure to follow any externally imposed design, justifies itself by what is done in its terms. To

B

break through the barrier it sets up is to find a world not at all remote. What Spenser is writing about proves to be bound by innumerable links to the human situation as we know it. In accepting his means of objectification we discover that he is, after all, exploring the world of all of us, in which we find our happiness or not at all.

This realisation takes the critic further into the problem with which this chapter opened, the puzzling nature of *The Faerie Queene*, its 'conception', its 'idea', its dream-like quality. It is to be regarded seriously as a consideration of what matters to humanity, while at the same time to be viewed as an example of a *genre* highly poetical. How these two subsist is clearly the point at issue. Poetry as magic of rhythm and phrase was always at Spenser's command; it is the first quality to which we respond, the last to which we return. In that sense Spenser was a great poet, and all members of his profession, even the most unlikely, have come under the spell of his verbal magic. But poetry as the impulse which drives a man's perceptions and compels him to transform them into things poetical poses another question. What was the impulse which gave *The Faerie Queene* its substance and its form, recognisable at all stages of the poem but responsible too for the problems of interpretation upon which criticism keeps foundering?

It appears that the only answer is to explore the concepts underlying this problematical text by accepting its variety and to pursue it in its fullness. The search for a starting point has to rely upon an apprehension of the constitution of Spenser's mind. Whatever critical path we take into the poem, its narrative, its allegory and of course its verse, the search finally ends up there. 'After all, Man is *not* a reasoning animal; he is a seeing, feeling, contemplating, acting animal. He is influenced by what is direct and precise.'[1] This perhaps points to the heart of the matter. For Spenser there is a preference for what is actual and immediate; his instinct leads him to create many different versions of particular images or events each of which embodies a concept like or unlike another. The effect is not tedium or repetition but a desire to establish a definite idea in terms of physical consciousness. This is why *The Faerie Queene* is so com-

[1] F. H. Newman, *A Grammar of Assent*, 1870, 1947, p. 72.

plicated in its impression. It seems to be asking more than it will ever perform because it is always producing images which keep dissolving into concepts and concepts which keep moving away into images. Spenser's habit of mind has done him little good with critics since he will not obey any of the established rules. Yet only when this habit is accepted can there be any hope of discovering how it is that he has succeeded in writing the great poem which *The Faerie Queene* proves to be.

Chapter II

CONSTRUCTION AND NARRATIVE DESIGN

CRITICS are born systematisers: it is their profession. To perceive and frame, in words not their author's, his intention and his performance of it, his success and his failures, to expound and to judge, to place the work in a literary, social and philosophical context, to connect it with the past and with the present—all these are what they see to be their business. They hope that even a minute piece of research will contribute to the system by its scholarship or by its interpretation of some part. Hence the search for sources, the assumption that everything a poet has experienced must be explicable and is discoverable in the books he read, the sights he saw, the life he lived. They collect, assess, and then shape. And the nearer the shape they make approaches to the shape that they find, the more satisfactory their labours have been.

This is their strength; but it is also their weakness. What of a poet like Spenser who read more than any single critic but less than all his critics put together, and who, capturing what he wanted from the endless variety of the world's experience, has made a poem which defies all attempts to impose a system on it? 'The Search for a Starting Point' soon brings us to a single conclusion of doubt upon Spenser's instinct for consistency.

i

It is easy to pick holes in the structure of the poem as it stands. *The Faerie Queene* is incomplete in the sense that it is unfinished, incomplete, too, in the sense that it does not resolve all its matter into any coherent design. Its stories are left with their ends ungathered, the virtues it proclaims are not wrought into any explicitly defined relationship with each other, there is no certain narrative scheme, no certain moral scale; as for the historical meaning, only the most blatant system-monger can find a way to make that apply in a regular and orderly fashion to the whole poem. And yet, in defiance of all principles, the poem does cohere: the unfinished stories drop away (although

36

we should like the added pleasure their endings give), the narrative scheme is based upon miscellaneous techniques and subjects, the moral values emerge with perfect clarity, there is in effect a consistency, though not one that is likely to please the hard-working critic.

For the moment, if we can abandon the proper literary terminology, it is fair to say of *The Faerie Queene* that it is as easily systematised as a life lived. Spenser carrying with him his inheritance from the past and his Elizabethan environment makes from them just such a job as a human being makes of his own personal inheritance and environment. The Books as he has designed them are temporary shapings of the experience of living; no more. But there is always a sense that none is complete without the others: that Holiness needs a fuller understanding of Love and of Justice than can be given to it in terms of its formulation in Book I; that Courtesy is the practice of what elsewhere was put on a higher plane, only there is time for knights to take the air and hear the thrush's song, and leave their steeds to graze upon the green. There is good reason for a minimal attention by Calidore to his quest, where all the other knights are condemned for their mistakes: Red Crosse, Guyon, Artegall inevitably have to pay for their failures, Calidore does not.

The experience of living as it was expressed in *The Faerie Queene* was the experience of living a good life, and a poet's, not a philosopher's version of it. There was little, or nothing, in Spenser's ethical theory that could not be found in some authority or other. The one thing he did give it, if this may be called a contribution to ethics, was his conviction that the nature and quality of any virtue could be defined only in its practice. He could have said to the moralists what the Duke said to Angelo in *Measure for Measure*, sharing with him the double intention of the pragmatic theorist and the questioning searcher:

Heaven doth with us as we with torches do
Not light them for themselves; for if our virtues
Did not go forth of us, 'twere all alike
As if we had them not. Spirits are not finely touched
But to fine issues.

I. i. 32-36

This is not a simple plea for the active life as against the contemplative. It is also a more complicated belief in the need for an ethical as well as an aesthetic basis in poetic practice. The form of Spenser's poem is in itself a contribution to ethical thinking: it is his way of saying that the nature of the good life is in nothing theoretical: it could only be found out in the process of living among all the incalculable variations of experience that life affords: it would never be exactly the same for any two individuals, and conclusions at its end would never quite cover all the facts of the case, just as every reading of *The Faerie Queene* never achieves an order that will hold good in every detail of the next reading.

Of course, it stood upon the ground of the great Elizabethan certainties about what are virtues and what are not, and perhaps it was the uncompromising definiteness of Spenser's belief in the rightness of Temperance, Chastity and Justice that earned him the recurring epithet 'moral'. But it was not that didactic feature only that was in Milton's mind when he praised Spenser for taking Guyon into the Bower of Bliss, for Spenser was not merely illustrating the virtue of Temperance in the face of temptation, he was formulating it, discovering something about it that he had not discovered when Guyon first encountered its appeal on Phaedria's island.

With such an ethical outlook, Spenser had necessarily to write a poem that was artistically complicated. He does not rely on the usual accepted simplifications; plot, character, structure are all subordinated to this belief that in its moral import the poem must express the good life in the process of being lived. Such a belief does not make for literary form of any regular kind. Temperamentally he repudiated any systematic organisation which the acceptance of a specific literary form requires. This is evident in poems other than *The Faerie Queene*. *Mother Hubberds Tale* changes its mode of expression four times, and *The Shepheardes Calender* has all the charm of a form which allowed him to put numerous different schemes into its design so that it can be read as a love story, or a series of comments on political and religious events, or a collection of pastoral lyrics. It is more than an anthology but rather a 'form' open to many types of interpretation so that the poet and the reader are left free to choose the emphasis that seems most appropriate.

Granted the general character of Spenser's vision, the structure and narrative design of *The Faerie Queene* is bound to be hazardous. Nothing schematic could stand for long in any consideration of what he had done. He set out to write a heroic poem, as an author of his calibre would do, and to make that heroic poem into 'a continued allegory or darke conceit'. Such a combination was also to be expected although not on the thorough-going scale with which Spenser carried it out. To an Elizabethan the epics of the past bore some kind of allegorical significance and no learned poet would wish to ignore the existence of that aspect of the 'kind' he was working in, however he chose to introduce it. Yet the problem of form as understood by Spenser soon began to exercise critics from the seventeenth century onwards, and not without reason. For the desire to systematise and the assertion of freedom to break down any system thus devised produced consequences that can be hopelessly confusing. It is only when Spenser's sheer distaste for obeying the rules he has set up and his tendency to abandon them for some more profitable standard of construction is accepted that we can begin to understand what kind of unity he eventually achieved in the poem.

ii

In the Letter to Raleigh which accompanied the first three Books, he set out the scheme which he appeared to think essential for the understanding of the course of the poem. Here, whatever the somewhat obscure relation between the prose summary and its poetic embodiment may be, he makes it clear that the poem's structure was not to be of one self-consistent simple kind. Twelve knights, each the patron of one particular virtue, were to issue on quests from the Court of Gloriana and to exemplify the virtue they represented in the process of fulfilling their quests. Arthur, the epic hero, with a quest of his own, too, representing the virtue of Magnificence was to enter all the Books by right of his rôle as hero and by the inclusive nature of the virtue he represented. Allegorically he was something more than they, and yet less in so far as they were specialists and he had only a share of their qualities.

It is difficult to see how this could work out practically, quite apart from the mathematical problem of one Book for each of the twelve virtues, and one final book for Arthur to achieve his quest and for the poem's beginning to be outlined, yet adding up to twelve books all the same—in effect Spenser ran into difficulties after the end of Book II and Arthur had to be demoted to an ordinary rôle in all the subsequent Books. This was a difficulty which the eighteenth-century critics recognised, and they went into the problem with some thoroughness.[1]

To Hughes the several books appeared 'rather like so many several poems', only slightly linked, and Arthur, although he occurs in every Book, has not a considerable enough part in any one of them: 'he appears and vanishes again like a spirit; and we lose sight of him too soon to consider him as the hero of the Poem'. Hughes attributes this fault to the influence of the Italians, especially to Ariosto, and to 'a bent in nature which is apt to determine men that particular way in which they are most capable of excelling; and, though it is certain he might have formed a better plan, it is to be questioned whether he could have executed any other so well'. This account of the poem as a whole conveys warm appreciation; and the faults do not in Hughes's mind outweigh the merits in the slightest degree.[2]

For Spence there was a strong feeling that *The Faerie Queene* could have been improved if Spenser had formed his allegories on the plan of the ancient poets and artists and had not mistakenly interpreted Ariosto as a serious poet. This attitude might have saved Spenser from the degree of fancifulness which damages his outlook and would have taught him to write more naturally. Spence, in his way, fastens upon the passages which seem to him peculiarly absurd, for instance the masque-like figures of Busyrane's house, and the transformation of the human body into a castle (the House of Alma, II. ix. 21). Even the seven deadly sins in Book I receive only a faint word of praise in that he finds the account of each particular vice

---

[1] See Henry John Todd, *The Works of Edmund Spenser*, in eight volumes, 1805.
[2] Mr Hughes's Remarks on *The Faerie Queene*, Vol. II, pp. xx-xxii.

'admirable' but complains 'that it is too complex a way of characterising Pride in general; and may possibly be as improper in some few respects, as it is redundant in others'. Collectively, Spence sees the allegorical figures as not being well invented.[1]

It is from Thomas Warton that the most stimulating critical comments can be derived. Observing the smallness of Arthur's rôle, he thought Spenser 'might either have established twelve knights without an Arthur, or an Arthur without twelve knights. Upon supposition that Spenser was resolved to characterise the twelve moral virtues, the former plan perhaps would have been best: the latter is defective as it necessarily wants simplicity'. Yet, Warton goes on, Spenser 'did not live in an age of planning' and he considers that much may be forgiven to a poet who makes up for the lack of epic severity by the wealth of imaginative appeal. 'If there be any poem, whose graces please, because they are situated beyond the reach of art, and where the force and faculties of creative imagination delight, because they are unassisted and unrestrained by those of deliberate judgment, it is THIS. In reading Spenser, if the critic is not satisfied, yet the reader is transported.'[2] Upon this matter of structure Warton has what seems to be the last word although other critics of his time tried to produce an argument in favour of the unity of the poem. Upton maintained that unity of action was achieved by Arthur, and Hurd considered that the poem held together allegorically because the narrative was subservient to the justness of its moral outlook. The part of Arthur considered in this scheme became in each Book *essential* and yet not *principal*. Hurd argued that Spenser knew very well that he could have adopted a classical design in which case a single adventure by one of the knights or a central part in the whole to Arthur would have provided unity to the fable but he chose a 'Gothick story' and consistently gave to his subject a form that should be all of a piece with it. It is not easy to agree with Hurd's opinion that it would have been possible for Spenser to write *The Faerie Queene* on classical lines, but his argument in favour of the allegorical form is well presented. The upshot of

[1] Dissertation on the Defects of Spenser's Allegory. Todd, xlvi.
[2] Observations on the Fairy Queen 1754. Todd, lx-lxv.

B *

the approach of the eighteenth-century critics determines that the poem will not hold together in terms of narrative, but perhaps it will in terms of meaning. Spenser was always willing to sacrifice externals in his design; the question remains as to whether he sacrificed inner coherence too.

The Letter to Raleigh outlines the plan as Spenser appeared to see it when Books I-III were to be published. It is noticeable that it says nothing of the content of Books IV-VI, and we could not guess from it that Friendship, Justice, and Courtesy were to follow. It is noticeable, too, that the account given of the first three tries unsuccessfully to show how the heroic plot is combined with the allegorical theme. The details of the plot do not conform with the action that takes place; and these details all concern the hypothetical, and presumably still unwritten, starting points of the quests. Guyon and the Palmer in Book II find the babe with bloody hands on the first stage of their journey, and from these circumstances the search for Acrasia begins; the Palmer could not, therefore, have arrived with it at the Court of Gloriana to ask for a knight. The Red Crosse Knight, Artegall and Calidore have pledged themselves to a quest, perhaps at Gloriana's court, before their action begins, Guyon and Britomart find theirs as they journey; and there is no single hero and no quest in Book IV. From this we may conclude that the epic structure was either imposed at a late stage or sketched out first and subsequently abandoned. If Spenser seriously intended the quest motive to form the backbone of his design, he would, one supposes, have altered the details of the opening of Book II to conform with the Letter, at least in the second volume, where the revised conclusion to Book III and many minor textual alterations were made. We cannot argue that Books IV-VI were written and published without reference to Books I-III as an independent second part, since the earlier Books were to some extent modified to harmonise with the later. Why were they not modified more completely and the Letter left to stand unaltered? Attempts to answer this question rely principally upon objections to the Letter as a source of information. The outline sounded complicated enough on Spenser's showing, and was made even more involved by the freedom with which the plotting was handled. In his account of Book III Spenser is saying that many other adventures are 'intermedled' with the central action, though these are introduced 'rather as Accidents then intendments', and in the subsequent Books (the themes and narrative outlines of which are not mentioned in the Letter), the complications begin to increase. The more we try to relate them to the scheme as laid down, the less satisfactory the design appears.

Regarded from the point of view of the heroic poem alone, *The Faerie Queene* presents diversities of structure which undermine any attempt to give a systematic account of it. Written on the lines of the classical epics mentioned in the Letter, it would be expected to have a single plot developed through a beginning, a middle and an end. Written on the model of Ariosto, also mentioned, it would be expected to have a cluster of plots interwoven with each other producing a number of subsidiary actions. Narrative event in both forms would provide the centre of interest. To Spenser the result was different, for neither alternative of organisation was in itself enough. The first gave a design for Book I, the second for Books III and IV, and for the poem as a whole, but in both he saw grounds upon which he might build his allegory. Plot and character, managed after the fashion of any of the authors listed in the Letter, were not ends in themselves. Spenser was willing to abandon each model and the demands of organisation implied in each for the sake of a multiple design in which allegory occupied the foremost place.

Chivalric action was in effect treated by Spenser primarily as a device to carry allegory, yet *The Faerie Queene* undoubtedly possesses a strong flavour of heroism. The virtues of Temperance, Chastity, Friendship, Justice and Courtesy, five of the virtues embodied in the Books, are what were always expected from knights. Moreover the life of action is what is emphasised most strongly in the scale of values underlying the plots. The rusty armour of Sir Verdant hanging unused in the Bower of Bliss and the abandoned shield of Sir Burbon both stand as instances, expressly deplored, of the failure to remain true to the knightly ideal. The Red Crosse Knight is not allowed to remain on the Mount near the House of Holiness gazing at the vision shewn him by Contemplation but is required to return to the world and fulfil his quest.

The virtues are those of Chivalry; all, even Holiness, are represented in terms of action. In that sense *The Faerie Queene* is a heroic poem. Yet the confusions and contradictions in its structure indicate plainly that Spenser was never wholly committed to an epic of the kind established by his predecessors.[1] Structurally, the consistency and interrelation of the narratives seem of small account.

Considered as allegory the poem runs into a similar difficulty. If the twelve Books with their twelve knights and their twelve several quests were complicated at the outset by the inclusion of Arthur and his search for Gloriana, the twelve moral virtues were elaborated by the fact that they had somehow to be at once less and more than the single virtue of Magnificence which Arthur was to embody. Spenser evidently did not regard his allegory as something that could run along conveniently upon two self-sufficing levels of narrative and moral meaning. The multiple structure in the allegorical as well as epical aspects suggests that he conceived his form as a framework in which many modes of meaning could have place. In it it would be possible to integrate the poetic experience that could be expressed only through metaphor and symbol with that for which other kinds of expression are best suited. Theoretically at least, the allegorical form allows opportunity for straightforward psychological portrayal as well as for methods of personification; it allows opportunity for direct representation of actions whose meaning is implicit and for indirect methods of symbolical journeys or battles. A fight with a monster can be an adventure of romance, in which case the knight's victory is the victory of the brave over the cruel, a victory of good over evil, as happens in the battles in *Orlando Furioso*: or it can be an allegorical episode *sui generis* when the knight is an embodiment of a virtue and the monster is defined specifically as some kind of evil. Thus in *The Faerie Queene* the Red Crosse Knight defeats

---

[1] Hallett Smith argues that the weight given to allegory in the Letter is due to Spenser's sense that that aspect rather than the heroic element was what would be new and difficult for his readers. But inside the poem the allegory is what matters.

Error, Calidore captures the Blatant Beast. Or it can be symbolical when there is no readily explicable meaning to which it can be confined. Monsters are for Spenser representatives of particular evils, though as in the case of the Red Crosse Knight's final conflict with the Dragon, they may be fairly comprehensive in meaning, on this occasion Sin, but such a battle as that between Britomart and Marinell is symbolical rather than allegorical in that no single interpretation presents itself.

The allegorical structure of *The Faerie Queene* is complicated by Spenser's assumption of its right to support multiple meanings. Allegory is, always, a difficult mode for a poet to sustain; he will find himself sometimes at the mercy of his medium and the need for narrative coherence may conflict with the need for consistency of thought. Something like this seems to happen at points in the poem. It would be better, we think, if the knight of Temperance had been allowed to defeat the rout that attacks the Castle of Temperance as well as destroy the Bower of Bliss; better if Arthur had been kept inside the rôle laid down for him in Books I and II, and had done only what the hero of the Book palpably could not do for himself. In contrast with Books I and II, we find any extension of Arthur's rôle puzzling; his appearances in later Books do not dispel the suspicion that Spenser is perhaps making use of any knight who happens to be available rather than the individual knight whose business it is. Arthur once in the poem has to be occupied. Yet his importance in Book II encourages the belief that Spenser may wish to convey a more profound significance through a reduction of Guyon's part in the Book. A criticism of Guyon may be implied, and this is the conclusion reached in a recent study of Book II.[1] If allegory is the centre of Spenser's thinking then the fullest explanation of the ideas conveyed through it must be made, however elaborate the structures through which it works may be.

A further difficulty, however, is the presence of certain imponderables about which no definite conclusion can be reached. The poem is not altogether coherent for reasons that are accidental and have more to do with the progress of its composition than with the nature of its form or with its thought.

[1] Harry Berger, *The Allegorical Temper*. New Haven, 1957.

We might analyse the allegory and estimate its meaning if there were not a lurking doubt about the unity of the whole. No one would wish to disintegrate Book I, nor perhaps Book II, though the problem of Arthur there suggests that Spenser may have made one plan and altered it, however we interpret the change. But in Books III and IV the question really has to be faced. Any critical judgment we make of the poem as a structure is built upon shifting sands because the apparent schemes may be accidental rather than deliberate.

How significant this textual difficulty proves is a matter of argument. Spenser published the poem in 1590 altering the conclusion of Book III so that it could be succeeded adequately in Books IV to VI and to that degree the final edition stands in the form in which he intended it. But it is evident that he did not always design the parts for the place they now occupy. The likelihood that the marriage of Thames and Medway in Book IV was written as an independent poem before 1580, when it is mentioned by Gabriel Harvey as *Epithalamion Thamesis*, is almost a certainty. Yet Spenser fitted it into the Book where it now stands and it is difficult to deny its right to be there even if it appears as a self-contained unit. It is attached imaginatively to the theme of the Book and we are perfectly sure that it could not have a place in I or II or in V or VI.

iii

A theory of piecemeal construction is one interesting solution to the problem at issue. It has been worked out with great thoroughness by Mrs J. W. Bennett who has made a full analysis of the poem's structure so as to map out what appear to have been different stages in its composition.[1] With her chronological reconstruction we may or may not agree: there are too many incalculable factors to make one feel altogether happy about relying on conjectures about Spenser's intentions at any given time or about his poetic development. But the analysis persuasively reveals features both of continuity and of changes in direction in the narrative which require explanation, some of which many readers have noticed with puzzlement; and these are certainly plausibly explained in terms of scissors and

[1] *The Evolution of The Faerie Queene.* Chicago, 1942.

paste, the incorporation of material designed in accordance with different schemes from that set out in the Letter to Raleigh.

The foundation of Mrs Bennett's argument is that *The Faerie Queene* was not necessarily conceived or expressed in the form in which we now have it, and that the Letter to Raleigh represents only the scheme as Spenser saw it at the time of the publication of the first three Books and not the plan from which he had begun to write. Her estimate of the course of composition is elaborate enough to allow for changing techniques of narration and allegory as well as for weaknesses of structural design in the poem as a whole; and it makes the earlier hypothesis of Miss Janet Spens appear too simple as well as lacking in sufficient evidence. According to Mrs Bennett, the poem began from a desire to overgo Ariosto in a chivalric romance which was to take the form either of a continuation or redaction of Chaucer's story of Sir Thopas's search for the Fairy Queen or of a narrative of the adventures of the knights of Maidenhead, members of that Order at the Court of the Faerie Queene. From this beginning, some of which survives in parts of the poem, Spenser made what was perhaps a fresh start with the formal illustration of the virtues of the kind contained in the Letter. A second period of Italian influence brought into the poem the romance of Britomart. Books I to III were put together for publication and it was at that late stage that Arthur was added and the more Aristotelian details in Book II. Aristotle and Arthur thus become afterthoughts: the failure of both to fit is the consequence of their belated introduction into a poem already well under way.

The striking advantage of this position is that it takes into account many of the difficulties that have exercised critics at all times. That Spenser did compose his poem piecemeal and join up the pieces for publication there can be no doubt at all; that some traces remain of such piecemeal working in the inclusion of seemingly independent, self-contained passages like the marriage of Thames and Medway and the encounter between Belphoebe and Braggadocchio, in the presence of loose ends, interrupted sequences, inconsistency of nomenclature, and inexplicable phrasing on occasion, there is also no doubt. Unfulfilled promises might have been supplied had the poem been completed. The ancestry of the Salvage Man, the fortunes of the baby adopted by Matilda, the subsequent adventures of Tristram, and, more important, of Serena and Calepine might have been provided in Books that were never written. How much these matter is debatable. But whether they are sufficiently numerous or consistent with each other for it to be possible to erect upon them a hypothesis about Spenser's plans at different times, to be able to say what he meant to do and what he abandoned, is not so sure. The inclusion of Thames and Medway and the Belphoebe-Braggadocchio episode can both be defended, granted Spenser's lavish far-looking treatment of his material in other less suspect parts of the poem (the scene between Una and the Satyrs for instance in Book I). Books III and IV are certainly more like a patchwork than Books I and II, but much of that patchwork may be deliberate. The difficulty is to know how far to attribute differences in narrative method and allegorical technique to distinct periods of composition, and how far to Spenser's habits of mind and preference for variety.

In Book II the narrative and allegory follow something of the same course as that in Book I. There is a single hero, accompanied by his ideal counterpart, and he has a definite quest which is made explicit at the beginning, mentioned in the progress of his adventures, and performed at the end. There is Arthur, who appears at the beginning of Canto VIII when he is urgently needed to rescue the hero and who performs one action as a defender of Temperance in Canto XI when he protects the House of Alma from the rabble attacking it. But these are superficial resemblances and scarcely prove that Book II is closely modelled on Book I or that Arthur is an unnecessary addition and an encumbrance to the poet who could have conducted this narrative in all its essentials without him. Spenser, it can be argued, regarded the theme of Temperance as a separate subject, requiring its own special mode of expression, just as in Book III Chastity required its own mode. The House of Alma may formally be comparable with the House of Holiness, but it is there in its own right, not because Spenser had created for himself a precedent in Book I. It is one method of allegorisation, working unnaturalistically by exact intellectual equations which make a limited impact upon the mind of its readers. The figure of Shamefastness stands out just as Contemplation became memorable in the House of Holiness but there is little else to keep it alive today. Yet it caught the interest of Sir Kenelm Digby and of Phineas Fletcher with regrettable results in both. It was evidently for contemporary readers what a handbook of popular psychology is for us, a somewhat inaccurate rendering of current theory. Mrs Bennett thinks it surprising enough that the same poet should have written this and the description of the Bower of Bliss, and finds it quite improbable that the two were planned and written as companion pieces.[1]

One of the arguments offered in support of this improbablity is the repetition of the motif of the Beast-headed men which occurs in the attack on the House of Alma and again in the Bower of Bliss. But this is precisely the kind of repetition which characterises Spenser's habit of mind. It occurs in single passages where there can be no question of patching and must have been conceived in the whole. A formulation once made lingers for a while to be tried out in the same or another context. It is, in fact, part of Spenser's style and language as well as of his general outlook. We see it constantly in repetitions of word and image; we see it in the chain of thought by which everything happens three times in the battle between Arthur and Orgoglio; we see it as something fundamental and serious in Spenser's poetic manner not the object of mockery made by Professor Raleigh in his critical comment on the angel that came to protect Guyon after his visit to the Cave of Mammon. Raleigh commented on Spenser's 'diffuser style' as follows:

> Beside his head there satt a faire young man,
> (This announces the theme, as in music.)
> Of wondrous beauty and of freshest yeares,
> (The fair young man was fair and young.)
> Whose tender bud was to blossom new began,
> (The fair young man was young.)
> And florish faire above his equal peers.
> (The fair young man was fair, fairer even than his equals, who were also his peers.)

[1] *ibid.*, p. 128.

The object of this passage of Raleigh's was to remark upon the compactness of Milton's mature style while allowing that in Spenser 'the whole stanza is beautiful, and musical with the music of redundance'.[1] Repetition in the appearance of the Beast-headed men in the House of Alma and in the Bower of Bliss is not an instance of useless extravagance. One might reasonably defend the stanza about the angel on the grounds that its design was a mode of emphasis and a means of providing a time-break while Guyon was unconscious and the rescuers began to hear and respond to the unknown cry. The presence of the Beast-headed men in this Book introduces a device for conveying the idea that sensuality brings men to the level of monsters. They give themselves up to each sense and to each of the seven Sins in Canto XI and to one, in particular, Lechery, in Canto XII. The monsters of the sea, encountered by Guyon on his voyage are expressions of the same association of ideas: they are derived from Tasso and have been transformed by Spenser into elements of nightmare, which is what the journey, in one aspect is. The others, from Ariosto and Homer, are formulations of sensuality. What is consistent throughout is the *idea* of monstrosity, and this is one of the dominant ideas in Book II. Mrs Bennett would have the repetition explained in terms of different periods of composition, an early one in imitation of Ariosto and a later following Tasso.[2] It is quite possible that the concluding parts of the Book were written separately and arranged finally in the order in which they now occur: the two are very casually linked with each other in retrospect at the beginning of Book III. But if so, Spenser has succeeded remarkably well in bringing the two episodes into the frame of his conception of the meaning of intemperance by carrying his image of it through the two technically very different modes of allegory, and as was pointed out by N. S. Brooke they are both prepared for in a preliminary stanza in Canto IX.[3]

What is not at all certain is that the allegory of the House of Alma was necessarily written earlier than the Bower of Bliss

[1] W. Raleigh, *Milton*, 1905, pp. 200-1.
[2] J. W. Bennett, p. 131, note.
[3] N. S. Brooke, 'C. S. Lewis and Spenser: Nature, Art, and the Bower of Bliss'. *The Cambridge Journal*, Vol. II, No. 7, April 1949, pp. 420-34.

episode. They differ in quality, but granted Spenser's varied methods of allegory we are in a state of uncertainty as soon as any assertions are made about his artistic development. Allegory of the House of Alma kind, if it is written at all, is in danger of becoming over-literal and didactic. The point at issue here and on many other occasions where there is seeming disparity of material is how much weight ought to be attached to Spenser's habit of working by analogy, repetition, and variation. Is it possible to disentangle the accidental from the deliberate when we encounter his changes in technique? Would Book III have been better constructed on Mrs Bennett's principles if Spenser had not been pressed for time in its final preparation for print? One can argue without hesitation that the Guyon who inexplicably recovers his horse at the beginning of this Book and charges the Knight of Chastity on it, is not the Guyon of Temperance, slow to anger in Book II, and that the tournament of Book IV might never have taken place for all the notice that is given to its upshot in the subsequent tournament in Book V, Canto ii, and that there are several confusions of persons [Red Crosse for Guyon (Book III, Canto i), Duessa mysteriously mentioned in a Canto heading in another (Book III, introduction to Canto i), and Archimago in a few lines of verse as the enemy of Britomart (Book III, Canto iv, stanzas 45-49)] all of which suggest the employment of material otherwise intended.[1] Some tidying up needs to be done to make the narrative consistent in points of fact, but the major task, that of creating a harmony of effect, Spenser has performed for himself. The poem certainly will not stand up to neo-classical criteria of form, nor to the demand that the allegory should be of one kind throughout, but if we concede the freedom of method Spenser proposed for himself in adopting the multiple structure adumbrated in the Letter to Raleigh we may discover greater coherence in the design of each Book and in the poem as we have it than analysis into strands of content can provide.

There certainly are 'submerged plots', but like the 'fossils' in

[1] J. W. Bennett, *ibid.*, pp. 145 and 181. 'It seems reasonable to suppose that the tournament in Book IV, ii, is a late interpolation in the story of Florimell, imitated from the tournament in Book V, and put into Book IV so that Florimell's part in that Book would not be limited to the last two Cantos.'

the text of Shakespeare they are too deeply buried to matter very much. Perhaps, too little weight is given to the fact that Spenser did after all print his first three Books and then reprint them with the second three in a form that satisfied him enough for publication. The joins are occasionally bad and the difficulties we meet then are better explained in terms of patchwork than on any other grounds. But to apply that explanation to other parts where it is less necessary makes in the end for little understanding of Spenser's achievement.

iv

An alternative approach to Spenser's construction in *The Faerie Queene* is that proposed by C. S. Lewis in *Studies in Medieval and Renaissance Literature*.[1] He here reinforces the distinction between the narrative techniques in Books I and II and those of the later Books. The difference, he argues, emerges from a prolonged tradition going back to Malory, to Boiardo, Ariosto and Tasso, presumably derived from Ovid's *Metamorphoses*. The technique is rooted in a peculiar method of recounting a story: in his lively, stimulating fashion C. S. Lewis labels this method as that of 'interwoven' or 'polyphonic' narrative. In it 'Spenser is obeying a method as well established as the fugue'.[2]

From this approach a defence of Spenser's structure is built up. It requires no support from any notion of piecemeal construction. The various episodes are disposed in a way that is 'highly formal and sophisticated'. Consequently Spenser is well aware of what he is doing. 'In a polyphonic narrative the weird, the voluptuous, the exciting, the melancholy scenes can succeed one another not where the exigencies of a single rigid 'plot' permit but wherever artistic fitness demands them.'[3] The effect results in considerable variety and also in the creation of the power of suspense. This is a positive approach which overrides difficulties and inconsistencies of the kind which Mrs Bennett found stumbling blocks and sails happily past them all. Spenser emerges more strongly as a story-teller, conscious of the

[1] Cambridge University Press, 1966.
[2] *op. cit.*, p. 133.
[3] *ibid.*, p. 134.

advantages of variety and suspense in the recounting of the sequence of events. Freed from the problems of 'the unity of *The Faerie Queene*', the critic can achieve a sounder appraisal of its narrative art.

At his best, Mr Lewis offers an acceptable summary of the imaginative response of the reader to the material before him:

> It [polyphonic narrative] adds to the poem what might be called depth, or thickness, or density. Because the (improbable) adventure which we are following is liable at any moment to be interrupted by some quite different (improbable) adventure, there steals upon us unawares the conviction that adventures of this sort are going on all round us, that in this vast forest (we are nearly always in a forest) this is the sort of thing that goes on all the time, that it was going on before we arrived and will continue after we have left. We lose the feeling that the stories we are shown were arbitrarily made up by the poet.[1]

This may be a light-hearted way of describing the nature of Spenser's narrative art; but as a summary of the process of reading it looks before and after and tells us more than we have observed. To compare small things with great, it is reasonable to link this passage with Johnson's account of the magnificent art of *Paradise Lost*:

> He [Milton] seems to have been well acquainted with his own genius, and to know what it was that Nature had bestowed upon him more bountifully than upon others; the power of displaying the vast, illuminating the splendid, enforcing the awful, darkening the gloomy, and aggravating the dreadful.[2]

C. S. Lewis admirably builds up an image of the slighter scheme of Spenser, adding much wit to his version where Johnson adds proper depth to his. From both we receive the impression of great achievement upon an imaginative and critical mind. Neither commits himself solely to impressionistic criticism but each in his own way recreates the sum total of the work upon which he is reflecting. From each we are given a topic for wider speculation, a clue to other aspects of his subject. When C. S. Lewis points out that changes occur in the narrative 'wherever

---

[1] *op. cit.*, p. 135.

[2] Samuel Johnson, *Works*. Ed. Arthur Murphy, 1816. Vol. 9, 'Life of 'Milton', p. 167.

artistic fitness demands them' we instinctively develop the suggestion, wondering what changes occur and where: when Johnson compresses the poetic power of *Paradise Lost* in a series of present participles we follow that suggestion with him into the details as they arise in his examination of character, plot and description. It is the reward of this type of criticism, that it at once creates a mental impression and at the same time asks a question. The intelligent reader is given part of the answer and can discover ways of supplying the rest or of asking other questions.

For this reason there is much more to explore when Mr Lewis's polyphonic narrative is placed before us. Its description implies the function of many aspects of Spenser's craftsmanship as a narrator. 'Variety' and 'suspense' have been mentioned: an occasion when the story first appears vague and slow enough to suggest suspense soon comes to mind. A group of knights are journeying in a friendly way in search of adventures; it is a dull muted scene until they reach a place where the atmosphere seems inimical:

> At length they came into a forrest wyde,
> Whose hideous horror and sad trembling sound
> Full griesly seem'd: Therein they long did ryde,
> Yet tract of living creatures none they found,
> Save Beares, Lions and Buls, which romed them around.

Something is expected in this barren setting, and something comes, making a singular dramatic impact:

> All suddenly out of the thickest brush,
> Upon a milk-white Palfrey all alone,
> A goodly Ladie did foreby them rush,
> Whose face did seeme as cleare as Cristall stone,
> And eke through feare as white as whales bone:
> Her garments all were wrought of beaten gold,
> And all her steed with tinsell trappings shone,
> Which fled so fast, that nothing mote him hold,
> And scarse them leasure gave, her passing to behold.
>
> III. i. 14-15

The management of tension has prepared for this brilliant moment. A pursuit ensues, an element recurrent in the sequence of the stories. Two knights follow the lady, dividing when the source of her terror (a foule forester) is discovered, one chases the forester, the other the lady. The distinctive feature of this event is its mysteriousness. It is long before the name of Florimell is revealed. Concealment of identity is an Ariostan device which Spenser adopts broadly in Books III and IV. He thus creates a degree of curiosity, which is a form of suspense.

An analogous situation is present in the adventure which befalls Britomart, the third knight in the group. She comes upon a knight fighting alone against six others. This happens in stanza 20, but the first reference to the name of the rescued man, Red Crosse, is made in stanza 62. Meanwhile, the castle has opened its over-hospitable gates, the tapestries on its walls have been described, and the household of dancing squires and damsels has been displayed. The narrative here is primarily allegorical through its indication of the character of its owner, Malecasta or the Lady of Delight. Again the names of the knights who have been attacking Red Crosse are kept secret: each is a personification of sexual pleasure reflecting a scale of relationship from Gardante to Noctante. In this episode the whole nature of Malecasta and of her knights is conveyed in the labels given to the characters and in the settings adorning the castle with their amorous associations.

Sudden action impinging upon static scenes is typical of Spenserian narrative. The storm at the beginning of Book I, the arrival of Orgoglio brutally when the Red Crosse Knight is idling with Duessa beside the enchanted well are obvious examples, each involving a complete change of tone. Indeed, suddenness is a vital factor in the reproduction of events in *The Faerie Queene*. The violence of the battles which emerge out of physical clashes of knights, or knights and monsters, creates one kind of drama. Another depends upon the sudden disappearance of essential figures—that of Archimago, for instance, after his conversation with Braggadocchio and Trompart, or, conversely that of the Angel when he has told the Palmer what he must do for Guyon. Each time the nature of the disappearance is pointed by the style. Archimago's departure upon the Northern wind leaves a sense of Satanic visitation; the Angel's final words are a benediction and a proof of his heavenly origin:

> Yet will I not forgoe, ne yet forget
> The care thereof my selfe unto the end,
> But evermore him succour and defend
> Against his foe and mine: watch thou I pray;
> For evill is at hand him to offend.
>
> II. viii. 8

The phrases which mark the conclusion of episodes such as these before the vanishing of the speaker both wind it up and open a door to the future. They create, in effect, yet another instance of the feeling of suspense.

The magical content of a plot is not wholly exceptional, although Spenser has plenty of space for more normal interests. He can concentrate upon human rather than devilish or angelic creatures. Outstanding are single portraits of characters in action: a man running—Pyrochles's servant Atin, for instance, arriving in a cloud of dust, 'panting, breathlesse, whot', Florimell's gentle Dwarf scratched and nearly lame from his efforts, the blacksmith hammering at his anvil, and the strange Malengin walking with his long staff and wide net for fishing in the brook. These portrayals all take into account people whose conduct carries on the narrative; none is separated from the growth of the action. Spenser's descriptions are here representations of individual members of the cast, not of figures outside the plot but of sharers in its progress.

This consciousness of mobility is part of Spenser's outlook upon the subject-matter out of which *The Faerie Queene* is built. His treatment is associated closely with its style which has the effect of fashioning the quality of the movement. When we are told how the false Una attempts to attract the Red Crosse Knight physically:

> So slyding softly forth, she turnd as to her ease
>
> I. i. 54

an appeal is made to the senses quietly. Spenser's line depends upon the implications of a visual effect. The gesture is both seen and felt. Even in the most straightforward piece of information there is an inconspicuous tendency towards defining action:

> They forward passe, ne Guyon yet spoke word.
>
> II. vii. 31

Plainness of statement conveys the grouping of Mammon, his fiend and Guyon on their way to the store of treasure. There are, of course, some moments when the movement is contrived in more self-evident terms; when, for instance, Maleger rides on his tiger, or Phaedria sails in her oarless boat, or Cymoent comes in her coach in search of Marinell. Such instances are more fully developed to create an impression upon the visual faculty. Yet it remains primarily an assumption that what is portrayed is still an object in motion.

C. S. Lewis ends his discussion of Spenser's narrative with a gesture towards allegory. It is hard to consider the art of story-telling without including that central element in *The Faerie Queene*. Any study of the arguments of Josephine Waters Bennett or C. S. Lewis must lead to that other aspect of the poem, however much or however little weight we may wish to give it. For all the narrative framework with which Spenser equipped himself, none stands as absolute. The form was regarded as essentially flexible, capable of being bent to fit whatever each episode was required to carry. The events do not impose their shapes upon the material, but are shaped to it in constant adjustment.

The apparatus of Book design, characterisation, and setting is regarded as nothing more than apparatus, ready to be discarded where the growth of the poem demands something else. Thus it appears reasonable that Books III and IV should follow a scheme different from those in Books I and II, and no inconsistency results unless the reader considers the first plan as a rule from which no deviations can be permitted. What matters more is the evolution of the ideas in the poem, and Spenser was evidently willing to leave on one side the design which had done its work successfully so far, and was not needed for the next stage. The scheme of a central hero and his absolute counterpart *was* going to be needed later for Book V; but in Book VI no partner accompanies Sir Calidore. Again, Arthur is never to take up the spiritual rôle he filled in the first two Books. Instead, the interests have changed: the heroic *genre* is sacrificed to the romantic in Books III and IV; something approaching heroic justice appears in Book V, but by the time Book VI is reached the emphasis has shifted to the pastoral.

The recurring factor in all six Books proves to be allegory, and if we have been forced to accept the presence of varying systems of narrative, we have learnt at the same time to accept Spenser's notion of allegory as the centre of his meaning and of the plot's action. The term offers a double interpretation and its duality is established upon literary and symbolic levels. Reflecting on this double approach, we have to discover a practical term in which this feature may best be defined. Briefly it may most fruitfully be labelled 'multiple allegory'.

Chapter III

MULTIPLE ALLEGORY

THE word allegory tends to arouse a sense of hostility in potential admirers of Spenser. They should be reminded of T. S. Eliot's observation upon the work of Ben Jonson, that it is 'damned by the praise that quenches all desire to read the book'.[1] It is hoped that the adjective 'multiple' will soften the objection and provide a link between the variety of narrative techniques and of allegorical forms.

The quality of allegory can be seen in any single example we may happen to choose. It is considerably extended as we move from one instance to the next. The impact of allegory becomes more powerful within the consolidating structure of a whole Book, and eventually of the whole poem. Analysis has to begin somewhere, but in any selected passage it soon becomes clear that certain methods remain typical and representative. The Red Crosse Knight's adventure in the Wood of Error is a useful example to choose. It is the first adventure in the first Book, and incidentally its material stands as a *caveat* for critics as well as for the knight.

*   *   *

The Red Crosse Knight and Una are driven into the wood by a sudden storm, lose their way, find a monster in a cave with which the knight successfully fights, and emerge again into the open to continue their journey. The whole episode occupies twenty-three stanzas and its allegorical sense is made clear from the outset: Spenser's canto head informs the reader that the knight 'Foule Errour doth defeate' and the explicit phrase of Una—'This is the wandring wood, this Errours den'—does the rest. Such information is essential to the poet's intention: the reader is not held up by puzzling out the underlying idea, nor

[1] *The Sacred Wood*, 1960 edition, p. 104.

does he read too fast in his anxiety to find out whether the Red
Crosse Knight is victorious. Spenser can count on his attention
being fixed on what is more important—the kind of error presented, and the progress rather than the outcome of the battle.

Ultimately these two things go together, the allegorical
meaning is caught up into the story, the story progresses as the
underlying idea, or perhaps we should call it the embodied idea,
is enlarged. But if we separate them temporarily we can see how
skilfully the narrative as narrative is conducted. There is
simplicity of statement that gives positiveness to the crucial
moments—'so in they entred arre'—'But forth unto the dark-
some hole he went, And looked in'—'Into her mouth they
crept, and suddain all were gone'; there is dialogue heightening
the suspense before the battle is engaged; there is a use of
character to afford some link between the experience of the
everyday world and the romance motifs out of which this episode is made—'Fly fly (quoth then the fearefull Dwarfe:) this
is no place for living men'; and current throughout, there is the
craftsmanship by which the *tempo* of the action and its weight
are controlled. The urgency of Una's exhortation is enforced
by repetition, alliteration, the epigrammatic phrasing; the
intensity of effort in the knight's response by a further and
harsher sounding alliterative scheme:

> . . . Now now Sir knight shew what ye bee,
> Add faith unto your force, and be not faint:
> Strangle her, else she sure will strangle thee.
> That when he heard, in great perplexitie,
> His gall did grate for grief and high disdaine,
> And knitting all his force got one hand free,
> Wherewith he grypt her gorge with so great paine,
> That soone to loose her wicked bandes did her constraine.
>
> I. i. 19

But what characterises Spenser's narrative more distinctively
than any of these, is its sequaciousness. The story flows on, and
the reader soon learns that he can trust Spenser to preserve that
movement so that even the static moments are swept along in it.
The wood spreads out before Una and the Red Crosse Knight
with its paths *'leading inward farre'*, *'And foorth they passe, with
pleasure forward led'*, the trees are listed in detail, *'Led with*

delight, they thus beguile the way' their wanderings are described until 'At last resolving *forward still to fare* . . . That path they take that beaten seemd most bare'. The battle and victory follows, and they find a way out.

The continuousness is further assisted by inconspicuous verbal repetitions, 'shrowd' twice in stanza 6, once in stanza 8, by the way in which the narration of events slides into a word that sums it all in and out again as with 'labyrinth' in stanza 11, and with the two epic similes both of which are at once retrospective and preparatory, linked to past and future by idea and phrase. They carry on the thread of the narrative while building up what appears to be a static image.

All this gives assurance of Spenser's wisdom in his choice of form. *The Faerie Queene* is from the start an imitation of an action and as such must be founded upon an understanding of the arts of narration. When we stop to analyse an episode we meet incontrovertible demonstration of Spenser's grasp of these arts in the precision of its record of fact, the relevance and vitality of its dialogue, comment seen to be within the power of character as well as of narrator, and in all the unobtrusive ways in which continuity is maintained. But we do not stop, and that in itself is a tribute to the peculiar continuousness with which Spenser has made his story proceed.

Yet separation into narrative and allegory must be only a temporary expedient of criticism for there is no such distinction made by Spenser himself. Indeed so closely are the two combined that they defy any system of 'levels' which critical thought attempts to impose. For even in an episode like this, and much more so in the whole mass of episodes which make up the poem, the 'literal' level and the allegorical levels shade imperceptibly into each other, and we experience them with various degrees of intensity as we read. The study of Spenser's allegory has been bedevilled by attempts to interpret it systematically: here, for instance, if the Red Crosse Knight represents Holiness, and Una, Truth, the monster Error, the Dwarf must also have a label. But Spenser has not given him one, neither explicitly nor by implication; he is a functional Dwarf, there to make himself useful to the characters (he carries Una's luggage, he goes to find her after the Red Crosse Knight's capture by Orgoglio), and to the poet. He brings a touch of humanity into the scenes where he appears: something would certainly be lost from the first image we have of Una and the Red Crosse Knight if he were not lagging behind, and from the episode in the wood if he were not there to echo Una's plea for caution. Any definition of allegory that we make must be wide enough to embrace him: but that he should be burdened with the weight of 'Prudence' or 'Common Sense' . . . 'the wisdom of the natural man who lacks the moral courage and spiritual stature of the militant Christian, that mind of the flesh which St Paul contrasts with the mind of the spirit',[1] or any other such load, is surely to sacrifice him to a conception of allegory more mechanical than Spenser ever intended. We misread *The Faerie Queene* lamentably if we try to force meanings where Spenser has suggested neither their existence nor their nature. His subtleties were of another kind. Here the Dwarf takes part in an action which is allegorical, the struggle between Holiness and Error, conducted in a setting which is allegorical, the wandering wood of mental confusion, with weapons which are allegorical, the Pauline panoply of the knight, the undigested books and papers of the monster; and when he speaks his remark is as allegorical or otherwise as you wish to make it. 'This is no place for living men' harmonises equally well with what Una says of the locality and with what Spenser says of the meaning, with 'the place unknowne and wilde' and with 'God helpe the man so wrapt in Errours endlesse traine'. But for all that this dwarf does not belong to the allegory in such a way as to be crammed into a pigeonhole of personification on the strength of one sentence.

The operation of Spenser's allegory is at once easier and more difficult than we are apt to suppose. It is easy in this episode in that its general drift is made plain, it is difficult in that it does not work by a simple equation but moves from one type of formulation, even one mode of perception to another, and we have to be ready to make the necessary adjustments of focus. To follow Spenser intelligently requires not only a capacity to see how the meaning is conveyed—only that will tell us what the meaning is—but also a readiness to accept all the methods he uses. Those which appear laboured, and limiting to the signifi-

[1] F. M. Padelford, *Variorum* Edition on Book I, p. 435.

cance of the matter in hand may well be justified in the long run; without them, perhaps, the great imaginative flashes, which we also meet, could not come about.

Something of this variety occurs in the treatment of Error here. The communication of meaning takes two forms, one tending to enrich the imaginative content, the other to impoverish it. The first works by suggestion and the evocation of wider and wider associations, the second by statement and ever narrowing applications. Spenser needs both to fulfil the whole of his intention, but it is upon the first that the mind is encouraged to dwell. What remains poetically memorable is the Wandering Wood and the knight's first sight of the monster in its depths; the conflict which follows confines that first experience within specified limits, informing us only of the nature of one kind of error and leaving all the rest, all the other forms of illusion and deception and ignorance, for the poem to discover in its own way later. But by some magic of phrase the image has been fixed, and the wood, 'not perceable with power of any starre', foreshadows the desolation of spirit that the Red Crosse Knight is to find in the dreams sent by Archimago and in the cave of Despair. It is one of those glimmering lines that remind us of the depths from which the poem sprang.

Such moments lift the allegory on to another plane of reality, and take it into the realm of symbolism. They cannot be sustained, but very near to them in imaginative power comes the prolonged wandering of the three characters in this perilous wood. In Spenser's poetry, syntax is an important medium for the communication of meaning and the long involved sentences here define the labyrinth more satisfactorily than any direct statement could do;[1] by the time Una's explanation 'this is the wandering wood, this Errours den' comes out we know what that means, for we have experienced it in the process of reading. Here, too, the monster 'with huge long tail . . . in knots and many boughtes upwound' all ready to wreathe round her foe, inevitably has her den. The wood is an extension of the figure, the figure a personification of the wood; there is an

---

[1] Witness the memories of Spenser's successors: Milton's fiends discussing metaphysical problems 'found no end in wandering mazes lost' and 'in mazy error wandering . . .'.

attunement between the two, verbal and visual, which gives the cue for the poet's comment. 'God helpe the man so wrapt in Errours endlesse traine' thus stands as the interpretation of an idea already apprehended, not an application of moral to episode arbitrarily imposed.

This close interpenetration of setting and figure is an essential feature of the allegorical method of *The Faerie Queene*. It does not always occur with such clarity as on this occasion but it is generally present in some way. The characters found in the forests or the characters of the sea belong to their own particular worlds; the Bower of Bliss is an expression of Acrasia—which is one of the reasons why Guyon has to destroy it in spite of its beauty—and Mammon lives in the black country next to Hell. But here the relationship is comparatively simple, one of preparation and extension (though it may be complicated retrospectively by the experience of other forests, other monsters, other kinds of error as the poem develops), the winding paths of the forest, the winding shape of the monster, are both identified with the winding thought of the confused mind.

The image of the wood is governed by the idea of mental confusion which it has to express, and is therefore very different from the wood in which Una finds the Satyrs or the one where the Salvage man dwells. And it has one feature which is not, happily, to be met again—a long catalogue of its trees. This is only indirectly connected with the concept of error—the information given about the properties of every tree has classical and Chaucerian authority and may be supposed accurate within its frame of reference; and it delays the progress of the story, and at first sight the allegory, for a stanza and a half, while reducing the mystery of the forest to a timber merchant's inventory. Why, we find ourselves asking, is it there? It can, of course, be accepted simply as a characteristically Elizabethan interpolation, written for its own readers and not for all time, comparable with the canto-ful of British Kings who invade the narrative of Book II. Judged by contemporary standards it was 'a praise' of trees occasioned quite justly by the need to divert the visitors' attention from their path until they were quite lost inside the wood. It was in that capacity that it was justified in Warton's view: 'it is highly consistent, and indeed expedient, that the poet should dwell for some time on the beauty of this grove, in describing its variety of trees as that circumstance tends to draw the Red Cross Knight and his companion farther and farther into the shade, 'till at length they are imperceptibly invited into the cave of error, which stood in the thickest part of it'. 'Beauty', however, was here a distinctly Elizabethan kind of beauty, vested in utility and in literary association. Many of the details have a long history: Spenser's immediate source was probably Chaucer's enumeration in *The Parliament of Fowles* where many of the trees occur with verbally identical or substantially similar properties, but this must have been supplemented by reminiscences from Ovid and other Latin poets and from emblem books such as Alciati's. As a display of learning it must make some intellectual appeal but as a scene of beauty, beguiling to the eye as well as to the mind, it is curiously deficient. Spenser is not in the least concerned with the visual appearance of the trees—the 'various dies' which constitute the charm of Dyer's list in 'Grongar Hill', or the shadowy trunks and foliage of Cowper's description in *The Task*, are not for him; and indeed it is odd that Warton should have allowed the grove any aesthetic quality at all considering how far from beautiful in any decorative, or more ordinarily Spenserian sense, it was. Yet Spenser has a gift to make it anticipate later meanings: the maple is inwardly unsound and the trees that Red Crosse is going to see in the next episode are deceptive in appearance and character. But Red Crosse and Una liked it enough to be 'led with delight' into it; and if that is granted, the reason for the catalogue form of its presentation is easily understood. It was out of this crowded close-packed mass of trees that the wandering wood grew, syntactical convolutions following upon an overpowering, unassimilated aggregation of facts. The Wood of Error must remain error of the mind not of the senses.

It is only when the progress of the battle between the monster and the knight is pursued in detail that the allegory begins to thin. The dark landscape, the figure which dwells there, 'where plaine none might her see, nor she see any plaine' have to be made to take an active part in the story, and the night of the mind dwindles to a repugnant vomit of books and papers and a serpentine brood of deformed creatures, black as ink, which drink their mother's blood and so die. We know more about error from this—and less: quantitively more, qualitatively less. Of course Spenser goes on allegorising and sparks of his original apprehension are struck off as he goes, witness the frogs and toads which

> eyes did lacke,
> And creeping sought way in the weedy gras,

but the process is principally one of interpreting or applying the first vision to a particular moment in the narrative. Nothing more is seen, and the disappointment we feel comes from this rather than from the nastiness of what takes its place, from the confinement of meaning and the discovery that, after all, this strangely limitless image of evil is reducible to a definite and rather commonplace cause.

Such a reduction is inevitable from the terms of the poem: the narrative structure demands, and will continue to demand, specifications of one sort or another. The poem cannot proceed without them, and far from being a hindrance, the narration gives Spenser the scope he needs for the evolution of his theme. The study of the poem becomes more and more rewarding as we appreciate its allegorical method, that narrowing and widening process, the thickening and thinning, by which meaning is expressed. Between the idea of error first glimpsed and its elaboration in the ensuing battle there is certainly a wide gap; but the particulars of this formulation, in a monster, will be surpassed in a greater and more treacherous version, Archimago, to which the Red Crosse Knight will succumb. There the gap will be smaller and something new added to the idea by the same mixture of suggestion and statement. As the narrative continues, the thought enlarges with its embodiment in the person and action even though each in itself is necessarily limited. This contraction and expansion of meaning is 'Allegory' in the distinctively Spenserian sense. Coleridge called it 'fancy operating under the conditions of imagination', which indeed it is; but it is equally, or at times, imagination operating under conditions of fancy. One occasions the other: the imaginative vision of error as a darkness and a confusion generates fanciful details and those in their turn lead to a fresh activity of the imagination. There is in fact no sharp division of categories, the operations of fancy and imagination are contained within the continuously flowing narrative form.

ii

If this is a valid account of the relation between narrative and meaning which constitutes Spenser's Allegory, several problems of interpretation and criticism begin to appear. At every point the story is penetrated with significance and the question of meaning is not only 'what' but 'how'. Indeed it is impossible to assess the content of Spenser's thought without taking into account its method of formulation. His technique gives many signs of expediency: he imposes allegorical ideas upon both symbolical and literal episodes and persons. It soon becomes evident that for him the imaginative passages are always potentially fanciful and, conversely, the expressions of fancy can be transformed easily into imaginative ideas. This is a condition of his thinking as a poet and it applies to the whole of *The Faerie Queene*.

It was Spenser's habit to multiply distinctions, finding particulars only as temporary shapings of his mind's experiences. 'To be still searching what we know not, by what we know, still closing up truth to truth as we find it';[1] this process was for him the continued activity of the poetic faculty. In Book I one kind of deception leads to another, and further discovery of what was first guessed at in a symbol is reached through the addition of more particulars, of other fables and of other characters. Thus theme grows out of theme. Book I leaves much to be discovered in Book II, Book III in Book IV, and so on until the business of closing up truth to truth is over. In his refusal to shut the door upon the variety of material appearances stood his belief that they collectively represented a form of truth. Unspeculative as Spenser's cast of mind seems to have been, he was convinced that intellectual exclusiveness was no way to achieve a sound conclusion about anything. Hence the copiousness of the allegorical matter and method in *The Faerie Queene* as a whole.

[1] Milton, *Areopagitica*, C.U.P., 1928, p. 49.

It may be suggested that the manner which came so naturally to him occasioned an unjustified degree of repetition. This impression has to be admitted. It was Spenser's habit to formulate his ideas looking towards shapes in which they had been expressed elsewhere. To read *The Faerie Queene* most profitably is to make a compact with its author and be prepared to accept the terms in which he chose to set out his thought. For him there was always a significant relation between the physical phenomena of the external world and the world of mental or spiritual expression. Thus images which were found for one episode, a moment in the character's life in the poem, may be recalled long after on a subsequent occasion. It is not by chance that Una when telling Arthur how she and the Red Crosse Knight were separated describes how he abandoned her,

> And other bywaies he himself betooke,
> Where never foot of living wight did tread,
> That brought not backe the balefull body dead.
>
> I. vii. 50

Her account re-creates a memory of that first episode when, in her company, he went into the Wandering Wood, and was warned by the Dwarf that 'this is no place for living men', reached Error through the labyrinth of paths, destroyed it in a successful fight, and found his way out when

> That path he kept, which beaten was most plaine,
> Ne ever would to any by-way bend.

His separation from Una caused by Archimago brought him to byways and to places that were not for living men.

The relations between the parts are rarely made obvious. They depend upon the flow of the allegorical narrative as a whole and to halt the flow and try to pin down the details apart from their context is to court disaster. Indeed, one constant factor that emerges out of extensive reading is that for all the variety of images and ideas, Spenser keeps their meaning firmly in their context. Apparent contradictions are many, but once the image and idea are preserved within their setting such contradictions prove fallacious. It has been objected, for instance, that the representation of Lucifera in her golden splendour misleads us into thinking that she will stand for Queen Elizabeth:

> A mayden Queene, that shone as *Titans* ray,
> In glistring gold, and peerelesse pretious stone.

and so 'we have to read on to discover that she is Pride, with a dreadful Dragon at her feet, and that no comparison with Elizabeth is intended, at least consciously, by the poet'. But the fluidity of Spenser's style makes it always necessary to read on. His account of the journey in the Wood of Error is threaded on an inescapable sequence of movement and it is the same with the House of Pride. Spenser has informed us in the epigraph that the scene is set in 'the sinfull house of Pride' and once that clue has been absorbed there is no reason to neglect the other damaging anticipations of the nature of the 'mayden Queene'. She lives in a house built upon sand, her porter is called *Malvenu*, 'Proud' is the repeated adjective for her before the Dragon is mentioned. It is difficult to agree with the comment that 'the imaginative excitement and colour-brilliance completely over-throws the moral allegory which limps along behind very much as an afterthought'.[1] 'Reading on' is precisely what Spenser's mode of allegorical expression expects.

The fact that the poem was described by him as a 'continued Allegory or darke conceit' is Spenser's way of defining the kind of reading it required. To read on is to absorb at once the story and the allegory; they are not separable and in both there is the common factor of movement. *The Faerie Queene* is one of those works of art which depend for their quality upon cumulative effects. Each event in the scene slides into the next, and ulti-mately needs the context of the whole poem to give it its full force. For those critics of classical inclinations who admire 'form' of the kind supplied by order, proportion, and outline, this is a distressing method of procedure; perhaps it is to every critic, whatever he admires, since it drives him to vagueness, half-truths, and tedious modifications of every statement he would like to make precise. But it is the only type of structure which Spenser found he could use satisfactorily if he were to say

---

[1] J. W. Saunders, 'The Façade of Morality' in *That Soueraine Light*. Ed. by William R. Mueller and Don Cameron Allen, Baltimore, 1952, p. 26.

all that he wanted to say in *The Faerie Queene*. The generous pattern of *The Shepheardes Calender* offered him a similar variety but when he attempted in other works more limited, stricter kinds of design he was defeated by the requirements of their plan. What he needed was a multiple form which he could shape to any purpose as it arose. Consequently the only kind of consistency we can look for is consistency of formulation to meaning, never consistency of formulation here with formulation there.

Allegory for Spenser has become a means of submitting an unsystematic habit of thinking to an imaginative type of expression. It enabled him to regulate the quantity, the quality, and the kind of significance he desired at any given stage in the poem. The last thing it was designed to be was a system in itself. This might imply a state of considerable confusion, but for Spenser multiple allegory was positive and constructive in its outlook. It offered a medium where many different kinds of material could find their place. It became for him a dimension, a mode of perception, never a fixed scheme to which all poetic thought had to be subordinated.

One of its merits lies in the freedom of range it allowed. Some formulations appear at first to be hardly allegorical at all. The presentation of the figures of Abessa and Corceca in Book I, or of Malengin in Book V, makes a strikingly realistic impression: both images and the setting in which they occur, have been rightly attributed to Spenser's memory of scenes in Ireland. Abessa is a girl carrying a pitcher on her head, walking slowly in a desolate valley, Malengin is a man dressed in rags with a fishing net on his back and a staff in his hand. And we might add other isolated figures to these—the old fisherman asleep in his boat while his nets dry on the sand, the old man counting his gold in the sun. Each is introduced in a way that appeals to the sense of sight so that every one appears realistic rather than symbolic in conception. What is uppermost is the human figure, though a human figure so strange that it carries in itself hints of some profounder significance. What this is, is conveyed by the names—only the fisherman has none, but in Abessa, Malengin and Mammon we are unobtrusively moved into an allegorical framework. Each acts as an *exemplum*, indicating a special meaning as the context suggests. Abessa runs with terror from the sight of Una to a hut inhabited by Corceca and Kirkrapine and the imagery remains a flat, equational, sign. Malengin turns into many unprepared-for shapes and proves to be a figure of guile whose abode runs down to hell and is, in fact, closer to Spenser's symbolic images, ultimately mysterious, only partially interpretable. The fisherman is the typical instance of the characters who make Florimell their victim and prepares the way for a more frightening successor in Proteus. Mammon, standing for all that his name is associated with, dives down to his lair in the underworld, and acts as his own interpreter speaking as an emblematist to expound what Guyon will see and to formulate the temptations which his world offers.

In these four instances, the shades between naturalism and the various degrees of symbolism which constitute Spenser's allegory are reflected. It is one of the inherent virtues of the framework he had adopted that so many different levels of meaning can be introduced easily without labour or repetition. He does not have repeatedly to point his morals in the fashion of the emblem book, but can trust the conception to run by itself once it is established. It is, therefore, a means of economy. Once set in this context in each Book, all become part of a changing story. Spenser has not left his form at the stage where a single isolated example stands alone. The assumption of a moral idea formulated in terms of narrative was for him only a beginning: the narrative will vary as the idea grows and will develop more branches; each Book will be different; there will be different relations between the literal and allegorical meanings; there will be different ways of indicating the relationship, from the most explicit (as in the Abessa and Mammon episodes) to the merest suggestion by context, analogy and contrast (as with Malengin); but always the allegory is there. *The Faerie Queene* is written in its shadow and belongs to its world.

iii

Once the constant pressure of *themata* is recognised, the use of different types of allegory is to be expected. Narrative and its interpretation continue together. "The sense is given us to

excite the mind' is Ovid's conception of the relation of imagination and intellect.[1] Spenser's application of this conception can
be deduced from the way in which he connects the forms of the
different features of *The Faerie Queene*. In it allegory follows a
method quite different from those of other Renaissance expressions of it, from those of *Orlando Furioso, Gerusalemme Liberata* or
Arcadia. In Ariosto it is fitfully constituted by the introduction
of figures which are abstractions and create scenes which cannot be accepted literally. In Tasso, its presence is a matter of
interpretation, imposed *post rem*. From Sidney it is completely
absent, but if it were supplied it would be like that of Tasso;
Basilius functioning as an incompetent king, Cecropia a villainess
who exemplifies the evil which comes to women in power.
One could surely allegorise Sidney just as Tasso allegorised
himself. *The Faerie Queene* is allegorical in its nature.

It is not so in the consistent fashion of medieval literature
because there is in it a continual shading and sliding from one
level to another. Spenser does not, of course, work out the
design deliberately—it would be impossible to carry out such a
process systematically. But by assuming that everything can
have more than one meaning he has transformed concepts into
modes in which the literal meaning is sometimes the most
important, sometimes the least, but are still present in the
exactitude of observation attached to them. This is true of the
range of allegorical senses: they may be conveyed through
personifications or emblematic figures, they may be expressed
in symbolical incidents or mythological narratives, or they may
come in debates on abstract topics, but the movement of the
story in which they occur carries the reader from one stage to
another with no sharp breaks between different methods.

It is not difficult to illustrate the ease with which Spenser can
handle various formulations of his meaning. The Malbecco-
Hellenore tale of Book III, for instance, provides a remarkable
combination of the extremely literal with the extremely allegorical. It begins with sharp realism in the arrival of Paridell,
Satyrane and the Squire of Dames outside the house of Malbecco, their inability to gain admission owing to Malbecco's
determination to hide his wealth and his wife from strangers,

---

[1] Chapman, Ovid's *Banquet of Sense*.

the storm that drives them to shelter in a shed, the addition of
Britomart to the group and her fight with Paridell. The
necessary information about the house they have reached has
been acquired through the Squire whose report places the situation before the reader clearly by description, and anticipates
what will follow. In this story we are presented with the
January and May situation, the Chaucerian scene which
reminds us of other references to the *Canterbury Tales* in Books
III and IV. The Marriage group was in Spenser's mind and in
some generalisations he quotes what was referred to in tales
which dealt with true love.[1] The character study of Malbecco
prepares the action which will follow. In the scene at dinner,
Paridell successfully entices Hellenore's attention. All this is
kept on the wholly social level. Hints of symbolism occur in the
subordinate tale of the fall of Troy in which Paridell describes
his ancestry; they are to be developed in the sequence where
the conduct of Helen is used as an analogy to describe the
conduct of Hellenore but they are kept well within the range of
normal conversation through the introduction of a similar yet
purely historical account by Britomart of *her* ancestry. The
story develops as a realistic tale of seduction and crime in
Hellenore's elopement with Paridell, their theft of Malbecco's
gold, and their setting fire to his house, his indecision in choice

---

[1] Examples of quotations from the *Canterbury Tales*:
    'Franklin's Tale.'
    'Love wol nat ben constreyned by maistrye
    When maistrie comth, the God of Love anon
    Beteth his wynges, and farewel, he is gon!'
                        'Franklin's Tale', 764-766
    'Ne may love be compeld by maisterie;
    For soone as maistrie comes, sweet love anone
    Taketh his nimble wings, and soone away is gone.'
                        The Faerie Queene, III. i. 25
    'Pardoner's Tale.'
    'And on the ground, which is my moodres gate,
    I knokke with my staf, both early and late,
    And saye 'Leeve mooder, leet me in!
    Lo how I vanysshe, flessh, and blood, and skyn!'
                      'Pardoner's Tale', 729-732
    'That every houre they knocke at deathes gate?
    And he that happie seemes and least in payne,
    Yet is as nigh his end, as he that most doth playne.'
                      The Faerie Queene, IV. iii. 1

C *

between saving his wealth or pursuing his wife, and finally his meeting with Braggadocchio and Trompart and the discovery of the now deserted Hellenore living with the satyrs. The interpretative elements which have lurked in the naturalistic characterisation of Malbecco—his avarice, his suspiciousness, his jealousy and, physically, his blind eye, his impotence, and the meaning of his name—are brought into the open by the plot until the narrative widens into the wholly allegorical situation in which Malbecco is transformed into a bird, a type of Jealousy.

The action opens on a realistic plane with characters recognisably human behaving naturally on a social occasion; it ends in typology and personification. But the earlier section contains features of the later, and a closely attentive reading supplies enough anticipation to enable us to accept the allegorical conclusion. It would be difficult to draw a firm line between the opening and the close: we are carried along by the flow of the narrative and there is no moment when we wish to break its substance up into categories.

In Books III and IV, the meaning is set between two extremes, the apparently entirely naturalistic and the symbolic. There is in both, more mythological material and more philosophical thinking than in I and II. In certain respects the imaginative quality, as distinguished from the fanciful, is more strongly present. Consequently, interpretation is more open to debate. Spenser gives the reader a considerable degree of help by introducing the episodes, or stages in the narrative, in preliminary explanatory stanzas where the ethical character of the action is made clear; but these cannot measure the emotional force with which the scenes are surrounded. There is, in fact, a poetic quality embedded in the rhythm, the images, and the diction which we recognise as peculiarly characteristic of Books III and IV. We are unwilling because of it to try to apply the standards of interpretation which held good for Books I and II. It was possible to translate the events in those into explanatory prose. The sequence could be followed, the parts logically related to the whole, and however inadequate the accounts of their content may have been they were not positively misleading. They provided a foundation upon which interpretations could be based. But Books III and IV do not lend themselves to translations of this kind. The meaning which emerges is more difficult to decipher because the imaginative force, which is necessarily our main clue, does not readily coincide with the sequence of the narrative. Britomart is the heroine of Book III, yet the seashore on which Marinell lives and the journey of his mother in search of him after his wounding carries much stronger emotional power than Britomart's meditation before she encounters him. That was a familiar form of expression, Petrarchan reflections by a lover in a series of resemblances between his heart and a ship. We have met them before and Spenser has nowhere given them the distinction which might have made them appropriate to that highly independent woman, Britomart. There are occasions, of course, when she stands out and becomes an individual who is more memorable than any other central figure in *The Faerie Queene*, except for Una. But the emphasis is not necessarily laid upon her only; and on this occasion the heightening goes elsewhere, to the Rich Strond and to Cymoent. Later it will fall on the Gardens of Adonis. Thus Spenser's imagination transforms Books III and IV into another type of allegory, nearer to symbolism, nearer to the products of poetic imagination.

iv

Granted the closeness of realistic narrative and characterisation to allegorical material we come gradually to discover the quality which is central to Spenser's cast of mind. Looking back over this chapter we can see that the visual scenes described in it are brilliant, clearly defined, and at the same time linked to their context in rhythm and movement. They are sections in which action and image combine. They may concentrate on symbolical or literal material, usually both, but in them we are led through surface description to concept. There is no pause or interruption, no requirement to linger over detail for its own sake because syntax and diction insist upon progress.

This progress, though often embodied in specific imagery is the most characteristic feature of Spenser's art. When Coleridge said that 'no one can appreciate Spenser without some reflection on the nature of allegorical writing' he was pointing out the principal element in his author's way of thinking. Allegorical writing involves the operation of the solid and the transient quality of all appearances. For this reason the key to its understanding lies in a readiness to respond to the mobility of its formulation. In responding, readers can recognise a shift from the realistic scenes in the household of Malbecco to the ultimate personification of Jealousy in its flat bird-like form. It is impossible to follow the narrative about Paridell's corruption of Hellenore and her elopement with him to its conclusion in the metamorphosis of Malbecco without absorbing the variousness of Spenserian techniques.

Spenser treats the ideas underlying his themes with some degree of detachment. In Book II the Palmer regards the experiences which he and Guyon undergo as illustrative of moral topics. He draws the conclusion implied in the study of Mordant and Amavia or in the episode of Medina, Perissa and Elissa in a way in which the separation between event and significance can be preserved. If there is no Palmer, another method is found for introducing an independent comment. Mammon in Canto VII is his own commentator, and in Book VI Colin Clout outlines the meaning of the appearance of the Graces and his personal reaction to it. A distinction between perception and idea continues throughout the poem as a whole and is conveyed in the assumption of the separation between substance and explanation.

This separation comes about in numerous different fashions. Personification offers a series of examples where the comment is clearly divided from its object. The personifications are not necessarily always successful, for they tend to rely on too great an emphasis upon only one side of the content. Furor, for instance, represents uncontrolled anger; this weakness is embodied in a human form and has to be suppressed by physical devices. Consequently, a padlock restrains her tongue, chains bind her to a stake, and by these means she is effectually silenced. Furor's son, Occasion, is subjected to similar detention, bound in foot and hand with a hundred iron chains tied in a hundred knots. The two figures do not convince. Clearly, allegorical thinking demands balance between each component element. Here the human side of the personification is sacrificed to its meaning. Sacrifices of this kind are prone to occur often. In Book II, although the Palmer emphasises the moral interpretation of the events in which he takes part, his presence tends to bring overmuch weight to the theoretical aspect of the allegory. Thus, faced by one of Furor's victims he seizes the excuse to embark on a thorough-going piece of exposition:

> Wrath, gealosie, griefe, love do thus expell:
>   Wrath is a fire, and gealosie a weede,
>   Griefe is a flood, and love a monster fell;
>   The fire of sparkes, the weede of little seede,
>   The flood of drops, the Monster filth did breede:
>   But sparkes, seed, drops, and filth do thus delay;
>   The sparkes soone quench, the springing seed outweed,
>   The drops dry up, and filth wipe cleane away:
> So shall wrath, gealosie, griefe, love dye and decay.

II. iv. 35

This passage of rhetoric was considered an admirable example and was quoted intact by Abraham Fraunce in his *Arcadian Rhetoric*. It can be so considered, but obviously it exists in its own right, not as a contribution to the narrative.

The faulty application of condemnation to character and the Palmer's elaboration of moral law expose the limitation of the device of allegory in Book II. Personification does not in its nature rule out the combination of the two features. Despair in Book I is an example where both are offered in perfect harmony. The character remains a type but is given the support of a setting and a power of verse which only extends the personification, deepens but in no way individualises it. The failure to observe the sensuousness of the embodiment of Furor and Occasion is here overcome, and Spenser carries off successfully everything which the narrowness of his form permits.

Allegory is open to many other hazards. The characterisation of the central knights, who are intended for personal rôles and need to be granted an opportunity for internal experience, the study of states of mind in minor characters, the concentration upon argument and points of view expressed by abstract figures, the parts played by other non-representational beings, and, of course, the upshot of the complicated narratives—all these are contributory to the Spenserian manner. Yet, resisting the chance to explore these topics, we can move beyond them to what they have in common. One can find this best in the words of Hazlitt when he was writing on the form Spenser was employing: 'His ideas seem more distinct than his perceptions.' From a critic strongly opposed to the presence of allegory in a poem whose appeal seemed to be so extremely romantic and magical, this is the most illuminating of observations. Hazlitt says that the scheme Spenser had adopted possessed the richest poetical and intellectual material for his genius. Yet, even so, for Spenser as a poet there was no complete commitment to that physical world. However sparkling its external representation in the descriptions and stories might be, and sparkling indeed they were, the perceived objects ultimately dissolve into abstractions. Spenser is one of the most sensuous of poets; but he is also one of the most conceptual, and it is in this paradox that his endless fascination lies. The physical world is a visionary world, and in the moments of greatest imaginative insight it proves after all to be largely a figment of the mind. Thus concept triumphs over actuality. The ideas *are* more distinct than the perceptions. And that, in truth, is the nature of allegory.

It is not necessary to pursue this point of view into particular examples because it applies widely to the whole scheme of *The Faerie Queene*. The concomitants of epic and of romance resolve themselves in the last resort into ideas, and the world of appearances becomes only a shadow of the world of reality. Here is Platonism, and Platonism so firmly maintained (as it was in many of Spenser's other poems) that it penetrates deeply into the conduct of the narratives and into the superficial features of the allegory. Beneath the epic pageantry, the variously obvious moral themes, the arbitrary equations and the personifications, there lies something else—a sense of the visionary.

This sense introduces what appears to be a contradiction. Spenser's extraordinary powers of visualisation led him to devise living scenes based upon instincts of sight and sound but these are not confined solely to physical impressions. In the whole poem perceptions are often abandoned so that their immateriality may be drawn out. Brilliant similes in single clauses or in complete stanzas often dissolve into abstract

notions once they are linked with their subjects. This is true of
the developed scene of the rising sun in Book I (vv. 2-5), of the
beguiling passages containing images from nature to define the
conduct of the characters in Book VI, or of a brief simile such
as that in which Cymochles is shown absorbed in the sensuality
of the Bower of Bliss:

> He, like an Adder, lurking in the weeds,
>   His wandring thought in deepe desire does steepe,
>   And his fraile eye with spoyle of beautie feedes;
>
> II. v. 34

The vigour and vitality of the first line, embodying Cymochles's
sinister intention in 'lurking' and 'weeds' is lacking in the
generalised lines which follow. The whole context is needed, so
that the evil atmosphere of the Bower can be built up through
another image till Cymochles, like Leda in the House of
Busyrane, creates a subtle kind of sensual enjoyment.

> Sometimes he falsely faines himselfe to sleepe,
> Whiles through their lids his wanton eies do peepe,
> To steale a snatch of amorous conceipt,
> Whereby close fire into his heart does creepe:
> So, them deceives, deceiv'd in his deceipt,
> Made drunke with drugs of deare voluptuous receipt.
>
> II. v. 34

Here the vivid image of the adder has been transformed into a
step towards the gradual discovery of the true nature of the
Bower of Bliss. This scene occurs well before the journey and
the arrival. It is only one stage and others will succeed in which
there will be similar shifts from the material to the immaterial,
until the concept of the Bower has become the alluring and
destructive vision that it is.

v

It is only in the study of individual Books that we can profitably follow the methods of allegory as Spenser carries them out.
Each Book, he tells us, possesses one central theme. We discover
quickly that the theme is expressed in a variety of forms. We
also discover that the central theme is not just the label given
in the title but depends upon the interpretation made of the

incidents and ideas contained within the Book. Naturally there is a certain amount of overlapping; the art of debate in the scene between the Red Crosse Knight and Despair will anticipate debates between Guyon and Mammon and that between Artegall and Burbon. In the same way, the series of personifications in the House of Pride and the House of Holiness look forward to those in the Garden of Proserpine and the House of Busyrane. But the tone and direction is so different that it may be more profitable to consider each in its own Book, taking into account the nature of the Book and the total interpretation we make of its form and structure.

There is an order in the sequence of the Books. Spenser began with the subject from which all moral beliefs start, man's relation with God. The Knight of Holiness is a knight who has to discover that relationship, and in the process he is led astray. His failures result from the power of illusion upon his mind: the plot of Book I is concerned with the degree to which he succumbs to illusion and with his gradual liberation from false seeming until he is capable of fulfilling his quest and triumphing over the Dragon of Sin. But the main topic is the various phases of illusion and its attempts to destroy him.

Book II deals with man's relation with himself, the achievement of an ideal of character through personal discipline and renunciation. Again, as in Book I, there is a central topic, the opposite of the virtue for which the hero stands. Here, however, the allegory contains more than one aspect of the evil the Knight has to fight against. Wrath, Avarice, and Lechery, cross his path. The sequence of the narrative follows Guyon's determination to free the knights who have become victims of Acrasia. The plot begins with one of her victims, encounters others on the way, and has for its climax her capture in the Bower of Bliss. There is a central core of evil to which men are submitted; it is not illusion but what may be called distortion. It is embodied in various examples where knights are failing to carry out their proper duties.

With Book III the thought widens to the world that surrounds man and his relation with others. Books III and IV treat of what is at stake in the connections between individuals, of love in the Platonic sense as the source of all being, Book V of what is at

stake in societies, the force of Justice. In some respects the profoundest part of the poem, Book III, is about solitude and
separation—Marinell persistently alone, Florimell fleeing from
capture and rescue, Scudamour parted from Amoret, his bride,
Hellenore abandoning Malbecco, her husband, Britomart
seeking Artegall, her promised lover. It is also about the world
of the imagination, fuller of mythological figures, reaching out
to the elements in the waters of the sea and the flames of the
House of Busyrane, and presenting its ideas in ways that belong
more to symbolism than to allegory. Yeats, regarding the vision
of Scudamour, or more accurately of Britomart, as 'the finest invention in Spenser', sees in the climax of Book III a quality 'full
of a sort of ghostly midnight animation'.[1] It is right that Book
IV should be on the same plane, completing and complementing
it, taking for its theme union and reconciliation instead of
solitude and isolation. The characters move in pairs and unite in
great scenes of harmony, in Scudamour's attainment of Amoret
and in the marriage of Thames and Medway.

Book V, thinner poetically, is narrower than these in that it
goes little to the metaphysical basis of its chief virtue, but wider
in that it deals with relationships which are not private but
public, with the rights and duties of man in the community at
large and with current political affairs. Here Spenser deals with
Spanish persecution in the Netherlands and with insubordina-
tion in Ireland as well as with sociological problems that spring
up in any contemporary town and village life.

One wonders what else Spenser can offer in his allegory, but
he contrives in Book VI to descend from heroic issues and epic
conventions to the plane of normal everyday living. The final
virtue is Courtesy. It facilitates all social relations and it is also a
personal quality, bestowed by nature as well as achieved by
effort. The form is pastoral, the tone leisured and easy. The
reader is returned to what he kept meeting in other books
although only in lines and sections. Now the whole tone and the
choice of imagery preserve a level that is natural. Spenser was
right in his decision in Book I to banish Mars as his Muse. He
preferred first to invoke the 'sacred Muse' as suitable for the

[1] W. B. Yeats, *Poems of Spenser*. Introduction, xlv. The Caxton Publishing
Co., London., n.d.

topic of holiness. Now he desires only the pastoral muse, interpreted as the voice of rural normality.

This was the end, yet not the end, of Multiple Allegory. It is all too evident that Book VI was not intended to provide the poem with a conclusion in the way it does. Any critical comment one wishes to make tails away in feebleness although the Book itself stands up in its own right. The addition it makes to the poem is insufficient: it is a stage but not a climax. Granting the whole as it stands, we have also to recognise that each Book is arranged in a chain which joins each to the next by an explicit link. By this it is made clear that Spenser is feeling his way from each Book to the next. Book I ends with a simile of a voyage which looks forward to the comparable opening image to Book II. Book II begins with a meeting between the Red Crosse Knight and Guyon, a meeting which proves courteous and hopeful and defeats the wiles of Archimago who is plotting against the activity of the knights. The Red Crosse Knight's words to Guyon indicate Spenser's attitude to the poem when he says 'You, faire Sir, whose pageant next ensues', for each hero is to act in an individual pageant. Book III begins with an allusion to Guyon's success against Acrasia and with the temporary quarrel between Britomart, the hero of Book III, and Guyon. At the end of Book III the uncancelled version in the text of 1590 foreshadows the unions that are to be found throughout Book IV. The opening of Book IV is comparable with those joining the earlier Books by the use of an explicit link in the reference to the rescue of Amoret and the evil conduct of Busyrane. Book V is joined with Books III and IV by the presence of the two major characters, Britomart and Artegall. There is also an explicit bridge in the Proem at the beginning by an allusion to the Golden Age, already mentioned in Book II, 7, and Book IV, 8. With Book V there is an overlap in that the hero of Book VI, Sir Calidore, meets the successful Sir Artegall, learns something about the Blatant Beast which constitutes his adventure, and receives heart-felt good wishes from the man who has achieved his quest to the one whose is yet to come.

Finally, there is one more Book not included by Spenser but probably so intended. This survives in only two Cantos, known as *Two Cantos of Mutabilitie,* owing its title perhaps to the author, perhaps to the printer. It was found after Spenser's death, and was published in a Folio edition of *The Faerie Queene* in 1609. It is difficult to sustain any sound objection to its appearance with the six complete Books. It has much in common with the ideas, the method and the outlook with which we have been concerned. Its manner is exceptionally mature; it includes the mythological, the philosophical, and the episodic features out of which the narrative of the rest is built. It does not in fact provide any conclusion to the unfinished events in Book VI nor to the poem as a whole in the design outlined in the *Letter* to Raleigh. Perhaps it does no more than offer the core of another Book, and yet its style and meaning suggest that Spenser was injecting into it the essence of what had given weight to the most powerful scenes in earlier Books. The two Cantos turn upon the virtue of Constancy, and in their imagining of the process of change they embody all the substance of *The Faerie Queene*. The acceptance and rejection of the power of Mutabilitie lead to the only summary possible. This is a Book about Truth.

PART TWO

Chapter IV

BOOK I. ILLUSION

BOOK I is usually regarded as Spenser's most successful treatment of allegory as a literary form. Perhaps it is. In it, certainly, narrative and allegory are most closely combined. The episodes may differ from each other in character and tone, ranging from comparatively static scenes of pageant or argument to vigorously effective action, but a close grip of their allegorical significance is maintained all through their narration and we never lose sight of what they stand for. The Canto-heads, the names of the actors, the poet's explicit comments, point the way to interpretation continually. This grip loosens as the poem proceeds through the other Books: none responds as faithfully to critical analysis as this. In Book I, also, each episode is built into a developing structure in a way that is attempted nowhere else: every stage in the story is also a stage in the meaning. Consequently the allegory acquires a certain self-sufficiency; at each point it looks before and after as it pursues the spiritual progress of its hero.

For these reasons Book I possesses a coherence which subsequent Books appear to lack. Its protagonists are characters in their own right as well as figures in the allegory; they gain forcefulness and some personal existence from the control governing their presentation. Spenser has more freedom in the structure of later Books and can draw a character like Britomart who appears in Books III, IV and V; but in this the tighter organisation of the plot gives him a different kind of opportunity enabling him to show how his hero learns and how his heroine suffers not only through direct characterisation but also through implication and contrast. Book I lays down the plan from which Spenser will diverge to a greater or lesser extent in the Books which follow. It is not independent of the whole poem but it is, what perhaps Spenser meant it to be, a prelude in which the form he chose is more easily grasped. In the first Book we learn how to read the poem and what may be discovered in its other sections. Archimago, Duessa and Arthur will recur, not necessarily in the same rôles, and they provide links to the sequence, but their contributions to Book I are complete and clearly defined. What we learn of them afterwards, adds to or modifies what they represent here. Their recurrence creates some of the problems of estimating the poem as a whole, but at this stage we are given a sample of the types of meaning Spenser will make his allegory carry.

The opening episode of Book I, which was discussed on pp. 59-67, defines the characters of the two protagonists, their relationship as champion and lady, and the nature of the conflict in which they are to be involved. It was Una who identified Error and warned the Red Crosse Knight of the danger awaiting him; it was the champion who plunged bravely into the attack unabashed by her warning. He successfully defeats Error in the narrow limited form it takes, and although the battle was carried on in darkness, he knew what it was he was fighting. The next form of error leads him to different darkness, a darkness of the mind where even Una cannot help him. They become separated. Una remains herself, Truth unaltered though deserted by her champion.[1] The Red Crosse Knight becomes the victim of Falsehood, falling into error after error which the Holiness of which he is patron proves too fragile to resist.

Archimago is the chief engineer of the knight's downfall and in him Spenser introduces one of the great figures of evil in the poem. His characterisation is fuller than Spenser tends at the outset to make it. When he is first seen, he appears as a kindly, friendly hermit, glad to accommodate the two wandering people who meet him. Benjamin Robert Haydon speaking of Fuseli says: 'I found him the most grotesque mixture of literature, art, scepticism, indelicacy, profanity, and kindness. He put me in mind of Archimago.' Not all these terms apply adequately to Archimago but his portrait is convincing enough to suggest a many-sided figure. On the narrative level he is recognisable as a person and as a wicked sorcerer into whose

---

[1] It is difficult to accept the view of A. C. Hamilton that Una's adventures apart from Red Crosse represent a series of falls counterparting his. A. C. Hamilton, *The Structure of Allegory in The Faerie Queene*, p. 86.

powers heroes of chivalry so often fall, the Atlante of Ariosto, the Red Ettin of Scotland, and like Sacripant he is disguised as a hermit. In the allegory he fills more than one rôle. Most obviously, he is associated with the unguarded faith which leads the Protestant knight away from truth: he tells his beads and slips in an *Ave-Mary* as occasion serves, through him Red Crosse leaves Una for Duessa, the Duessa who with Orgoglio will ride the seven-headed beast and be crowned with a triple crown. This is one element in the significance of the narrative and the one where the allegory most evidently thins as it did in the spewing forth of pamphlets by Error. Archimago stands for something wider than this. In the Canto-head he is simply labelled 'Hypocrisie' which confines his wickedness only to the moral sphere. 'A bold bad man', a guileful character, he certainly is: but his wickedness is more sinister than that, hedging the Red Crosse Knight round with intangible deceits until he is lost in a world of spiritual and intellectual evils.

Archimago is the cause and originator of the Red Crosse Knight's wanderings, and in the poem as a whole (he reappears plotting in Book II) he stands for much more than Spenser's drawing of his character at first suggests. When he begins to devise tempting dreams for his visitor, the world to which he really belongs eventualises: the spirits he summons are messengers of hell and he is at home in the hellish Underworld, can arouse Morpheus to do his bidding, and dares call by name:

> Great Gorgon, Prince of darknesse and dead night.
>
> I. i. 37

Only the action of the whole Book can show how profound the wickedness is which he represents. Spenser's way of defining it lies in the illusory dreams he sends to Red Crosse; the gradual deterioration of the knight illustrates it more completely. Here again the allegory stretches towards the symbolical vision of evil and yet also dwindles into the narrow plotting of a mere deceiver adopting a disguise.

Archimago through his contact with the world of darkness and night is able to summon spirits who will work upon the mind of the Red Crosse Knight in sleep and dreams. They bring first sensual dreams to him in general terms of sexual

desire, and next the specific image of Una beside his bed
appealing for his love. Both he is able to resist, but the third
stage when Archimago in his disguise as a hermit rouses him to
see the same false image of Una in bed with a squire destroys his
faith in her, and he leaves the hermitage shocked and jealous.
Archimago has been successful in dividing him from Una. It
may seem that the Red Crosse Knight is the victim of a magical
power against which he could hardly have protected himself
since his misconception of the conduct of Una arises from hostile
deception. But Spenser makes it clear that his incapacity to
resist such influences is to be attributed to a failure within himself. Una had advised him to accept the offer of hospitality and
rest before he followed Archimago's suggestion to begin another
quest. Sleep is required for him, and the tempting dreams
which allure him are wholly deceiving. The nightmare sequence
is distinguished openly from the value which he sets upon her
during the day:

> Her, whom he waking evermore did weene
> To be the chastest flowre, that ay did spring
> On earthly braunch, the daughter of a king.
>
> I. i. 48

Una's dignity and virtue are in themselves enough to shame
him to allowing such illusions to take hold of him. His dreams
have been shot through with sensual desires and when he sees
Una, as he supposes, subject to the passions which are his own,
he condemns her for the desire he should have controlled in
himself. 'The eye of reason was with rage y-blent.' He leaves her
and rides away accompanied by the Dwarf:

> Still flying from his thoughts and gealous feare;
> Will was his guide, and griefe led him astray.
>
> I. ii. 12

Una herself has already shown the truth of her love for him in
her concern with his exhaustion after his first struggle with
Error, and Spenser underlines this by his account of her
immediate search for him after his departure and by her direct
reflection that it was he 'whom she loved best'. Such plain
statements are never used about Duessa's relation with him

which has always an element of duplicity about it. Indeed, during the battle with Sans-joy at the House of Pride she is represented as encouraging the winning side and offering herself as reward, and she can change her support as quickly as the chance of success changes. And as openly. Una's fidelity is present, unremarked, through all the scenes in which she appears alone—in the hut with Abessa and Corceca and in the wood among the satyrs—and it is defined explicitly and personally in her account to Arthur of Archimago's machinations. By this time the Red Crosse Knight has wandered far in the byeways foreshadowed in the first scene in the wood, and Una's summary goes straight to the heart of Archimago's evil power. It has to be formulated in a number of allegorical episodes, each of which has its own particular quality of spiritual destruction, but it belongs in its nature to a realm of mysterious darkness. For all its exactness and limitation, detail by detail, it has its roots in a formless mode of being which only a word here and an image there can suggest. The narrative that pursues the knight down his disastrous path springs from and returns to that vision of evil of which Spenser's poetic imagination is so constantly aware. It is in the story a destructive power, and in the allegory a metaphysical negation.

Illusion is the recurring term for this negation in Book I. It is the result of the deception to which the knight is exposed by Archimago and it spreads to the atmosphere and feeling of the episodes in which he is involved. It begins with the poetic impression made by the description of the Cave of Morpheus with its blurred sounds and lack of sharp definition; this is a matter of style, of course, but it is the style which Spenser uses for all incantatory effects in the Book and it will appear again in the allurements of Despair. It is carried on into action, first in the dreams which haunt the knight and then in the meeting with Duessa under the enchanted trees.

The effect of illusion is created by Spenser through a kind of false perspective. The dream had followed a sequence recognisable in dreams—vague shapelessness first, then close attachment to a particular person or place, then a sense of being now awake and finding the experience a matter of actual truth—yet it was in fact still a dream. The knight's deception results from

his taking the last phase of his experience as reality; but readers
outside it have no difficulty in keeping fact and dream distinct.
More subtly, the episode of Fradubio and Fraelissa is enclosed
within the analogous situation between the Red Crosse Knight
and Duessa. She, disguised as Fidessa, has already told him her
unfortunate story, but he was too easily attracted by her appearance to allow any doubts to enter:

> He in great passion all this while did dwell,
> More busying his quicke eyes, her face to view,
> Then his dull eares, to heare what she did tell;
>
> I. ii. 26

Consequently, he is little prepared to recognise that all Fradubio
tells him is true, and capable of being applied to his own
situation. Fradubio talks of his Fraelissa in words that recall
the beauty of Una, 'Mine, that did then shine as the Morning
starre', but the knight is past seeing the connection: Duessa's
false name and her physical charms prevent his recognising that
the event in the past is only a prognosis of what he is now
experiencing. He is incapable of noting the difference in
appearance between Una and 'Fidessa' although hints have
been offered by the details of the story. The past deception is
being realised in the present, and the actual presence of Duessa
during the telling of the tale subtly reinforces its effect. Illusion
is increased for the reader by just this dual action; the rôle of
Duessa is the same, so is the rôle of her victim and of his lady,
but the deception is multiplied in depth. Duessa on this second
occasion pretends again to be different from her real being, and
the appearance of innocence is twice distorted. The result is a
more complicated falsification in which nothing is but what is
not. The illusion which binds the knight leaves no sure fact that
can be grasped.

To emphasise this impression, Spenser uses two devices.
First he repeats the word 'seeming' in connection with Duessa.
She appeared in 'seeming glorious show' when Red Crosse first
encounters her; she became 'a seeming simple maid' after the
death of Sans-foy, and in the story of Fradubio, who knows
what she is, 'seem' appears as verb and adjective to multiply the
idea of falsity associated with her:

So doubly lov'd of Ladies unlike faire,
  Th'one seeming such, the other such indeede,
  One day in doubt I cast for to compare,
  Whether in beauties glorie did exceede;
  A Rosy girlond was the victors meede:
  Both seemde to win, and both seemde won to bee.

I. ii. 37

Secondly, Duessa achieves her triumph by summoning a deceptive mist to dim Fraelissa's beauty and give her the appearance of ugliness. This, too, is part of the truth about Duessa and it anticipates what occurs in the House of Pride. There, after leaving the enchanted trees and after an interval where Una's adventures are described, the Red Crosse Knight and Duessa are received by Lucifera. With her and her 'sage counsellors' they drive out into the country 'to take the solace of the open air'. The fact that 'a foggy mist had covered all the land' remains unnoticed by those taking part.

Duessa is constantly associated with false appearances and with darkness. The language used about her points this out openly and her conduct in relation to the Red Crosse Knight enforces it psychologically. Thinking that Sans-joy is successful she cries out to him 'Thine the shield, and I, and all', and afterwards, seeing the event going the other way switches her allegiance to the apparent winner in an equally proud gesture 'The conquest yours, I yours, the shield, and glory yours'. This is one of Spenser's typical moments of realism which keeps Duessa on a natural plane although we, as readers, know that she has used magic to put Sans-joy out of the victor's reach.

Deception is what Duessa represents all through her dealings with the Red Crosse Knight. After the Fradubio episode we are prepared to read critically the account of the next stage of their journey. Duessa is known to the courtiers in Lucifera's household, but the knight is received so loftily by the Princess that even he becomes suspicious of her court. The House of Pride is splendid in appearance but Spenser indicates its pretentiousness in showing how it is covered with golden foil, its walls are high 'but nothing strong nor thick', and it is built upon sand. None of this is apparent to the knight yet, it is only after the joust and the disappearance of Duessa as well as of Sans-joy that he decides to leave it.

Meanwhile he has experienced the delights of the scene to which Duessa has brought him. The narrative is suspended for prolonged description, an example of Spenser's instinct to invest with fuller interest an analogy once it has been introduced. The labels attached to this place, as in the Wood of Error, invite extensions of the concept underlying it, and occasion what Yeats called 'the elaborate ritual of his poetry'. A preference for expanding the ideas first suggested, an enjoyment of increasing the central parallel, topic by topic, is brilliantly reflected in this particular Canto. The framework has been established, and now Spenser can multiply the allegory without needing to include any further action but simply by bringing a power of description, stanza by stanza, to enlarge this first abstract idea from which it began. The concept of the Seven Deadly Sins incites a series of grotesque embodiments to accompany Lucifera on her journey. The fact that there is an obvious link between the physical image and the idea it reflects supplies fixed points, moments of rest. Thus Sloth comes forth riding upon an ass; he is dressed as a monk, carries a little-read breviary, and is marked with diseases associated with a riotous life. Thus, too, comes Gluttony, mounted on a swine, clad in Bacchic greenery, carrying a 'bouzing can' and suffering from dropsy; he is in appearance 'more like a monster then a man'. Both provide Spenser with a chance to elaborate the vice each stands for. In three stanzas, each Sin creates an effect that is bizarre and repulsive, and leaves an impression of the cloying society within which Lucifera keeps her court.

Spenser is free here to create allegorical expansion by accepting the framework and then setting up resemblances in the incontrovertible demonstration of something definite in the world of sense joined with something equally plausible in the world of conceptual experience. It is a technique which allows his genius full liberty by providing him with occasions upon which to work. Coleridge's remark about fancy operating under conditions of imagination seems to mean precisely that; and we never know when what begins as fancy may not spring into imagination. Nor the other way round. The Seven Deadly Sins are comparable with the episode in the Wandering Wood in the sense that they tend to rely upon equation; each, apart from Lucifera, follows an exact pattern in which an appropriate beast, a typical dress, a representative property, and a characteristic disease, unite to furnish every one with individual appearance and state of mind. The rigidity of the design increases the fancifulness of effect, and yet Spenser finds a chance to invent, or borrow, details of unforeseen originality. Avarice, for example, riding upon a camel (presumably for its Biblical implication) is described in a series of critical terms. He makes his God of wicked pelfe—a word which Spenser uses for Mammon (II. vii. 7), Malbecco (III. ix. 4) and Munera (V. ii. 27), all figures of grasping possessiveness—he is one of this 'faire' band, and his meagre way of living is summed up in the alexandrine concluding the third stanza where

> He led a wretched life unto him selfe unknowne.
>
> I. iv. 28

Such in the ironic phrasing is one of the six 'sage Counsellors' who accompany Pride in her clumsy, pointless expedition.

Lucifera stands out among them as the worst of the seven deadly Sins and the only one whose appearance is not grotesque but misleadingly splendid. Her chariot is drawn by these repellent caricatures of humanity. Their steeds are contrasted with the peacocks of Juno, in a simile which heightens their repulsiveness. Beauty and mythological associations inevitably accompany the image, and since the peacock is an emblem of pride it strengthens the conception Spenser is creating. The simile is there to be rejected for its classical association and at the same time to be preserved for its link with the quality Lucifera represents—one of the throw-away images of which Spenser is a master.

Duessa's journey to the Underworld is part of the epic design which provides one feature of Book I. Readers are reminded of it by the description of the coming of dawn to give brilliance to the progress of time in the narrative (V. ii). Literary convention invites Spenser to introduce scenes in the Underworld and he gives them as much relevance as he can. Duessa is at home in darkness; she claims, as daughter of Deceipt and Shame, a relationship with Night, and drives with her through Hell, to prevail upon Aesculapius to heal Sans-joy. Here begin subordinate stories as a mode of emphasis upon the main action. This is the story of Hippolytus who perishes because of the jealous love of Phedra for him. It is something of a stretch to bring Hippolytus into the Duessa-Night encounter. Hippolytus has been damaged by two monsters and has been protected by Diana; his fate is not unlike the dangers into which the Red Crosse Knight is running and his chastity is the virtue for which Diana defends him and in which the Red Crosse Knight has been conspicuously deficient during his association with Duessa. In effect, the whole of the visit to the Underworld carries less force to the plot than the earlier scenes gave and in that way we become conscious of slackening grasp upon the story for the moment.

The troubles of the Red Crosse Knight have been punctuated by the suffering of Una, parted from him, and the loyalty with which she seeks for him sharpens the impression made by his forgetfulness of her in his satisfaction with Duessa's company. That this company lacks any of the true joyfulness that was given to him by Una is evident from the allegorical comment upon it by the presence of the pagan called Sans-joy and from the nature of the society into which she has brought him. It is further conveyed by the contrasting poetry in which Una's adventures are described. First of all, Spenser directs emotion into another channel by an intervention in his own voice. It is the poet, not the knight, who recalls Una and creates a transition from the Fradubio episode to an analogous situation in which Una's beauty is represented as genuine in the way that Fraelissa's was, and her background shown to be all that Duessa pretended hers to be. The transition is achieved through a direct appeal for the compassion which must be felt for the deserted solitary heroine whom the knight had undertaken to protect and whose Kingdom he was to rescue. It brings the reader back to the ideals Una stood for at the beginning—her royal birth, her fidelity, and her religious grace. The narrative increases this memory through the coming of the lion which as King of Beasts recognises royalty when he sees it and replaces the knight as Una's protector; the contact with Abessa, Corceca

and Kirkrapine carries further the falsity (this time political)
of the world now surrounding Una's champion, and the appearance of Archimago disguised as the Red Crosse Knight leads
Una into greater unreality. She cannot recognise hypocrisy—
how could she?—and it is only the attack by Sans-joy that is
needed to reveal his identity. Sans-loy destroys her sole support
by mortally wounding the lion and carries her off as his victim.
The reader remains wondering at her fate at the end of the
Canto, and the narrative shifts to the House of Pride and the
continuing infidelity of her protector.

At the end of the House of Pride episode, Una's story enters
its second stage. Again there is a change of atmosphere. The
heavy sumptuousness of the Renaissance court surrounding
Lucifera and the dark solemnity of the scenes in Hell both
require a contrast in feeling. Una reaches another world, one
in which Sans-joy is unknown. where Sans-loy is frightened from
his cruelty, and where simplicity and primitive animal vitality
have a place. Spenser describes this world through an innocence
of style which relies on rhythm and repetition and avoids the
sinister vocabulary of Cantos IV and V. The satyrs and wood-
fauns are not virtuous in themselves, but are capable of some
elementary degree of virtue and are responsive to Una's beauty
and to her attempts to teach them goodness. Seen through Sans-
loy's eyes, they are a 'rude, misshapen, monstrous rablement';
seen through Una's, they are humble and compassionate. They
come to her rescue out of the natural world as the lion did
through wholly miraculous intervention. Sans-loy's attack on
Una is described in language heightened to define the allegorical meaning: it is a violation of truth, the action of evil
attempting to destroy the order of the universe and it outrages
the sun and the stars. The appearance of the satyrs brings unassuming gaiety which belongs only to the world of nature.

The verse creates this effect by its dancing movement which
is Spenser's way of expressing the value he sets upon the rural
and spontaneous. The satyrs try to express their sympathy for
Una's grief in their rough fashion because

> The salvage nation feele her secret smart,
> And read her sorrow in her count'nance sad;
>
> I. vi. 11

D

and when she rises to join them they show their unspoiled happiness in a pastoral scene:

> They all as glad, as birdes of joyous Prime,
> Thence lead her forth, about her dauncing round.
> Shouting, and singing all a shepheards ryme,
> And with greene braunches strowing all the ground,
> Do worship her, as Queene, with olive girland cround
>
> And all the way their merry pipes they sound,
> That all the woods with doubled Eccho ring,
> And with their horned feet do weare the ground,
> Leaping like wanton kids in pleasant Spring.
>
> I. vi. 13-14

The repeated present participles and the recurrent 'all' give the rhythm a quality of gladness which lightens the situation and brings a gentle feeling of comedy to Una's relation with them. Her allegorical rôle provides her with a hope of acting as a representative of true faith:

> her gentle wit she plyes,
> To teach them truth, which worshipt her in vaine,
> And made her th'Image of Idolatryes;
> But when their bootlesse zeale she did restraine
> From her own worship, they her Asse would worship fayn.
>
> I. vi. 19

Spenser can never avoid an instinctive sense of the behaviour of humanity, and here the satyrs' inability to distinguish between the truth Una represents and the person of Una herself has to be carried a stage further: if Una will not accept their adoration the ass must take her place. This is a characteristic emblematic scene[1] but Spenser turns it to his own purposes in bringing the satyrs close to his heroine within the story. A comparable event occurs in the introduction of Satyrane. He recognises and has respect for truth, and when he finds Una teaching the satyrs he remains with her to learn the true religion.

Satyrane represents Spenser's belief in the natural goodness of human nature. He is like the Salvage Man in Book VI who was reared in wildness and yet possesses instincts of virtue. He

---

[1] See Alciato *Emblemation Liber*, and Whitney *A Collection of Emblems*.

takes Una away from the primitive environment where he had
found her to continue her search for the Red Crosse Knight.
This scene is a scene of simple beauty and peace but Una cannot stay there long and her search with Satyrane leads her back
into Archimago's world of illusion. He appears disguised as a
Pilgrim, tells another of his lies, and leads Satyrane and Una to
find Sans-loy who is alleged to have slain the Red Crosse
Knight. Una flees when Satyrane fights Sans-loy, and is pursued
by Archimago who hopes to bring her to further disasters.

It is at this moment that the reader is brought back to the
Red Crosse Knight and to his fate. He and the Dwarf have left
Lucifera's abode after the joust and the disappearance of Sans-
joy. It is not surprising, however, that Duessa can still successfully follow him and exercise her charms more dangerously
outside Orgoglio's castle. She finds him resting by a fountain
having removed his armour and leaving his steed to graze
beside it. That he had discovered the character of the House of
Pride is made clear when he and the Dwarf decide to leave it;
that he should have discovered Duessa's falsity is also pointed
out by Spenser's introductory stanza to Canto VII; but he is not
prevented when she rejoins him from making love to her. He
has lost his vigilance and is unprepared for the attack that will
come. He is now

> Pourd out in loosnesse on the grassy grownd,
> Both carelesse of his health, and of his fame;

I. vii. 7

His weakness is reflected in the subsidiary story of the Nymph
who also 'sat down to rest in middest of the race' and whose
well would enfeeble whoever drank of it. His incapacity against
Orgoglio is not the consequence of his having drunk from an
enchanted well, but the well itself is a symptom of his mental
and physical condition. This *epyllion* is a further example of
Spenser's methods of allegory, giving objective narrative form
to the state of mind the knight has now reached. Orgoglio finds
him 'forlorne And left to losse'; he is hopeless and knows himself
to be

> Disarmd, disgrast, and inwardly dismayde.

I. vii. 11

Only heavenly grace can now save him from destruction, Orgoglio sweeps him away unconscious into a dungeon and accepts Duessa's offer to become his mistress.

Orgoglio is typical of another aspect of Spenser's allegory. He is a Giant and in this form represents one kind of violence. The noise he makes is that of thunder; and epic simile elaborates an idea of warfare by reference to cannon, explosion and smoke. He is less easily classifiable as an allegorical figure. He is not labelled in the way Lucifera was. From his name he is identifiable as a form of pride and from the information given about him it is possible to deduce what kind of pride he represents. He is the son of air and earth, who catches the Red Crosse Knight when he has taken off his spiritual armour. In the verbs linked with him, we can associate him with other Giants that stand for ferocity, with Argante and her twin Ollyphant in Book III, and the Giant with the scales in Book V. He puts Duessa on a seven-headed beast, Ignorance is his foster-father, and there has been slaughter of innocent children, Christians, and martyrs at a marble altar within the princely rooms inside his castle. From all this we can draw a strong distinction between the kind of pride Orgoglio stands for and that of Lucifera. Lucifera embodies worldly pride, Orgoglio a limited version of spiritual pride.

Lucifera's pride was decorative in itself and its method was the method of seduction. The pride of Orgoglio captures and destroys by brute force. If it is spiritual pride it is limited to one kind of faith, the kind that in Spenser's view was the result of ignorance and the cause of the Inquisition. The allegory is political allegory, whereas the allegory of Lucifera has a general ethical application. The success of Arthur and Una is the success of the Anglican church against the Roman Catholic, and the exposure of Orgoglio depends upon historical interpretation and only upon that. There have been other interpretations of the meaning of the allegory in this section but all imply that none of it is altogether clear.[1] Since it is the method

[1] 'Lucifera, the pride of Luxury and worldliness, and Orgoglio the pride of brutality.' *The Faerie Queene*, Book I. Ed. F. W. Kitchen. Oxford University Press, 1905, p. 193.
. . . 'Not the pride of life, spiritual and subtle, but the common or vulgar

of allegory with which we are principally concerned we must relate the techniques Spenser is using here to the techniques he uses in other Books and it is evident that Giants never assume so convincing a rôle as regards good or evil as human figures or monsters. Archimago, Duessa and Lucifera on the one side, Mammon and Guile in Books II and V, the monster Error and the dragon Sin on the other, make a greater imaginative impact than Orgoglio. Yet, at this stage in the narrative Orgoglio has gained complete conquest of the Red Crosse Knight. Only Duessa's appeal saves his life, and the Giant is glad to cast him into the total blackness of a dungeon. The gentle knight whose story had begun so hopefully in the journey across the plain into the Wandering Wood, and whose first trial had ended so promisingly, has been reduced to a state of utter destitution.

ii

All that can now be done is to pick up Una's part of the story and to make the Dwarf who has been with the knight until his final disaster the juncture between the two. He brings Una to Arthur and takes both to Orgoglio's castle where the Red Crosse Knight is imprisoned. Like Lear's Fool, that is the last we see of him. A minor, always trustworthy figure, he is paid the last tribute for his rôle at the end of Canto VII:

So forth they went, the Dwarfe them guiding ever right.

He has led the abandoned horse and carried the knight's armour, 'missing most at need', his silver shield 'now idle, maisterless', and all 'the rueful moniments of heavinesse', to Una. It is to Una that the plot must now shift. She rapidly interprets the message of the Dwarf's burden, and, concluding that her knight is dead, begins a lament for him which becomes an impersonal, generalised lament by Truth for man's fall. Her grief is grief for all mankind as well as for her own lost

pride in the power of this world; and his throwing of the Red Cross Knight into the dungeon is a type of the captivity of true religion under the temporal power of corrupt churches . . . and of its gradually wasting away in unknown places, while carnal pride has pre-eminence over all things.' Ruskin.

lover, and the Dwarf restores the tale to the main plot by giving a brief retrospect of what has occurred since her parting from her champion during the night in Archimago's cell. Together they set out through the romance landscape—'High over hils, and lowe adowne the dale' (or, as Tennyson was later to write, 'over the hills and far away')—with Una absorbed in her feeling for the knight 'For greater love, the greater is the losse'.

It is at this point that Arthur makes his first appearance and Spenser now finds the moment to describe him fully and write of him in a style which will both fit him into the context of Book I and into the whole poem. The description is fine enough to outweigh that of any other figure so far seen, for here is a man of greater stature than the rest, whose person is marked by a splendour which gives him immediate prominence. Gold shines on his helmet and sword hilt, ivory implants richness in its sheath, precious stones twinkle like stars over his armour, and dancing colours enliven the hairs above his crest. An enchanting simile is introduced to create a scene of natural beauty in this world of artifice. The armour is the armour made by a great designer; it includes a famous magical shield containing one central stone shining like Hesperus among the lesser stars, and an elaborate crest of a dragon made up of a fiery sparkling mouth and a long scaly tail hanging down the surcoat. Yet the simile strikes a new note:

> Upon the top of all his loftie crest,
>   A bunch of haires discoloured diversly,
>   With sprincled pearle, and gold full richly drest,
>   Did shake, and seem'd to daunce for jollity,
>   Like to an Almond tree ymounted hye
> On top of greene *Selinis* all alone,
>   With blossomes brave bedecked daintily;
>   Whose tender locks do tremble every one
> At every little breath, that under heaven is blowne.
>
> I. vii. 32

It is a note which impressed Marlowe and was borrowed by him in *Tamburlaine* to increase the glory of the picture Tamburlaine draws of himself as 'Emperor of the three-fold world'. Marlowe's version is more hyperbolic and lacks the Spenserian surprise of 'all alone'.

Like to an almond tree ymounted high
Upon the lofty and celestial mount
Of ever green *Selinis* queintly dect
With bloomes more white than Hericinas browes,
Whose tender blossomes tremble every one,
At every little breath that thorow heaven is blowen.[1]

The individuality of Spenser's simile lies in the spellbinding quality of the isolation of the tree, and in its avoidance of the repetition which occurs in Marlowe's phrasing—i.e. 'ymounted —mount' and 'bloomes—blossomes', not to mention the vagueness of 'queintly dect'.

Arthur is outstanding both within the frame of the allegory and in the story. Allegorically, he reflects all that the Red Crosse Knight ought to have been as patron of Holiness, and, fictionally, he is the courteous understanding stranger to whom Una can define her own background. From her account more is learnt about the quest which the Red Crosse Knight is fulfilling. Una's world is the world of Eden where her parents as King and Queen

Did spread their rule through all the territories,
Which *Phison* and *Euphrates* floweth by,
And *Gehons* golden waves doe wash continually.

I. vii. 43

(Duessa's parents ruled over a different world as Emperor of the West, we may remember.) Attacked by a huge dragon, it needed the rescue from a 'fresh unproved knight' such as would be discovered in the court of Gloriana. All others had failed either for want of faith or guilt of sin, and this failure was now demonstrated in the knight whom she had chosen. Her own emotion about him was firmly expounded to Arthur. His

[1] *Tamburlaine*, Part II, 4096-4103. The Marlowe-Spenser link has been debated since the eighteenth century when critics noticed the similarity between the two passages. Todd defended Spenser from plagiarism on the grounds that Book I had been handed about in manuscript and that Abraham Fraunce had quoted accurately II. 4. 35 in *Arcadian Rhetoric*. Other passages have also been quoted to suggest that it was Marlowe who did the borrowing rather than Spenser. See *Variorum* I, pp. 252-253 and discussion by T. W. Baldwin, ELH 1942, pp. 156-187, and W. B. C. Watkins ELH 1944, pp. 248-265.

allegorical and personal quality enabled him to grasp both the
force of her religion and the power of her love:

> Be judge ye heavens, that all things right esteeme,
> How I him lov'd, and love with all my might,
> So thought I eke of him, and think I thought aright.
>
> I. vii. 49

Her continual sense of what is appropriate comes out in her
characteristic plain statements. Una here refers to the religious
theme borne by the allegory and at the same time can speak
with moving simplicity as a woman. Arthur also responds
allegorically, for he will later come to life as a human being
sharing with her the capacity for extreme love. At this stage,
however, he indicates to her the importance of seeking help
from one who can supply it. Spenser depends on stichomythia
as the basis of their dialogue, a style which produces stiffness
and lack of humanity and is not usually to be found as Una's
natural mode of expression. Arthur invites her confidence (vii.
40) on the grounds that no one finds help who does not impart
the ills he has suffered, and the debate that follows anticipates
the later scene in which the Red Crosse Knight and Una
encounter Despair. We may conclude that out of this formalised
dialogue, Una (and Spenser's readers) have learnt something
which will emerge more powerfully during the scene with
Despair:

> O but (quoth she) great griefe will not be tould,
>   And can more easily be thought, then said.
>   Right so; (quoth he) but he, that never would,
>   Could never: will to might gives greatest aid.
>   But griefe (quoth she) does greater grow displaid,
>   If then it find not helpe and breedes despaire.
>   Despaire breedes not (quoth he) where faith is staid.
>   No faith so fast (quoth she) but flesh does paire.
> Flesh may empaire (quoth he) but reason can repaire.
>
> I. vii. 41

The source of despair which the knight is to discover after his
rescue and its final banishment by faith and reason in the House
of Holiness to which Una will lead him are both prognosticated

in this stanza. Arthur plays many parts in *The Faerie Queene* and here he is not only looking forward to the Despair scene and its sequel from which he will be absent, but also to the solid character of the Palmer in Book II.

Una, well aware of the disastrous power of the flesh acting against the faith and reason of the Red Crosse Knight, accepts Arthur's argument and is ready to ask him to bring deliverance to Orgoglio's victim. Arthur, the hero of the poem, shows himself physically and morally stronger than the hero of Book I, just as he will outshine Guyon in Book II. His battle with Orgoglio is a typical struggle between Giant and knight. What distinguishes it is the scale and the interpretation it enables the reader to put upon this particular Giant. Simile after simile creates the impression of violence: Orgoglio brings the force of a thunderstorm into the battle, his wounded arm pours out blood like a stream from a rock, he roars like a herd of bulls, and in a last ferocious effort he tears aside the covering of Arthur's shield and thus dazzled can fight no more. Then he tumbles 'as an aged tree' or 'as a castle'. Each metaphor and simile is given sound and weight until collectively a scene of uproar and tremendous vigour is built up. Then the huge roaring body dwindles into the little thing it truly was,

> and of that monstrous mas
> Was nothing left, but like an emptie bladder was.

One of Spenser's remarkable powers lies in his ability to change tone without producing anti-climax. The battle has been crude and fierce and has left in the reader's mind a recognition of what Orgoglio or Pride stood for and what Duessa chose for her lover in place of the knight he had captured. It is followed by the simple plain language of Una's gratitude, her 'sober gladnesse' and 'myld modestie', and by the account of Ignaro discovered by Arthur in the desolate castle where the Giant had carried on his murderous activities and had furnished as a royal palace for himself and Duessa. Ignaro is portrayed as a ludicrous figure, a further means of reducing the arrogance of Orgoglio to its unworthy level. When Arthur enters the castle he finds it mysteriously silent and undefended: in atmosphere it looks forward to that other sinister place,

D *

gorgeously decorated, where Britomart forces an entrance. Both appear beautiful and evil. Only here, in Book I, the villainy is openly defined in signs of human sacrifice conducted by ecclesiastical tyranny upon Protestant martyrs slain at the altar of the false faith of Orgoglio and Duessa. Here too lies the Red Crosse Knight, groaning in a dungeon.

Arthur's share in the allegory is set out clearly enough in his defeat of Orgoglio and his exploration of the Giant's castle. It will be carried further in his exchange of presents with the patron of Holiness. Meanwhile his more realistic aspect is not neglected; it is brought out in his dealing with Ignaro and will emerge later in his account of his personal contact with Gloriana. Ignaro is devised on the principles of emblem books but he is also portrayed naturalistically. From one point of view he derives from unrealistic personification:

> But very uncouth sight was to behold,
>> How he did fashion his untoward pace,
>> For as he forward moov'd his footing old,
>> So backward still was turnd his wrincled face,
>> Unlike to men, who ever as they trace,
>> Both feet and face one way are wont to lead.
>
> I. viii. 31

Yet Spenser treats him as if he were a credible human figure, and Arthur regards 'his reverend haires and holy gravitie' as objects for respect until his mental condition becomes obvious. Gentle enquiry draws a total blank: each question Arthur asks —where the occupants of the castle are, where the Red Crosse Knight is imprisoned, which way he might go—produces an identical response 'he could not tell'. Arthur, foiled by this stupidity, realises that his appearance of aged gravity belies him. Possessing himself of the rusty keys the old man is holding, he goes through the castle alone. On this occasion Spenser is introducing an arbitrary conception which he also treats naturalistically for a special effect. The name, Ignaro, provides one clue, the curious appearance and absurd mode of progression another, but as soon as Arthur in his heroic aspect comes into contact with such a creature Spenser develops all the laughable qualities and makes him the object of scorn and mockery. Ignaro is an abstraction when he is first encountered,[1] but appears to behave like a human being, thus creating wrath in the mind of Arthur and mirth among the readers.

A comparable use of comedy also occurs in Book I when the Red Crosse Knight has killed the Dragon, finally achieving his quest and destroying the Sin represented by the beast. After this, a religious struggle interpretable in terms of faith and doctrinal history, the crowd gathers to see the creature which has long brought terror into their lives and to their rulers. Ignorant of all that the Dragon represents, they treat it just as a crowd will treat a danger now made harmless and now in part attractive:

> Some feard, and fled; some feard and well it faynd;
>   One that would wiser seeme then all the rest,
>   Warnd him not touch, for yet perhaps remaynd
>   Some lingring life within his hollow brest,
>   Or in his wombe might lurke some hidden nest
>   Of many Dragonets, his fruitful seed;
>   Another said, that in his eyes did rest
>   Yet sparckling fire, and bad thereof take heed;
> Another said, he saw him move his eyes indeed.
>
> One mother, when as her foolehardie chyld
>   Did come too neare, and with his talants play,
>   Halfe dead through feare, her litle babe revyld,
>   And to her gossips gan in counsell say;
>   How can I tell but that his talants may
>   Yet scratch my sonne, or rend his tender hand?
>   So diversly themselves in vaine they fray;
>   While some more bold, to measure him nigh stand,
> To prove how many acres he did spread of land.
>
>   I. xii. 10, 11

The Ignaro scene is less psychologically far-ranging than this but it achieves something of the same bizarre effect, through depending upon one repeated phrase. For the crowd, Spenser has introduced his considerable knowledge of human weakness, cowardice, pride, social superiority and general habits of knowing better than anyone else, ingenious theories about the 'many dragonets', maternal instinct, and masculine interest in factual

---

[1] The source is unknown to us. The figure can be associated with 'January' which looks before and after, but Spenser's comment on it seems to suggest that a definite emblem is being recalled.

information; the strife with the dragon is over and the poet is able, as he was at the end of the Orgoglio incident, to bring his allegorical world into the ordinary state of being and prove that after all the people who have experienced great terror are the normal, rather self-satisfied persons to be seen in all times and places.

Duessa after the defeat of Orgoglio and the release of his prisoner is in the power of Arthur. Stripped of her glamour, she is revealed as the evil figure whom Fradubio long ago had prepared readers to see. Here, at last, Una has the decisive phrase to sum up all that the Red Crosse Knight has committed himself to. Fradubio could only say that he had once seen her as a witch (I. ii. 40 and 41); Una, whose truth and honour have been demonstrated so often during her separation from her hero, has free choice as to what should be done with Duessa now that her protector is dead. She chooses, wisely and unforgettably. Duessa is to be seen once more as she really is. The inevitable logic of the plot winds the deceptiveness of Duessa to its close, and Una rightly formulates what the narrative has been recounting all the while:

> Such then (said *Una*) as she seemeth here,
> Such is the face of falshood, such the sight
> Of fowle *Duessa*, when her borrowed light
> Is laid away, and counterfesaunce knowne.
>
> I. viii. 49

Even though the literalness and the physical ugliness as described by Spenser diminishes the repugnance he intends to create, the power of Una's dismissal brings a strong conclusion to the tragedy of delusion in which Duessa had embroiled the Red Crosse Knight. Now he is free to find his way forward supported by Arthur and Una.

The time for parting arrives. Arthur tells them of his upbringing and his dream of the love which will come to him, and each presents to the other gifts appropriate to their allegorical rôle. Arthur's personal story gives solidity to his function in the entire Book while his search for the Queene of the Faeries underlines his comprehension of the emotion Una has described to him on their first meeting. Spenser can make a magic episode out of a love story in the way reminiscent of Coleridge's account of a man's dream of his visit to Paradise.[1] Arthur describes how the royal maid came to talk with him and lay down by his side speaking words unheard by living men. When he awoke in the morning he found 'nought but the pressed grass where she had lyen'. The story comes across in that memorable phrase just as Coleridge's man wakes to find himself still holding the flower he had been given in Paradise—'Ay? and what then?' Both tales leave a proof and a mystery. Arthur will continue his search preserving a lyrical assurance in his decision:

> From that day forth I lov'd that face divine;
> From that day forth I cast in carefull mind,
> To seeke her out with labour, and long tyne,
> Ane never vow to rest, till her I find.
>
> I. ix. 15

This was what made him the source of the knight's salvation and the ready interpreter of Una's plight. The pledges each presented to the other again sum up what each stood for; from Arthur was handed a diamond and gold box containing drops of curative liquid, perhaps a sign of heavenly grace that can heal all sin or perhaps a sign of the love that motivates all his actions; and from the patron of Holiness was handed a New Testament, evidence of the nature of the Holiness that the Red Crosse Knight still seeks.

iii

Una, recognising the physical weakness of her protector, remains unwilling to press him forward towards the fulfilment of his quest. Her caution is justified in the incident which follows. It is, in fact, the scene with Despair rather than the fight with the Dragon which creates the greatest emotional intensity in Book I. This is because the various elements out of which Spenser's allegory is made meet in a single occasion, coincide, and cohere. In the narrative, regarded solely as a romance adventure, a different kind of climax is reached: the knight has been in danger of death before, when fighting with Error at the beginning, in single combat, with Sans-loy, then with Sans-joy,

[1] Coleridge, *Anima poetae*, p. 238.

and on his capture by Orgoglio. Each time his escape was narrower and each time his victory was only partial; he slew Error only to fall into a greater error with Archimago, he slew Sans-loy only to win Duessa, Sans-joy vanished from him in a black mist, Orgoglio imprisoned him. This time the danger of death comes from within, not from outside, and through the agency not of a human being, not of a monster, nor of a giant, but of a 'a man of hell'. We know from the experience of this particular book and from the whole poem that the most formidable figures are neither human beings nor any kind of personification, but creatures that look like men, Archimago, Despair, Mammon (in Book II), Guile (in Book V) and prove to be fiends. This incident, too, is prepared for by Sir Trevisan's story and the reality with which his terror is presented. 'For loe he comes, he comes fast after mee.' His hesitating acceptance of the knight's assurances, 'And am I now in safetie sure', indicates the blank fear within his mind. All that Despair may do, and the way he may do it, is foreshadowed in the image of the snake 'creeping close' and in the recollection of the enfeebling fountain which had put the Red Crosse Knight into the power of Orgoglio:

> His subtill tongue, like dropping honny, mealt'th
> Into the hart, and searcheth every vaine,
> That ere one be aware, by secret stealth
> His powre is reft, and weaknesse doth remaine.

I. ix. 31

As Upton observed, 'No one had ever such a power of raising visions and images as Spenser' and the sense of extreme fear experienced by Trevisan is a remarkable illustration of this observation.

If one wished to read the poem apart from the allegory, these two elements would be enough to indicate that the impending scene is to become critical. But the development of the plot has led us to expect Despair: the knight has already encountered Sans-joy, has already longed for the 'happy choyce of Death' in his dungeon, and Una and Arthur have already heralded the conflict in their conversation. Moreover, the career of the Red Crosse Knight as the Knight of Holiness, has been that of progressive failure: he has moved further and further away from his vocation, through the House of Pride and its deadly Sins, to his dalliance with Duessa, from positive, recognisable worldliness to its spiritual consequences in his loss of his armour of Faith and the strength to fight an obviously wicked Giant. Devotionally, the meeting with Despair marks the final stage of his downfall.

The scene itself is presented in a way consistent with its allegorical intention. In contrast with the splendour of Lucifera and with the monstrous brutality of Orgoglio, Despair is a desolate, meagre figure dwelling 'low in an hollow cave' and surrounded by an equally desolate landscape.[1] The setting is, as in the Wood of Error, an extension of the character: a wasteland of rocks and leafless trees, a place that contrasts not only with the partial beauty of Lucifera's house, but also with the real beauty of the woodland where Una spent time with the satyrs.[2] In its minor details it may appear theatrical,[3] as Spenser's borrowings from classical portrayals of hell are apt to be, but its main function of creating a visible image of a mental state within the medium of allegory is successfully carried out. This is an experience of the mind, set out partly in the personification of the concept of despair, and partly in the guileful train of argument which the knight is to encounter. Our recognition of its sterility is sharpened by the memory of the life brought into the poem by the forest world of the satyrs

[1] Despair was personified in Higgins's contribution to the *Mirror for Magistrates* in the tragedy of Cordelia and the analogue between this and Spenser's episode was first pointed out by Warton. Higgins's *Despair* is represented by a ghostly figure of a woman who approaches Cordelia in her prison 'with stealing steps', calls herself Cordelia's friend, offers her a choice of means of suicide, and fortifies her argument by recalling past joys and present misery. Yet there is nothing of the sophistry of the Spenserian argument, and Higgins raises none of the particular issues which concerned the Red Crosse Knight. His narrative is a straightforward statement of the familiar contrast between past and present of the Fall of Princes with the introduction of Despair to motivate suicide and to deny hope. See Lily B. Campbell's edition of *Parts added to the Mirror for Magistrates by John Higgins and Thomas Blenerhasset*. C.U.P., 1946, pp. 145-160. It was printed in 1574.

[2] See Spenser's use of trees as symbols of life and death in Chapter III, pp. 64-5.

[3] Spenser's failure to give reality to such borrowings is pointed out by Douglas Bush in *Mythology and the Renaissance Tradition*, pp. 86-123.

where Una finds a sense of joyful abandon, natural and legitimate, full of pathos, perhaps, because primitive and non-human, yet more desirable than anything the knight saw in the House of Pride for all his victory over Sans-joy. Spenser makes no explicit contrast: it is not within his programme to underline such a difference, for the satyrs are incapable of the more exalted kinds of joy open to the Knight of Holiness and to Una. But the difference is none the less there. It exists inside the frame of the allegory so that the gaiety of the earlier scene makes the grey lifelessness and the solitude of Despair's world with the languorous clinging movement of his speech more distinct for the reader. It is truly a 'universe of death', spiritually as well as physically; and Milton in a differently organised poem, suggesting a greater contrast, could remember Spenser's unstated comparison and find for it open expression in the phrase 'Oh how unlike the place from whence they fell' (*Paradise Lost*, I. 75).

The scene with Despair belongs to a sequence of states of mind as well as of events, and it is defined in part at least by its position in that sequence. It makes a comment on all that has passed: the House of Pride appears more evil when we judge it by its consequences; the scene in the forest more nostalgic when we regard it as a lost world never to be experienced by the Red Crosse Knight. But apart from that relation with the whole Book, the persuasiveness of the arguments of Despair, are as I have suggested, given weight in the anticipatory study of their effect upon Trevisan. In the extremity of fear to which they drive him and have driven his companion, we have a means of measuring their power. Despair's arguments are seductive and insidious; in what precisely their incisiveness consists we have yet to see, but we readily absorb the surroundings in which they occur. 'Every estate and vocation should be known by the differences of their habit' was Puttenham's notion of the connection between appearance and reality, and the ragged clothing of Despair and its patching by *thorns* conveyed a meaning to Elizabethans accustomed to conceptions not said explicitly.[1]

What this evil creature does in fact do is to interlace an emotional appeal with arguments based upon half-true religious

[1] Puttenham, *The Arte of English Poesie*, ed. G. D. Willcock and Alice Walker, 1936, p. 283.

doctrines, linked with each other by only the appearance of logic. He drives them home by skilful placing of references to the knight's personal life, so that his case is at once an account of the human condition in general and that of the Red Crosse Knight in particular. By this means he plucks away hope and leaves only desolation. The particular arguments are a summary of what has already been exposed in the course of the narrative and are corroborated by what the hero knows only too well and what the readers have witnessed. The general arguments are those which Spenser will return to in other parts of the poem: they turn on mutability, on justice, and on human suffering, ideas which are elaborated elsewhere in the action of *The Faerie Queene*. If one wants to concentrate on one single aspect of Spenser's imaginative greatness, one can rightly set these discussions in the tenor of the whole poem. Intellectually and emotionally expressed debates reign unforgettably in scenes between Guyon and Mammon (Book II), between Artegall and the Giant (Book V), between Artegall and Burbon (Book VI), and in the Mutability Cantos, and if Despair is demonstrated wrong by Una, part at least of his case is raised elsewhere in terms of virtues other than Holiness. Artegall does in fact reproduce one of Despair's arguments, that of the ultimate ordering of the universe and with it the destiny of man, in order to vanquish the Giant of equity. And in the final assessment of Book VII, Mutability is shown to be both right and wrong.

Consequently, here in Book I, we meet for the first time a recurring feature of Spenser's allegory. His method of exposing the arguments of the wicked is to question their premises and to concede to the representative of virtue a simplicity of statement which cuts across the tortuosity of the tempter. Thus Guyon can say 'All otherwise I riches read' and Artegall will counter Burbon's defence of temporising by offering another conception of truth which excludes double-dealing. This is a distinction which only virtue can draw because its representative removes the argument into a different field and finds another mode of expression. Here we can notice one of the lessons which Milton learned from Spenser. Comus seems to possess all the literary rhetorical arts, yet it is the Lady's simplicity of style which is victorious. Similarly, Satan offers a specious subtlety of argument and we know that Eve has no weapon against it. The Red Crosse Knight equally has no answer to Despair, and it is Una who ultimately destroys his case by setting against his doctrine of God's justice the orthodox statement of the atonement, thus conveying the incompleteness of the thesis demonstrated by her antagonist.

Despair's methods of reasoning may well have been acquired by Spenser during his years at Cambridge for it is just the kind of sophistical argument which suggests an interest in the techniques of logic and an experience of induction and deduction which these involve. The knight makes two propositions each arising from the particular circumstances of the dead knight outside the cave, and Despair appears to concede the premises and then builds up an argument in the opposite sense, partly by bringing in fresh propositions which are not within the scope of the original theory and partly by making unwarrantable deductions from the premises he has granted. In form as well as in content, his argument is fallacious and when to this speciousness is added an art of presentation which annuls the critical faculty by its lingering rhythm, its strongly evocative phraseology, and a vocabulary charged with emotional associations, there enters upon the mind a consciousness of another realm of thought altogether, one that can never be more than adumbrated by suggestion and is known in dreams and trances with greater certainty than in the conscious operation of the intellect. Thus when the Red Crosse Knight maintains that eternal justice will never permit the slaughter of Sir Terwin, the term 'justice' is snatched up and twisted into the idea that it can always be rightly applied against those whose conduct does not merit their continuing existence. And from this point Despair moves to the idea that the dead man is better off than the Red Crosse Knight because:

> He there does now enjoy eternall rest
> And happie ease, which thou doest want and crave,
> And further from it daily wanderest.
>
> I. ix. 40

He creates an emotional appeal and drives it straight home to the Red Crosse Knight's life. When the knight tries another line, that a man may not decide on the length of his life any

more than a soldier may abandon his watch until his captain
gives him permission, Despair again twists the notion in a number of different directions, slipping from point to point to make
an alluring image of the advantage of death. On the logical side,
he seizes the knight's characteristic military analogy and maintains that a sentinel is always permitted to leave 'at sound of
morning droome', and he ascribes the time of death to the order
of destiny so that when the hour comes 'let none aske whence,
nor why'. All this creates an effect of inexplicability, and Despair
moves to the attractions of self-destruction: the longer the life,
the greater the sins perpetrated by man and the more terrible
the punishment; further, living itself has so little in its nature
to invite man to remain alive, for

> Feare, sicknesse, age, losse, labour, sorrow, strife,
> Paine, hunger, cold, that makes the hart to quake;
> And ever fickle fortune rageth rife,
> All which, and thousands mo do make a loathsome life.
>
> I. ix. 44

The knight has no verbal equipment to meet the voice of this
lotus-eater. A picture of escape has been drawn which is hard to
avoid, and the arguments are pressed through the recollection
of all that his victim has done and so fatally thought since the
beginning of his quest. That there are contradictions in his
argument, that the idea of the peace of death is totally inconsistent with the idea of punishment in hell, tends to be obscured
by the strange spell-binding quality of the words. The poetry, in
fact, contains some of Spenser's most memorable generalisations springing out of a powerful application to all that we have
seen and shared in the narrative. Upton suggests that a parallel
should be made between this and Eve's plea for suicide in
Paradise Lost, X. 979, but the real likeness is surely reflected in
Adam's soliloquy, with its sad, nostalgic rhythm and recognisable wrongness of thought:

> How gladly would I meet
> Mortalitie my sentence, and be Earth
> Insensible, how glad would lay me down
> As in my Mother's lap? There I should rest
> And sleep secure;
>
> (*Paradise Lost*, X. 775-779)

Despair is one of Spenser's great imaginative figures, coming from a world alien to humanity, not necessarily hostile, nor friendly, but simply alien. He is hung about with mystery and lurks on the fringe of the unknown and unknowable. However irrational his arguments prove on examination to be, he creates an impression which the knight's belief in reason, in duty, in the path of the true warfaring Christian, cannot wholly gainsay. The most deadly of the temptations that assail Spenser's heroes in all the Books is the creeping consciousness of the limitations of human perception. The only guides he has to grasp are his virtues—that is why Guyon meditates upon them during his journey in pursuit of Acrasia. Hence the real villains in *The Faerie Queene* are protean: in person, figures like Archimago, Proteus and Guile, masters of physical delusion; and in thought, those like Despair and Mammon, who keep shifting their ground to make the argument appear to be about something different from the agreed premises from which it started.

On the other side are the virtuous characters, primarily women, who can cut across the subtleties of the wicked and take the topic on to another plane. In this episode, Una not only brings to the Knight a different outlook, but also a strong rebuke to shock him out of his susceptibility to Despair's infectious vision. The appearance of scriptural authority based on Mosaic dogma is countered by her with Pauline interpretations. Her only response to Despair's doctrines must be vision of a different calibre. She reminds the Knight of the obligations undertaken in his profession, the battle for her against the 'fire-mouthed Dragon, terrible and bright'; she reminds him of the nature of heavenly justice which is independent of Despair's misused term of 'great grace' because:

> Where justice growes, there grows eke greater grace,
> The which doth quench the brond of hellish smart,
> And that accurst hand writing doth deface.
>
> I. ix. 53

and she couches her reminder in dramatic language deliberately contrary to the slow lyrical movement of the verse to which Red Crosse is succumbing. Una fiercely ignores the poetic skill upon which her antagonist has built his enchantment and replaces it with a vigorous plea for action. Speed breaks down the passivity she has to meet. 'Fie, fie, faint harted Knight', and 'Come, come away, fraile, feeble, fleshey wight' bring a new scornful vocabulary into the situation. Una's intelligence and her fidelity has been seen throughout the narrative and here Spenser can draw on it plausibly and economically. Characteristic at this moment is verse that can with complete simplicity outweigh the magic of the poetry which has preceded it. This is one of Spenser's triumphs, for it hardly seemed possible to introduce a stronger power to defeat that of Despair's poetry. That he succeeds in doing just this is proof of an ability to free himself from his own poetic gifts, and replace them with others.

Each separate incident in Book I provides a distinct introduction to Spenser's style in *The Faerie Queene*, and it has seemed useful to spend some time upon each. The scene with Despair makes an especially strong impact because it depends upon so much of Spenser's art. It is, after all, the genius for poetry which makes the whole book endlessly readable and, unlike Una, we cannot ignore the richness of the invocation to death which marks this episode. Despair is clearly condemned, but *as* poetry, his speeches are unforgettable. No other passage in Book I is remarkable in the same degree, because the use of the stanza form, the metre, the metaphors and vocabulary, the variety of rhetorical devices all add up to that melancholy rhythm which becomes so haunting in Spenser's work. We can find it briefly in other sections, in the quiet of Morpheus's sleep, in Cymoent's lament for Marinell, in Belge's sadness for her captured country, but it is in this single part that the essence of his style is present at such length. It was naturally a temptation to regard it as the climax to the Book, in place of the final triumph of the Red Crosse Knight in his defeat of the Dragon.

iv

Spenser, however, has ensured due continuous reading by giving Una the rôle of a forward-looking character so that her energy may sweep the story onward. He also insists on the necessity for a cure for the knight's moral debility and readiness to lapse from his purpose by recalling all that has occurred during his past. It had been in the House of Pride that the

knight's service to Duessa conspicuously took place and therefore the introduction of another House is properly required to
balance that. The House of Holiness observes the same allegorical pattern as that of Lucifera. Caelia occupies a central position, and a number of personified figures are comparable in
technique with the personifications in the House of Pride.

Granted this parallel in structure, there is no strong departure
from the content in the previous episodes. We must be brought
back to those by reminiscences of what the Red Crosse Knight
longed for in his desperation in Orgoglio's dungeon and by the
description of the single figure of Ignaro who is an old man,
much like Humilità, the ancient Porter of the House of Holiness. Yet a distinction in method divides them sharply. Ignaro
is:

> An old old man, with beard as white as snow,
> That on a staffe his feeble steps did frame,
> And guide his wearie gate both too and fro.
>
> I. viii. 30

Humilità appears similarly:

> He was an aged syre, all hory gray,
> With lookes full lowly cast, and gate full slow,
> Wont on a staffe his feeble steps to stay
>
> I. x. 5

None the less, they are kept far apart. Ignaro, as we have
already seen is presented partly in caricature with his back-
ward-looking face, his bunch of rusty unused keys, and in his
inability to answer the questions asked by Arthur. Humilità has
a function which fits into his character. He looks humbly to the
ground and he can lead his visitors through the symbolic
entrance which is straight and narrow, like the path to heaven.
The figures they are to meet recall technically the appearance
and manner of those in Lucifera's court; only none is on the
edge of caricature as were the Deadly Sins. Nor is there any
recognisable iconography for them, but each possesses the
merits of his nature: Zele is known by courtliness and vitality,
Reverence by modesty and unpretentiousness; while Caelia,
heavenly in name and nature, welcomes Una as one of an
admirable race. Her children, embodiments of the theological

virtues, are dressed in emblematic attire and accompanied by representative devices. These are inevitably linked typologically with illustrations in Emblem Books and in Natalis Comes and Ripa, and from *The Faerie Queene* they have acquired circulation as Peacham's *Compleat Gentleman* indicates. Fidelia, dressed in white, carries a golden cup enclosing the serpent of wisdom and a book containing doctrines of faith. Speranza, dressed in blue, always the colour of hope, rests upon an anchor.

The knight is impelled to learn from Fidelia what Una had attempted to make him understand so that she could withdraw him from Despair's temptations. These are matters:

> Of God, of grace, of justice, of free will.

The power of faith is demonstrated through its wide influence over the universe. The Red Crosse Knight becomes too well aware of his unworthiness in the sight of God, of his absence of grace, and of his mistaken use of the free will which had been granted to him. Speranza can only help by enabling him to forget the theological learning Faith has set before him. He has, therefore, to gain inward improvement based on patience, amendment, penance, remorse and repentance. This amounts to the catholic foundation of the Anglican church, for which monastic regulations formed the basis, not a puritan set of assumptions. It is only after physical and mental suffering that the knight achieves due qualifications and becomes in consequence worthy to meet the third daughter, Charissa, who stands for true love. She, like her sisters, is described in terms of symbolical imagery. Her garment is yellow, she wears a coronet of gold and is seated in an ivory chair, with a pair of turtle doves as a device beside her. As in Ripa, she is surrounded by a group of children, the embodiment of perfected love, and she is able to teach the aspects of faith and hope which Fidelia and Speranza had had to omit: the quality of devotion and of ideal goodness. The operations of the seven works of mercy are subsequently employed, demonstrated in the actions of seven Beadsmen which Mercy leads him to witness at Charissa's request. Finally, the knight, in the care of Contemplation, progresses to the vision of Salem.

The House of Holiness is designed to balance the earlier

House of Pride, but its allegorical method is concentrated primarily upon ideas rather than upon appearances as such. Fidelia, Speranza and Charissa are iconographic figures, dependent upon familiar, early recognised, formulae.[1] Apart from them, the individual characters are absorbed into the themes of the allegory, and the emphasis rests upon the development of moral and spiritual conceptions. For this reason, Spenser is prepared to write in direct narrative style. The seven works of Mercy are described as religious actions. The three Mounts to which Contemplation leads the Red Crosse Knight express the highest reaches of human experience; they are Mount Sinai, the Mount of Olives and Mount Parnassus, the contribution of the Old Testament, the contribution of the New Testament, and the contribution of poetry. This juncture is not in any way blasphemous. Spenser would not allow his opportunism to lead him astray but links the three together because they are naturally consistent with his most profound sense of values. Similarly, the new Jerusalem is rightly connected with Cleopolis, its earthly parallel, and the knight is truly identified as Saint George but also properly addressed by Contemplation as 'thou man of earth'—the Greek term of γεώργιος. After his vision he is required to carry on his pilgrimage and to gain his title and his claim for entry to the new Jerusalem from his success against the dragon of Sin.

Allegory in Book I varies in power, and although the House of Holiness is artistically far less impressive than the House of Pride it possesses an ability to draw together literary methods which have been employed throughout the plot. There is nothing contradictory in its technique, only a change of emphasis. The religious element becomes more prominent and in that sense it prepares for the piety in the final battle which St George must conduct against the embodiment of Sin in the Dragon. The articulation of the narrative depends upon Spenser's consciousness of what is primarily important to the plot of the entire action. Consequently, the climax underlines the elements presented in the House of Holiness as well as those included in the previous scenes where the Red Crosse Knight became involved during his first sinful adventures.

[1] See quotations from Peacham in R. Freeman, *English Emblem Books*, p. 81.

The concluding section of the Book makes heavy demands upon Spenser's ability to control the material out of which the allegory has been constructed. The knight's quest has been directed against the Dragon of Sin and it must be an enemy worth destruction. It must be more powerful than the monster fought at the beginning, and more powerful, too, than the Giant who captured the knight at his weakest state. It has to be evil enough to threaten the peace of the country ruled over by the King and Queen of Eden and satanic enough to require a sojourn in the House of Holiness before the knight can hope to kill it. Moreover, it must be portrayed on a great enough scale to manifest the total impact, both of the plot and of the allegory.

Of course, the difficulties are enormous and Spenser's capacity to meet them is not altogether sufficient. There is genuine success in his realisation that the plot is part of an epic as well as of a morality. His voice is heard appealing to the Muse to assist him just as Homer and Virgil begin their epics with an address to Clio. Here, however, the Muse is sacred, ready to empower the Knight of Holiness. Mars might have been included but is rejected as fulfilling too military a rôle for this purpose, yet Spenser acquires a double advantage in suggesting a god not relevant to a religious struggle but introducing his presence in this rejection. He gains in using both ways. Other epic qualities are brought in on the same principle. The watchman on the tower is a religious guardian and also the conventional protector of a besieged city. The descriptions of sunrise and sunset which make the timing of the battle recall epic precedents and are reminiscent of other dangerous occasions in the allegorical action—the coming of night in Archimago's cell and the dawn before the joust with Sans-joy in Lucifera's palace, for instance. Spenser is deliberately transforming the fight with the Dragon into a heroic battle.

Yet there is so much that is peculiar to the design of the Book and so much that the allegory drives Spenser to take into account that the impression is not altogether heroic. As soon as he can draw upon his instinct for poetic effect, all is well. When the hugeness and ferocity of the Dragon comes across, a genuine excitement comes with it. But when the physical details

of the size of the beast and when the facts of the progress of the
fighting are introduced, the result can end in hyperbole and,
occasionally, in a degree of absurdity.

At its best, the appearance of the antagonist is wholly successful. When the Dragon is awaiting the attack, its 'roaring
hideous sound' is what might be expected, and the sight of it
brings imaginative surprise:

> Eftsoones that dreadfull Dragon they espide,
> Where stretcht he lay upon the sunny side
> Of a great hill.
>
> I. xi. 4

The creature seems natural in its behaviour, and when it
gathers itself for defence against its attacker it moves,

> Halfe flying, and halfe footing in his hast,
> That with his largenesse measured much land,
> And made wide shadow under his huge wast.
>
> I. xi. 8

This is something that has been seen, both the movement and
the shadow. It was a description that Milton never forgot and
found a useful phrase to borrow for Satan's passage out of hell.
Again, when Spenser wishes to portray the Dragon's hostile
descent upon the Red Crosse Knight, he relies upon his great
art of making pictures:

> Then with his waving wings, displayed wyde,
> Himself up high he lifted from the ground,
> And with strong flight did forcibly divide
> The yielding aire, which nigh too feeble found
> Her flitting parts, and element unsound,
> To beare so great a weight: he cutting way
> With his broad sayles, about him soared round;
> At last low stouping with unweldie sway,
> Snatcht up both horse and man, to beare them quite away.
>
> I. xi. 18

Here is narrative poetry at its best. It creates suspense, supports
the picture with vigorous energy, and translates the gigantic
wings of the beast into sails which enable it to hover over the
plain with its burden. If Spenser could only have preserved this
metaphorical vision for the whole conflict, he would have left a

permanent description of the knight's struggle and victory. But there were, as he realised, further items to be recorded and it is these which necessarily diminish the poetic force of the scene.

He preferred to add more to the description by supplying factual information. The Dragon is covered with brazen scales, it has a long curling spotted tail ending in a pair of stings, it has huge scratching claws, its mouth contains three rows of iron teeth, its jaw is capable of pouring out smoke in clouds, like the mouth of hell, and finally it possesses blazing sparkling eyes which send out flames of fire. All these details indicate how useless the knight's weapons are going to be. The fight will be an operation requiring bravery and skill, and it will need more than purely knightly strength to conduct it.

The list of the features which constitute the Dragon's alarming appearance hardly assists in keeping the creature alive in the reader's mind. Its pleasure when lying in the sunshine on the hill and its readiness to leap into action,

> often bounding on the brused gras,
> As for great joyance of his newcome guest

I. xi. 15

certainly puts it well within the sympathy of the reader. 'Brused' is a vivid term, and the suggestion that it enjoys the prospect of a new fight makes it appear a likeable kind of enemy. Spenser has, too, another device to bring it into the ordinary world. He frequently introduces familiar Elizabethan imagery which recalls habits of daily life. The sparkling eyes are linked to it by a simile of beacons which are lighted to send messages of danger to the shires; its flight made with the knight and his horse is as long as 'Ewghen bow a shaft may send'; and the weight of the prey forces it to be dropped just as a hawk finds itself unable to carry the bird it had hoped its claws would be strong enough to bear off. Images like these relate to the nature of the struggle facing the knight. They make it credible by bringing it within the comprehension of those who have experienced such events—the beacons, the archery, methods of hawking to which they refer. Their careful treatment contrives the enlargement of the beast, and they do not reduce the atmosphere of gigantic terror it creates. There might be danger in bringing down the scale of the battle but this Spenser manages to avoid. The epic scale remains, and if the fight is made intelligible by naturalistic analogies, it does not lose its vastness. The imagery, in fact, preserves a distance between the man and the Dragon. It does not even bring its own nature into the scene in the way that references to daily life in Book VI were designed to do.

It is easy to repeat examples of the number of ordinary images used in this scene, especially because they often take the form of lengthy similes, but they are not the only type Spenser employs. Mythical and classical allusions are introduced to keep the episode within the Renaissance framework. The flames which exude from the wounded Dragon's jaw burn the knight's armour giving him the anguish felt by Hercules when he was wrapped in the poisoned garment. The grasp upon the knight's shield is compared with the grip of Cerberus upon a bone; and the eruption of Aetna is the best likeness Spenser can find for the fire and brimstone which the Dragon poured out when its paw was chopped off, shield and all. These similes are inserted beside the more naturalistic examples and leave the somewhat mixed impression a battle creates.

A mixed impression, too, is attributable to the content of the progress of the fight. Since this is a Christian epic and since the Red Crosse Knight is engaged in a struggle against Sin, Spenser includes some straightforward Christian material. On the two occasions when the hero is on the verge of defeat, he is preserved by a miracle. On the first, he retreats in a state of complete exhaustion, desiring death, though not in the yearning fashion he desired it in the cave of Despair:

> Faint, wearie, sore, emboyled, grieved, brent,
> With heat, toyle, wounds, armes, smart, and inward fire
> That never man such mischiefes did torment;
> Death better were, death did he oft desire,
> But death will never come, when needes require.

I. xi. 28

Spenser's generalised verse here includes several nouns and adjectives, and lengthens the lines by avoiding most unstressed syllables and replacing them with two heavy stresses at the opening of each foot so as to produce an impression of unwilling-

ness to take up the fight any more. On this occasion the hero
finds unexpected salvation when the Dragon pushes him into a
well. *The well of life* is as magical as any well can be through the
addition of Biblical and geographical allusions. The purpose is
not only to endow it with miraculous virtues but also to provide
a religious answer to Una's prayer. Its quality may at first sight
seem overstated:

> Both *Silo* this, and *Jordan* did excell,
> And th'English *Bath*, and eke the german *Spau*,
> Ne can *Cephise*, nor *Hebrus* match this well;
> Into the same the knight backe overthrowen, fell.
>
> I. xi. 30

But Spenser needed to range as widely as he could to establish its divine nature. The knight is 'new-born' from entering
it, his sword was hardened from 'the holy water' and his
'baptised hands' became stronger against the Dragon. Granted
a living concept underlying Spenser's description, it is perhaps
easier to accept his method of presenting the knight's release
from the embodiment of Sin which is about to destroy him.
Similarly, at the end of the second day's fight, the Dragon's
advantage is countered by a second liturgical element. Here,
the tree of life, planted in Eden by God, has poured forth a balm
which, like the eucharist, promises 'happie life to all, which
thereon fed, and life eke everlasting'. It saves the knight from
death and frightens the Dragon from any approach to it.

We can read the incidents of the well and the tree in terms
of romance or we can recognise the allegorical meaning in the
presence of the two sacraments. In either way we are ready for
the success achieved by the hero. Much of the battle is over-
written. The noise during the fight seems excessive, the Dragon
'loudly brayed', it clapped its iron wings after what it thought
was its first victory, it roared like a hundred ramping lions, threw
down trees, and tore rocks to pieces. More imaginative is the
cry of the monster after its wing was wounded:

> He cryde, as raging seas are wont to rore,
> When wintry storme his wrathfull wreck does threat,
> The rolling billowes beat the ragged shore,
> As they the earth would shoulder from her seat,
>
> *   *   *

> Then gin the blustering brethren boldly threat,
>   To move the world from off his stedfast henge,
> And boystrous battell make, each other to avenge.
>
> I. xi. 21

This passage is interesting on account of its poetic scope, based
doubtless upon Spenser's knowledge of storms off the Irish coast.
Its vitality, with the description of the rest of the Dragon's noise
is evident, and its allusion to the destruction of the earth terrifying. The reader regards all this uproar as a melodramatic
summary of what has been happening. Undoubtedly it is; yet
it is piled up in order to prepare for the final slaughter. The
Dragon is more than a physical enemy; it is also 'the damned
fiend' and 'the hell-bred beast', capable of shaking the world in
its foundation. When the knight gains his victory at the end of
the three-day struggle, Spenser describes it in verse which
becomes a triumphal chant, combining relief and glory. The
stanza form allows for a choric effect dependent upon the long,
sonorous, repeated phrases which convey jubilation and
certainty:

> So downe he fell, and forth his life did breath,
>   That vanisht into smoke and cloudes swift;
>   So downe he fell, that th'earth him underneath
> Did grone, as feeble so great load to lift;
>   So downe he fell, as an huge rockie clift,
>   Whose false foundation waves have washt away,
>   With dreadful poyse is from the mayneland rift,
>   And rolling downe, great *Neptune* doth dismay;
> So downe he fell, and like an heaped mountaine lay.
>
> I. xi. 54

The little that remains for Spenser to close Book I is largely
celebratory. We return to the watchman who can now announce
the death of the Dragon, we are shown the King and Queen
descending from their castle accompanied by a procession of
courtiers and a group of joyful virgins dancing and singing to
their timbrels, we see Una crowned with a garland as 'a
Maiden Queene', and we hear the satirical tone of the description of the crowd coming to see the cause of their sufferings.[1]
The joy at the end of the story is not wholly unqualified, for

---

[1] See p. 107.

the appearance of Archimago in disguise bearing a letter from Ducssa, modifies it. Evil is still active, and although Una promptly recognises the false messenger and has him imprisoned, the Red Crosse Knight's insistence that he must return to the court of the Faerie Queene to carry out his obligations is given stronger force by this intervention. Una and her knight officiate their marriage rites in the formal Roman style but the knight cannot stay for long. The Book ends on a serious note with Una left to lament his departure, and the forward-looking image of the boat that is to carry the story into new realms and other enterprises.

Chapter V

BOOK II. DISTORTION

THERE are many resemblances between Book II and Book I, and Spenser had found several ways to instruct his readers in the understanding of his allegorical techniques in the first Book which proved helpful in the second. Both possess a hero with a quest to fulfil; both endow him with an ideal counterpart who clarifies the virtue of which he is patron and assists him in the discovery of its nature. But Book II lacks a single developing plot and relies upon a series of different aspects of its central virtue. On the other hand, its action begins with an instance of the quest in the subtle enchantment of Acrasia causing the deaths of Mordant and Amavia and introduces something of the urgency felt by Guyon when he hears Amavia's story with its touching comment: 'For he was flesh; all flesh doth frailtie breed'. Acrasia's power of corruption is inescapable both to the innocent like Mordant, and Verdant in the final Canto, and to the naturally sensual like Cymochles. The narrative of the Book is punctuated by references to her activity, first in the scene in the Bower of Bliss in Canto v, then in a parallel scene with Phaedria, who is her servant, in Canto vi, and a further account of her by Guyon to Arthur in Canto ix. We are prepared consequently for his final encounter with her at the end: her sensuality and luxurious idleness are situated in enticingly beautiful surroundings, but the hero has seen by then too much of her wicked influence not to call her and her victims to account.

Even so, Acrasia does not occupy the whole concern of Book II. Her story provides the main thread, but there are other opposites of Temperance, in Wrath and Avarice. Wrath is embodied episodically by the appearance of Pyrochles, a knight, of Furor and Occasion, two personifications, and of Phedon and Philemon, whose subsidiary self-contained romantic tale, derived from Ariosto, illustrates the power of Furor and Occasion. None of these scenes is particularly memorable, but the Canto dealing with Avarice stands out as exceptionally imaginative since it is focussed upon the failure of humanity to achieve a good way of life. It takes place in the cave of Mammon next door to the entrance to Hell. Guyon first sees Mammon as a miserly old man counting his wealth and descends with him to the world out of which his gold has been brought. He is to be exposed to the temptations of worldliness. It is significant that the Palmer has been left waiting behind, for man cannot serve God and Mammon and therefore the temptation of wealth and worldliness is left to Guyon to face alone. This scene is unusually forceful, and one realises that the episodes in Book II are arranged in two climaxes where the greatest strain is imposed on the hero and where the strongest emotional effect is felt. Perhaps Guyon does not progress in the discovery of Temperance as the Red Crosse Knight had progressed; but the reader still may sense a scale of ascending evil. For Guyon, the period underground is exhausting enough to make him lose consciousness. Moreover, his emergence has been marked by the arrival of Pyrochles and Cymochles prepared to seize his armour and by the coming of Arthur to protect him. More impressive had been the cry 'come hither, come hither, O come hastily' which is a call to the Palmer in his religious capacity. This is one of the occasions when Guyon's rôle as a hero within a religious context becomes most prominent. It is supported quietly by the extensive degree of Old Testament allusions during the fight between Arthur and Cymochles and Pyrochles.

The episodic structure of the first sections of Book II creates an occasion for Spenser to introduce each Canto with a moral commentary. In Book I the voice of the poet had been heard less frequently because the chief concern had been with narrative as it developed; but here in Book II there is less development of narrative as such, and the introduction of a fresh episode is best indicated by a direct pointer from the author. Thus the beginnings of each Canto from IV onwards are marked by an evident change of tone so that the reader can appreciate the new topic. These subjects vary from moral observations in V, VI, IX and XI, to a long seafaring simile in VII, and to the lyrical, much admired, passage on the power of heavenly love in VIII. For Spenser this variety of technique provides a considerable

E

range of poetic opportunity which is what seems especially needed in a Book so much confined in the scope of its principal topic.

Book II inclines to regard the two representatives of Temperance in more intellectual terms than those in Book I. The Palmer is undoubtedly drawn from an abstract rather than human point of view. No one can delight in him in quite the same spirit as in Una, and the reader will not regret the separation between Guyon and his companion as he is likely to regret the separation between the Red Crosse Knight and Una. This is partly a matter of characterisation. There is compassion in our minds when we witness Red Crosse's gradual fall and a similar compassion when we witness Una's sorrow and her danger when she is without the love and protection of her knight. The relation between Guyon and the Palmer is scarcely of the same order. We cannot feel much sympathy for Guyon when he is forced to travel across the lake in Phaedria's boat without him and to explore the cave of Mammon alone. In fact, he has absorbed the principles of the Palmer so completely that he speaks like him and is in no danger from Phaedria or from Mammon. He is well equipped to deal with the temptations that he comes into contact with and acts calmly as the mouthpiece of Temperance rather than as the victim of the tempter. As for the Palmer, he regrets Phaedria's refusal to transport him over the Idle Lake, but we have no inkling of how he occupied himself until he 'passage found elsewhere'. Una had her own kind of life while the Red Crosse Knight was going his way independently, and her experiences are set before the reader from her point of view.

A contrast of this kind inevitably puts the hero and his partner in Book II at a disadvantage. The two are portrayed in a way that gives them less individuality or vigour than their predecessors in Book I, but they are not for that reason dull. Spenser rarely commits himself to fully developed studies of people, and what is interesting about the characterisation of Guyon and the Palmer is the degree of humanity they contrive to obtain while preserving their functions as types. The Palmer is particularly difficult to regard apart from his pedagogic aspect. He is a survival of the medieval morality figure, the doctor or presenter; he is characterised by a propensity to preach and most of his reactions are frankly didactic. As a result he habitually theorises upon the details of the plot. When, for instance, Phedon tells the story of his life, the Palmer moralises in a set speech, the speech which was previously quoted by Abraham Fraunce as an example of Spenser's logical skill. More interesting because less ethical is his account of the secret virtues in the world of nature. The occasion for this is an explanation of the well which preserves its purity and cannot clean the blood from Ruddymane's hands, but it is still an intellectual exposition such as one might expect from the Palmer. He does occasionally escape from his improving rôle. He has something personal to say, for instance, when he implores Pyrochles and Cymochles to leave the apparently dead Guyon's armour for his funeral because they are 'relicks of his living might', and he displays an agility unexpected in the 'Reverend Sire', when he seizes Guyon's sword and hands it to Arthur who is having the worst of it in his fight with the Saracens. Spenser, too, gives him appropriate and individual epithets to define his speech: he is 'suppliaunt' to the pagans, and 'grave' to Arthur when describing Guyon's physical condition. Moreover, in his religious character he is the person who arrives in time to speak to the guardian angel beside Guyon and to receive the heavenly commission to preserve his safety.

Guyon is obviously given more humanity than the Palmer and this is particularly evident when he is in contact with other typical figures, with Huddibras and Sans-loy, for instance, in the house of Medina, or even with Pyrochles and Cymochles. This depends, of course, partly upon the share of the Book allotted to him since Spenser has greater room to develop several aspects of his nature, but it depends also upon a more subtle treatment of typology. More dialogue is allocated to him and when we see him and the Palmer together in the opening scene of the Book, it is he who responds with the strongest feeling to the 'pitiful spectacle' which awaits them and he who extracts from Amavia the cause of her fate. Her story stops when she reaches her own share in it:

> Which when I wretch, Not one word more she sayd
> But breaking off the end for want of breath,

> And slyding soft, as downe to sleepe her layd,
> And ended all her woe in quiet death.
>
> II. i. 56

Sir Guyon, constantly labelled 'the good Sir Guyon', weeps for her and insists that she should be buried with her husband, not, as the Palmer suggests, be the only one provided with an honourable tomb because she had died of grief and not of wickedness like Sir Mordant. It is he, too, who is ready to act in the way that is scarcely expected of a knight dressed in full armour. He picks up Amavia's child, makes it smile, senses the pathos of its situation and, indeed, the pathos of the whole human condition when he says:

> Full litle weenest thou, what sorrows are
> Left thee for portion of thy livelihed,
> Poore Orphane. . . .
> Such is the state of men: thus enter wee
> Into this life with woe, and end with miseree.
>
> II. ii. 2

He kneels down by the well to wash its blood-stained hands, and having sworn during the funeral rite when he uses its father's sword to lop off locks of hair from its dead parents, he commits himself to carry out proper vengeance against Acrasia. This is the knight who will face the temptations of Mammon, will fight the enemies of Temperance outside the House of Alma, and will capture Acrasia at the end of his journey. Guyon represents 'great Temperance' in all his activities but none the less when he is humble enough to think of Amavia's child.

He is not unique in this combination of tenderness and heroism. In Book VI Spenser deals with a similar matter when Sir Calepine has an opportunity to look after the child he has rescued:

> From his soft eyes the teares he wypt away,
> And from his face the filth that did it ray,
> And every litle limbe he searcht around
> And every part, that under sweathbands lay,
> Least that the beasts sharpe teeth had any wound
> Made in his tender flesh, but whole them all he found.
>
> VI. iv. 23

One side of Spenser's originality as a poet emerges in his introduction of such incidents reflecting so much personal understanding into an epic poem. Book VI is primarily pastoral, and Sir Calepine is not wearing armour since he has been recovering from a wound. He is now strong enough to come out into the fresh air. When he finds the baby unharmed, he wraps him up in his bands again and carries him through the forest, conscious all the time of his cries for food. In even so a domestic a scene, we do not forget Sir Calepine's knightly prowess. In the case of Sir Guyon Spenser is more anxious to emphasise the humanity which can remain side by side with the dignity appropriate to knightly grandeur. There the scene shows how close the chivalric world is to the world of normal life.

A streak of imagination is the psychological feature which distinguishes Guyon from the Palmer and from the limitation of his dominating virtue. He is something more than a mere representative of Temperance and at different moments in the narrative adds an unexpected quality to the virtue he stands for. For instance, he teaches his horse to keep in time with the Palmer's slow tread, a merit the more conspicuous because we later see the horse expressing its independence when Braggadocchio rides it, and later still in another Book its affection for its true owner when the Knight of Justice sees that it is returned to Guyon. Temperance inevitably appears dull and negative, but at best it includes thoughtfulness, kindliness and courtesy. Guyon's attitude and conduct to the orphan child, his thoughtfulness towards the Palmer, and his patience in carrying Sir Mordant's armour after he discovers that his horse has been stolen are all positive and personal aspects of his interpretation of what Spenser calls 'the great rule' by which he lives.

In the sequence of events after the burial of Sir Mordant and Amavia Spenser transforms his narrative into a number of episodes where the evil of Acrasia is not altogether forgotten but is largely replaced by other types of intemperance. Journeying on, Guyon and the Palmer reach the first house where they stay as they will later stay in the House of Alma. This is occupied by three sisters, two representing extremes of character and the third, Medina occupying the moral centre. Medina is, in fact, the feminine version of Temperance and has been identified by some critics with the lady Sir Guyon mentions to Mammon in Canto VII. She stands for the mean: the virtues of modesty and gravity which balance the scowling ill-temper of Elissa and the excessive gaiety of Perissa. The two admirers of the women are also extremes: Huddibras is a malcontent of considerable rashness of temperament, and Sans-loy brings the lustful constitution already demonstrated by him in Book I in his attempts to rape Una. The presence of Perissa and Sans-loy refer again to the sensuality on which the whole Book turns but this is only a side issue in this particular episode. Huddibras and Sans-loy are naturally quarrelsome and seize the chance of Guyon's arrival to begin a fight with him and with each other. Medina offers a different standard of conduct: she appeals to them for justice and the rightness of a cause before any conflict should begin, and she dismisses their assumption that malice and bloodthirstiness are sufficient reasons for fighting. The quarrel, supported by the sourness of Huddibras and the lawlessness of Sans-loy, develops into a thorough-going conflict emphasised by long poetic similes which call attention to the vigour of Guyon's contribution to it.

This chapter has been called 'Distortion' because all the figures who are the opposites of Temperance create an impression which is in some way or another distorted. This will be demonstrated more fully later but even in the references made by Amavia to what had happened to Sir Mordant and in the contrast between Sans-loy and Sir Huddibras and their respective mates, the notion of deformity is beginning to grow. Amavia says of Sir Mordant that he was enthralled by Acrasia.

> And so transformed from his former skill,
> That me he knew not, neither his own ill;
>
> II. i. 54

Here is the beginning of corruption and distorted judgment, Sans-loy and Huddibras each represents extremes of temperament which are, in fact, distortions of human nature, while the function of Medina is to suggest the over-reaching in the make-up of Perissa and Elissa. So far, the opposites of Temperance have been indicated, if only faintly.

Canto III has been described as a 'conspicuous irrelevance' and it may well seem so in view of the approach we are making. It deals with the theft of Guyon's horse by Braggadocchio, his meeting with Trompart, and, more important still, the portrayal of Belphoebe. What, we might ask, has this to do with 'distortion'? Fundamentally it has a close connection with the theme of the Book, for in Belphoebe we meet the only good character who stands in her own right and is not obviously governed by the needs of the theme as is Medina, and Alma later on. I think that if we are to grasp the fullness of the concept of 'distortion' we need to come into contact with one figure who is untouched by the whole idea. Belphoebe possesses real beauty and innocence, she possesses youth and vigour, wonderfully apart from the atmosphere of the lasciviousness and sexuality of Acrasia's Bower of Bliss, equally apart from Mammon's worldliness and from the emotional extremes of Pyrochles and Cymochles. Belphoebe brings into the Book what no one else can bring, not even Guyon and the Palmer because they are both too close to the central topic. And she has probably never heard of Temperance, for she is too innocent to need it.

Spenser is right to spend some time on her, even if she is not related directly to the Acrasia plot. Each item of her appearance is given its own heightened loveliness which relies upon visual hyperbole and the associations of classical analogy. And it properly calls attention to itself:

> How shall fraile pen descrive her heavenly face,
> For feare through want of skill her beautie to disgrace?
>
> II. iii. 25

Spenser answers his own question by finding a series of poetic images which can be combined with an exalted commentary. Thus her face was too beautiful to be made of flesh but seemed a 'heavenly pourtraict of bright Angels hew' and was 'cleare as the skie', its Petrarchan quality of lilies and roses is not left as the familiar cliché, nor is her ivory forehead, for

> All good and honour might therein be red:
> For there their dwelling was . . .
>
> II. iii. 24

Similarly, her hair, 'crisped, like golden wyre' acquires individuality in spite of so obvious a phrase because it 'waved like a penon wide dispred' and was scattered with flowers and leaves out of the forest where her vigour had led her to hunt. How charming is the effect contrasted with Medina's tidy coiffure where 'no looser heares did out of order stray about her daintie eares'. The glow of Belphoebe leaves Medina and the Aristotelian virtue of the mean quite out of competition. Spenser describes her dress in the same kind of vivid detail and clinches the whole matter in an image which sums up all that the Renaissance studies of classical poetry meant to the Elizabethans:

> Such as *Diana* by the sandie shore
>   Of swift *Eurotas*, or on *Cynthus* grene,
>   Where all the Nymphes have her unwares forlore,
>   Wandreth alone with bow and arrowes keene,
>   To seeke her game: or as that famous Queene
>   Of *Amazons*, whom *Pyrrhus* did destroy,
>   The daye that first of Priame she was seene,
>   Did she shew her selfe in great triumphant joy,
> To succour the weake state of sad afflicted *Troy*.
>
> II. iii. 31

Romance and Virgilian sadness colour the simile as well as the Spenserian feeling for beauty which has been running through the whole lavish series of stanzas written to describe the 'irrelevant' heroine. She will, of course, occupy greater space in Books III and IV, and one might defend the elaboration of the description in Book II on the grounds that Spenser is simply carrying out the scheme he began in Book I with his lengthy presentation of Arthur.

That is not, however, the only reason, for one has to take into account the fact that this impressive presentation—one of 'the finest things in Spenser' as Hazlitt called it—occurs in a surprising context. The scene in which Belphoebe arrives is deliberately comic. The description of her, of course, is not, but the appearance of Braggadocchio, his attempt to ride Guyon's horse, his acquisition of Trompart as a squire, are absurd. They are, in effect, parodies of chivalric standards of conduct. Braggadocchio demands homage from Trompart, and he addresses him in what is obviously a low style—'vile Caytive' and 'dead dog'. They set off, 'a well consorted pair', until they meet Archimago whose flattery is well received by both. Archimago frightens them with his story of two murderous knights (Red Crosse and Guyon) and by his Satanic disappearance. Their fear prepares them to meet Belphoebe, and after a notable change from the highly decorative style we are returned to the ludicrous in Braggadocchio's concealment in a bush. The mean style accompanies his emergence:

> with that he crauld out of his nest,
> Forth creeping on his caitive hands and thies,

II. iii. 35

as does also the mean simile of a 'fearefull fowle', which had hidden itself from a hawk and now 'peepes forth' to see that the danger is over and then forgets its previous cowardice. In the dialogue which follows, Belphoebe crushes Braggadocchio's suggestion that she should seek life in the Court away from 'this wilde forrest where no pleasure is', with a defence of a search for honour:

> Abroad in armes, at home in studious kind
> Who seekes with painfull toil, shall honour soonest find . . .
> In woods, in waves, in warres she wonts to dwell,
> And will be found with perill and with paine;

II. iii. 40-41

It is an aspect of Spenser's freedom in handling his medium that he can place Belphoebe and her view of life in a context which inserts one of the rare satirical sections into Book II. Of course, he can without difficulty write a single line which is deliberately intended to parody his own serious style; for instance, Guyon's reply to Archimago's appeal is clearly designed for the reader's recognition of Archimago since Guyon is quite unaware of the evil sorcerer he has met. Archimago says:

> Vouchsafe to stay your steed for humble misers sake

II. i. 8

and the narrative continues on the same note as a comment:

> He stayd his steed for humble misers sake
> And bad tell on the tenor of his plaint,
> Who feigning then . . .

E *

After the splendour of the description of Belphoebe we are presented with Braggadocchio's lustful desire for her, and the scene returns to the context of Archimago's wicked world. Spenser has so much control over his narrative that he can slide from one level to another without creating any disharmony. Braggadocchio reacts to Belphoebe's physical appeal just as a crude, boastful man might be expected to do, which is dramatically correct, but Spenser is able to preserve the total impression of their encounter as a mixture of visionary idealism and caricature. The emphasis comes out most strongly upon the visionary element, but the satire is deeply rooted in the language attached to Braggadocchio and Trompart.

The fourth Canto adds to the impression that so far the Book has been dealing with preparatory matter, illustrating the triumph of passion over reason and the destruction of the virtue of Temperance which should keep passion in its proper place. Here there is a more emphatic version in that the figures who constitute it are formulated in a dehumanised way. Furor and Occasion have been designed upon the familiar principles of the emblem book. Occasion has a recognisable iconography in her long hair in front and her bald head behind; like every opportunity in time she must be taken by the forelock otherwise she is gone. Spenser adopting this well-known image attaches it to a decrepit, lame, ill-spoken old woman who will use every means in her power to urge Furor to attack his victim with more ferocity. Furor is not traceable to emblem books to the same degree; he appears to be a mad man allowing all the freedom he can to the passionate rage which consumes him. Spenser's verse creates dramatically how his madness is expressed. He

> With beastly, brutish rage gan him assay,
>   And smot, and bit, and kickt, and scratcht, and rent,
> And did he wist not what in his avengement.
>
> II. iv. 6

Such a monosyllabic line occurs often in Book II, and here it creates an impression of animal wildness. Furor possessed great strength but was incapable of directing it, and so in an alexandrine the monosyllables draw out his purposeless action:

> And where he hits, nought knowes, and whom he hurts,
>   nought cares.
>
> II. iv. 7

The problem of making use of these dehumanised figures in a narrative is the problem of giving them any plausible action. Spenser's embodiments of the Seven Deadly Sins in Book I are impressive because they are not absorbed into any kind of plot. They appear, grotesque and repellent, in a pageant. But here, in Book II, such figures are carrying on an action. The Palmer expounds to Guyon something of their meaning when he urges him not to attack Furor before he has disposed of Occasion:

> Not so, O *Guyon*, never thinke that so
> That Monster can be maistred or destroyed:
> He is not, ah, he is not such a foe,
> As steele can wound, or strength can overthroe.
>
> II. iv. 10

The answer was, as we saw in Chapter III, to padlock Occasion's tongue and bind her hands; then they would be able to fetter Furor and tie him up in a hundred iron chains. The difficulty with this treatment of personifications is that the effect is too visual. The ideas they represent are skilfully conveyed but the handling of their form is disastrous. It is probably true that conceptual figures of this dehumanised kind contribute generously to processions or to static scenes—much of *The Faerie Queene* is made up of them—but when they are required to move about and originate parts of the plot they are plainly out of their element. Pyrochles and Cymochles are much more successful as people who have to act, although they also represent Wrath, and Pyrochles grows nearer to an abstract figure when he literally burns in flames of fury.

Pyrochles is first heard of through his squire, Atin (strife), who enters bearing his knight's shield emblazoned with a flaming fire upon a bloody field and the motto '*Burnt I do burne*'. Spenser combines this information with an account of the pedigree of Pyrochles and his brother Cymochles and links them with the hellish stock of Sans-loy, Sans-joy and Sans-foy, who are Night's 'nephews'. It is his formal method of suggesting the characters of the two. They are the sons of Acrates (intemperant love of pleasure) and Despight (malice), grand-sons of Phlegeton (a river in hell and according to Spenser a son of Herebos and Night) and Jarre.[1] It is typical of Spenser to set an object in Greek mythology, the river in Hades, beside the English word 'Jarre'. The two brothers have inherited the characteristics of their line. Pyrochles (*pyr*, fire, *ochleon*, to move, disturb) manifests 'the irascible, contentious, or passionate element of the soul: the wrath that burns without cause, that wilfully seeks "occasions" '. Cymochles represents 'Passion fierce and fickle as the sea waves, characterised by long fits of sensual indolence'.[2]

Guyon soon observes Pyrochles riding fast over the plain. Spenser beautifully creates the vividness of his sudden appearance on the scene. Guyon first notes the speed of his approach and the brightness of his armour:

> That as the Sunny beames do glaunce and glide
> Upon the trembling wave, so shined bright,
> And round about him threw forth sparkling fire,
> That seemed him to enflame on every side:
> His steed was bloudy red, and fomed ire,
> When with the maistring spur he did him roughly stire.
>
> II. v. 2

The image makes a decorative impact but Spenser will not leave the portrayal at this stage. The next two lines may be ornamental but they are also suggestive of meaning. By the time the horse is described there is no doubt as to what the meaning is. A blood-red horse begins to convey the notion of anger and by the end of that line it is foaming *ire*. It is almost as if Spenser thought that 'ire' was visible just as Night's black horses had been seen 'foming tarre'. He does not draw any hard and fast line between what the eye can see literally and what it cannot. His description of Pyrochles is studded with references to flames, he shews that his conduct is marked by the dominance of wrath, and his movement violent and unhesitating. Thus when Guyon, on foot, attempts to defend himself from an attack from this mounted knight and succeeds without inten-

[1] *Variorum F.Q.*, II., pp. 231-232.
[2] R. E. N. Dodge. *Spenser's Complete Poetical Works*, 1908, quoted by Harry Berger. *The Allegorical Temper*, 1957, p. 59.

tion in killing the horse, Pyrochles unlike his normal habit 'slow uprose' and returns to his ferocity by abuse and recourse to his 'flaming sword'. Pyrochles is, in fact, very different from the abstract personification of Wrath previously displayed. He really acquires genuine vigour both in his verbal fury at the death of his horse and in the intensity of his fighting on foot. When he is eventually at Guyon's mercy and has to plead for his life, he becomes more of an individual. And so does Guyon, who makes a solemn speech to him about his proneness to 'outrageous anger and woe working jarre', then smiles, not without patronage, when he hears the cause of the attack made by Pyrochles against him, and permits Occasion, and consequently Furor, to be released. He subsequently is ready to succour Pyrochles against Furor, but the Palmer intervenes and successfully warns him not to be moved by pity.

Cymochles also comes into the scene which had opened with Pyrochles. The elasticity of Spenser's allegory enables him to move easily from the flames and furious action between Guyon and Pyrochles to the sensual beauty of Acrasia's Bower. Atin is the link, who seeing his knight in serious straits hastens off for help to Cymochles. Cymochles is where his nature has led him, in the Bower of Bliss, and thus we acquire the first direct description of that evil place being enjoyed by an evil character—which Sir Mordant was not. Here is extreme refinement of sensuality imparted to the 'fraile eye' of humanity. Cymochles versed in all the voluptuousness that the Bower can afford, seeks the subtlety of its pleasures, 'mingled amongst loose ladies and lascivious boys'. Atin finds him lying, half asleep, in an arbour which in itself appeals to all the senses in its heavily scented flowers and its murmuring soporific stream. Worse information is given about the Bower in the way which anticipates what Guyon is later to discover. Acrasia can transform her lovers into monstrous shapes and can imprison them eternally in dark prisons where they never again see the light of the sun. This perhaps refers literally to imprisonment such as the Red Crosse Knight suffered from Orgoglio, but it may possibly refer simply to their transformation into beasts such as Guyon will witness when he reaches her island. Cymochles is spared this fate but has become totally enslaved by the lasciviousness

of Acrasia's world. Atin finds him and urges him to rescue
Pyrochles. He calls for his armour and speeds guiltily ahead
pricked 'with spurs of shame and wrong'. But he is not to get
far because when he takes a ferry across the lake and is
required by Phaedria to abandon Atin, he finds in her, the
servant of Acrasia, an enthralment just as powerful as he succumbed to in the Bower of Bliss.

Phaedria is a lively figure who enjoys travelling in her boat
and makes every effort to amuse her passengers. We are not
intended to sympathise with her yet she has many of the attractions of her name (Mirth). Her laughter is frequent and entirely
empty of reason. The shaking of the leaves and the dancing of
the water round the edge of the boat are enough to stimulate it.
The rocking movement over the lake distracts Cymochles from
his ostensible goal:

> Whiles thus she talked, and whiles thus she toyd,
> They were far past the passage, which he spake.
>
> II. vi. 11

Phaedria has been making garlands from flowers for her head,
and plaiting rings of rushes to entertain herself. She is recognisably a type character but a surprisingly successful example of
one. She truly comes to life as a person both in her Tasso-
inspired song, which has its source in the biblical parable of
the lilies, and in her firm rebuke to Guyon on his complaint at
having been brought off his course. After all, she says:

> Who fares on sea may not commaund his way,
> Ne wind and weather at his pleasure call.
>
> II. vi. 23

This is a lesson which the virtuous Guyon can do no harm to
learn. Her charms and the charms of her island are strong
enough to keep him cautious of being misled by its attractions.

The *Idle lake* is interesting for its various impressions upon
those who voyage over it. Cymochles, Guyon, Pyrochles, and
Phaedria herself, all react differently towards it. For Cymochles,
his was a pleasant voyage in which the port he had asked for
was missed unnoticed. His intended revenge upon Guyon and
his succour to Pyrochles were forgotten; Phaedria interested
him more, and he enquired her name and that of the lake; and

upon their arrival he gladly walked with her on to the island.
The scene before them is described in a pattern which drugs
him by the regularity of its design:

> No tree, whose braunches did not bravely spring;
>> No braunch, whereon a fine bird did not sit:
>> No bird, but did her shrill notes sweetly sing;
>> No song but did containe a lovely dit:
> Trees, braunches, birds, and songs were framed fit,
> For to allure fraile mind to carelesse ease.
>
> II. vi. 13

Its appeal to a man susceptible of sensuous pleasure rapidly
follows. Cymochles falls asleep in this enchanting garden with
his head on Phaedria's lap and the sound of her song in his ears.
In time Phaedria sets off again in her boat to meet Guyon and
the Palmer. As in the case of Atin the Palmer is rejected, and
she starts along on her customary course. This time her merri-
ment fails to attract Guyon and they sail 'Through the dull
billowes thicke as troubled mire' (II. vi. 20). The water reflects
Guyon's attitude to Phaedria and the journey she takes him.
He is angry with her for disobeying him while he had obeyed
her in leaving the Palmer behind, although the beauty of the
garden and the sweetness of its owner were apparent to him.
Only after the awakening of Cymochles and a fight with him,
was he able to prevail upon Phaedria to take him back over the
'dull' waves where he wanted to go.

Pyrochles also found the water different from what he had
expected. Driven to the end of the fury which he had released
he had reached a state of burning with intensity of fire. He had,
in effect, reached the symbolical situation implied in his motto.
He is conscious of burning in flames 'yet no flames can I see', and
leaps in desperation into the lake. Atin, standing on the bank
still waiting for the ferry, leaps after him to save him from
drowning. For these two the waves were slow and sluggish, and
so thick with mud that neither Pyrochles nor Atin had any
chance against sinking to the bottom. To Archimago, who
arrived to see the two struggling in the water, the lake appeared
to be an ordinary lake in which, as he said, the two seemed more
in danger of being drowned than burnt.

The lake is in effect what those who come to it want it to be. For each it is a mirror of his own expectation. Cymochles finds it and its ferrywoman beautiful, Guyon finds it dull and heavy, Pyrochles the promise of restoration, Atin and Archimago nothing in particular since neither has a bias towards its quality nor towards its ferry. Archimago identifies the serious condition of Pyrochles and saves him from death by treating him with a curative balm. He remains the sorcerer who sides with the villainous parties in this Book and he hopes to do some damage to Guyon by putting Pyrochles back in circulation once more. He is also equipped with Arthur's sword which he had promised to Braggadocchio, but Pyrochles is obviously the more useful agent for his evil intentions and his immediate object is to heal him so that he can attack Guyon when opportunity occurs.

ii

Guyon, having returned to the mainland with Phaedria's unwilling assistance, walks through the desert in search of some new test which will draw out his own capacities as a soldier. He finds one in his encounter with Mammon. His interview with this essential figure is in some ways reminiscent of the Red Crosse Knight's interview with Despair. Both scenes are debates; both possess considerable emotional power, relying for their effect upon the force of their language. They are peculiarly memorable because the poetry swings the whole episode along, creating a sense of terror and mystery. Guyon, unwarned and alone, comes upon a shabby, dirty old man surrounded by his wealth just as the Red Crosse Knight comes upon Despair surrounded by the bones of his victims. But Red Crosse has Una with him and he has been warned of what he will see by Trevisan. He is prepared for the danger he is to meet, whereas Guyon in solitude has been contemplating his success and, one may suppose, his Temperance. This is an aspect of his self-sufficiency against which Professor Lewis is critical; but Guyon cannot achieve his aim unless he remains constantly aware of the virtue of Temperance.

This scene is distinguished by its skilful narrative and its powers of description as well as by the quality of the argument

between Mammon and Guyon. Mammon when he is first seen
has at once the appearance of a human being and of a god.
There is naturalism in the setting: it is a 'gloomy glade covered
with boughes and shrubs from heavens light', and naturalism,
too, in the appearance of the man hiding within it:

> An uncouth, salvage, and uncivile wight,
> Of griesly hew, and fowle ill-favour'd sight;
> His face with smoke was tand, and eyes were bleard,
> His head and beard with sout were ill bedight.

> II. vii. 3

What impresses one quickly is the way in which the description
moves on to the symbolical. The next two lines report that:

> His cole-blacke hands did seeme to have beene seard
> In smithes fire-spitting forge, and nayles like clawes appeard.

This person is obviously a miser and a man who has devilish
attributes in his possession of claws. Perhaps, as Guyon thinks,
he is more than a miserly blacksmith and his preference for
secrecy and a place far from *heaven's light* encourages his suspicion. The account continues in a mixture of the realistic and
the symbolical. He is wearing an 'yron coate all overgrowne
with rust' but beneath it is a golden robe which suggests far
more than its literal appearance:

> A worke of rich entayle, and curious mould,
> Woven with antickes and wild Imagery.

Here is the fascination of meanness and prodigality. 'Wild
imagery' arouses curiosity, and looks forward to all that Mammon will offer to Guyon in his temptations.

It is appropriate that Guyon should doubt whether he really
is a man and should ask him why he is keeping his heaps of
wealth apart:

> From the worldes eye, and from her right usaunce?

The question is pertinent from the knight of Temperance, for
'right usaunce' is at the basis of his standards of goodness.
Throughout the Book he sees, and we, too, see distortion
developing in the lack of the proper use of mental or physical
qualities or of riches, and here on the edge of Mammon's underworld he makes the point which will guide him through the

temptations before him. It gives the readers a clue to the debate that is to follow.

Mammon's reply to Guyon's question is first of all an assertion of his godhead: he possesses all the goods for which men work endlessly, 'riches, renowme, and principality, Honour, estate. . . .' all the things which constitute him the god of the world and worldlings. And he follows this statement by a recognisably scriptural temptation:

> Wherefore if me thou deigne to serve and sew,
>   At thy commaund lo all these mountaines bee
>
> II. vii. 9

This Guyon rejects on the grounds that his view of riches is not what Mammon supposes but is the glory of knightly virtue. Mammon immediately pursues his offer with a fuller account of what his wealth can buy—'sheilds, steeds, and armes, and all things for thee meet'—and boasts about his power:

> Do not I kings create, and throw the crowne
> Sometimes to him, that low in dust doth ly?
> And him that raigned, into his rowme thrust downe,
> And whom I lust, do heape with glory and renowne?
>
> II. vii. 11

Guyon's rejection of such power is again scriptural:

> Ne thine be kingdomes, ne the scepters thine:
>   But realmes and rulers thou does both confound,
>   And loyall truth to treason dost incline;

It was not for nothing that the author of *Paradise Regained* commented on the visit of Guyon to the cave of Mammon as well as to the Bower of Bliss for Milton recognised the New Testament references in the phrases used by Guyon in his refusal to be swayed by Mammon's arguments. The parallel with Christ's temptation in the wilderness is evident. The knight had been walking through desert ground when he came upon the world's tempter and he found then what he had sought, 'a worthy adventure'. Spenser hardly needed to expound the reason for the broad road which they came upon in their descent to the Underworld. It led to the house of Richess which was 'a little stride' from the widely open gates of Hell.

Part of Guyon's temptation occurs on the earth and already the style firmly establishes the quality of the argument. The melancholy nature of the movement of history emerges in Mammon's boastfulness of what his strength can do, and of Guyon's certainty of the fatality of acquisitive wars and their effect upon rulers and their possession:

> The sacred Diademe in peeces rent,
> And purple robe gored with many a wound
> Castles surprizd, great cities sackt and brent:
> So mak'st thou kings, and gaynest wrongfull governement.

Spenser, despising all that Mammon stands for, yet inspires his poetry with a sense of lament. This is a case of the medieval 'sic transit gloria mundi?' which both Guyon and Mammon recognise. The poetry produces this feeling and it includes also condemnation of the power of making money. When Mammon speaks of his riches as 'pretious pelfe', Guyon promptly translates it into 'worldly mucke' and later into 'mucky filth'. He has the better of the argument because his vocabulary is more concrete and incisive. The adjectives he introduces supply connections of ideas in, for instance, the '*sacred* diadem' and the '*purple* robe' and the images are concerned with the struggles of those who undertake explorations in little known seas, the Caspian and the Adriatic. He can also portray the golden age when men lived gratefully upon the gifts of the Creator. For Mammon this means little:

> . . . leave the rudeness of that antique age
> To them, that liv'd therein in state forlorne:

and he replaces the notion with the belief that in later times men must acquire wealth by their own abilities or by the acceptance of the gold that he is offering. Guyon meets this repeated temptation with a refusal that in its content and abrupt phrasing anticipates the refusal made by Christ to Satan in *Paradise Regained*. He will not receive anything offered 'till I know it well be got' and he doubts whether wealth on such a scale as Mammon possesses can be kept in any safe secret place.

Mammon's brief word 'come thou and see' dramatically begins the descent into the Underworld, and the rest of the temptation occurs in various places below the earth. Guyon still preserves his conviction of the evil which his companion represents. He speaks no word as he is conducted through the realms of Mammon until Mammon himself tries further temptations and he then dismisses them in the terms he has used before:

> Another blis before mine eyes I place,
> Another happinesse, another end.

and directly abuses Mammon as 'thou Money God'.

Spenser's allegorisation achieves great effect in this unknown world and it is more powerful than the visit of Duessa to the Underworld in Book I because the arrival of Guyon is that of a stranger and a heroic figure in whose responses we are more closely involved. The realm is reached by a dark path

> And was with dread and horrour compassed around.

The Virgilian personifications are fully explored. Spenser does not merely make a list but brings them to life. The familiar adjectives are present: cruel Revenge and hart-burning Hate are expected, but Feare and Sorrow become something different. Spenser can never leave Feare without some imaginative perception; it appears thus:

> And trembling Feare still to and fro did fly,
> And found no place, where safe he shroud him might.
>
> II. vii. 22

and Sorrow from the poet who was always so eloquent over grief becomes

> Lamenting Sorrow did in darkness lye.

Since he has so vivid a sense of personification Spenser transforms Horror into a bird, always soaring and 'beating his yron wings', followed with lugubrious Owls and Night-ravens who carry tidings of death with them, and Virgil's harpy, *Celeno*, who

> A song of bale and bitter sorrow sings,
> That hart of flint a sunder could have rift.
>
> II. vii. 23

Guyon passes through all these, gazing at the strangeness of the scene until he is led by Mammon into his own dwelling where they are followed by an ugly fiend. Inside Mammon's house he sees a mixture of gold, which in a Keatsian fashion 'with rich metall loaded every rift', and has a huge web of blackness and smoke hanging over it. There is twilight, 'a faint shadow of uncertain light' which obscures any clear impression of the first room, scattered with dead men's bones. Guyon has gone through a vision of mystery and death yet is still able to respond negatively to Mammon's statement that 'here' is the 'worldes blis'. Spenser sums up the hope that Guyon would not succumb to temptation with a generalisation comparable with that used in the Wood of Error—'Eternall God thee save from such decay'. Guyon is safe, and is ready to move to the next room in which the mining activities are taking place. The description of these is technical in a way reminiscent of the making of gold for Pandemonium in *Paradise Lost*, and both are conducted by deformed creatures who have never seen a human being before. Mammon is 'their soveraigne Lord and sire', and Guyon is appalled by their repellent appearance and is only too ready to reject in strong terms the suggestion that he is now witnessing 'the fountaine of the worldes good'. If we are not already conscious of the distortion of Mammon's appeal Spenser makes it plain in his account of the source of the world's wealth. Mammon acts as interpreter to the archetypes of wickedness which are stretched before us.

What Guyon sees in this horrible place is nothing that could attract him. What the reader sees in it is an example of Spenser's art of making poetry out of things that are wholly unpoetic in their character. The descriptions of the process of melting the gold, the keeping up of the furnaces, the skimming of the dross, the stirring of the metal as it is separated from the ore, are remote from what the poet's poet normally describes. It recalls the making of steel in the film of *Major Barbara*, or the instinct of a modern poet to bring his work close to contemporary experience. And why not, one asks? But Mammon is mistaken in allowing Guyon to see the ugliness of the Underworld: because he assumes that such a revelation will create a temptation to Guyon, he exposes his own scale of values.

He is outraged by the failure of this particular trick and tries another which he hopes will prove more enticing. This involves taking Guyon to see Philotime, his daughter. To reach her they pass a Giant, called Disdayne, who acts as a guardian at the gate to Philotime's splendid abode. He is a living creature, made all of gold (he was 'of yron mould' in the text of 1590) and armed with an iron club. By nature he is accustomed to the darkness of his environment, better acquainted with fiends than with men, as Spenser points out, and the brightness of Guyon's armour makes him spring to attack. Mammon, however, holds him back and leads the knight forward into a room adorned with golden pillars hung with the glory of past greatness. Here Philotime holds court among a crowd of people who hope to obtain the 'crownes and Diademes and titles vaine' that are in her gift. They press towards the throne where she sits holding a chain that reaches up to 'highest heaven' and down to 'lowest hell'. This is the chain of Ambition which is in its way another version of distortion. Philotime has the appearance of beauty, but it is only what has been presented as 'seeming' in Book I in the description of Duessa—the appearance not the reality. Ambition draws forth the habits which Spenser constantly attributes to the world of the court, habits which derive from the worst instincts of social climbers, of men ready to make themselves successful along immoral paths, using cruelty and falsity to make their way. *Mother Hubberds Tale* and *Colin Clouts Come Home Againe* create similar portrayals of the destructive uses of ambition, illustrating the psychological effect of its influence upon humanity. Mammon offers Philotime to Guyon to be his wife, and Guyon refuses this offering in terms which are ironic. He thanks Mammon for his generosity but explains that as a mere humble man he is not worthy of a marriage of this exalted kind. This is the sole occasion when he says that he is already committed to another lady—the first time we have heard of this—and cannot as a knight break his promise. The suggestion that Medina is the lady (see page 134) is based upon this statement.

The final attempt by Mammon is his display of the Garden of Proserpine. This needs considerable interpretation because although it is possible to trace the mythological references, the reason for their collocation is by no means apparent. The best study of the Cave of Mammon is that by Frank Kermode[1] and

---

[1] F. Kermode 'The Cave of Mammon', in *Elizabethan Poetry. Stratford-upon-Avon Studies*, 2, 1960, pp. 151-173.

anything I say about what happened in the Garden of Proserpine is largely derived from that. Spenser has portrayed his Garden as a reverse of the gardens he celebrates elsewhere in *The Faerie Queene*, that of Adonis in Book III, and, of course, those of Phaedria and of Acrasia in Book II. The plants are black and are associated with death and danger. Typically Spenser fills a stanza with the names of poisonous plants culminating in *Cicuta* (hemlock) and a reference to the death of Socrates. He then describes a silver seat placed under an arbour and beside it a tree of golden apples. The apples have a mythological history which is recognisable to those familiar with Renaissance classical thought. According to Spenser they were planted there by Hercules when he obtained them as one of his twelve labours from the daughters of Atlas; they are the apples which defeated Atalanta, one of them was also used by Acontius to obtain Cydippe for his wife, and another was thrown by Ate to the three goddesses, whose claims to it were granted by Paris to Venus in opposition to those of Athene and Juno, a decision which was rewarded by the gift of Helen of Troy and resulted in the Trojan war. Spenser introduces these stories out of his liking for Ovid and Natalis Comes but, according to Kermode, they also all represent 'intemperance of mind not body'. This view is supported by a definition of the apples of the Hesperides as 'emblems of astronomical knowledge'; and the story of Atalanta as 'a warning against blasphemy'. As for the offering by Ate of the apple to the three goddesses, that is, according to Comes, 'the symbol of an insane contempt for the divine wisdom'. For most modern readers the allusions are obscure. The one that seems most familiar is that of the goddesses because they figure elsewhere in Elizabethan literature and painting. The best known treatment of the topic is in *The Arraignment of Paris* by Peele where the climax is suitably achieved by the presentation of the apple to Queen Elizabeth, a compliment which implied her possession of all the virtues symbolised by the goddesses. A painting by Hans Eworth (1569), now in Hampton Court, portrays the same subject where the Queen is represented holding the orb to the dismay of the three claimants. Spenser has, of course, many ways of introducing Elizabeth into *The Faerie Queene*—as Belphoebe and as Gloriana—and would not in any case bring her into so evil a setting as the Garden of Proserpine.

The Garden is edged by the river Cocytus, black and deep, full of damned souls. Two of them Guyon invites to recount their past. One is Tantalus who could never drink the water in which he is submerged nor eat the fruit which hangs over the river. To his appeal for help Guyon only replies that he must remain for ever as an example of an intemperant mind. The other is Pilate, endlessly washing his hands and always remembering his guilt in committing Christ to death and saving Barabbas. Guyon, after the sight of these two instances of extreme classical and Christian failure, knows more profoundly about damnation and has no hesitation in refusing Mammon's suggestion that he should take some of the fruit and sit down upon the silver chair. Of the chair, Kermode has some explanation to offer. Following Upton, he maintains that it represents forbidden mysteries. It 'fits the general pattern of the Garden temptations; they are all associated with the sin of forbidden knowledge, and the related sin of revealing or perverting divine knowledge'. This is the final stage of Mammon's temptation and Guyon's ability to extricate himself from them all is a tribute both to his will and to his intelligence. For him Temperance is a stabilising quality, and his merit rests upon his consistent adherence to it. Three days and three nights have constituted his experience of Mammon's worldliness. No man may spend longer in the Underworld and no man may suffer longer there without release. Mammon is therefore forced to return Guyon to daylight, and the knight, enfeebled and exhausted, is brought back triumphant to the world from which he came.

iii

How much Guyon has learnt from his struggle with his enemy has yet to be seen. His strain has been physical, as well as spiritual and intellectual; and he faints in the freshness of the open air into which he re-enters. His return is marked by the arrival of a Guardian Angel and by the summons to the Palmer, who responds as fast as he can to the divine voice he has heard.

The two stanzas describing the heavenly compassion which sends succour to man 'all for love, and nothing for reward', are

two of the most moving passages in the Book (viii, 1-2). They
are cast in the form of humble enquiry, not statements, and do
not apply only to Guyon but to all mankind. Euphonious and
beautiful, they convey a sense of religious wonder at the mercy
of God, wholly undeserved yet always protective of men at
need. The stanzas bring an assurance that there *is* care in
heaven; Guyon has preserved his integrity throughout the
darkness of Mammon's world, and it is good that he should now
be preserved by an Angel who descends from the world of light.
The Palmer is reassured that his appearance of death is only
temporary and that he will soon return to his normal physical
strength. Meanwhile danger is at hand, but the Angel will continue to cherish him whatever evil befalls.

Guyon is a hero wholly confident in the virtue he represents
and gives little sign of being tempted by Mammon as we understand the term. He has not had to fasten upon the weaknesses of
Mammon's arguments, but only to produce positive opposi-
tions. His situation was very different from that of the Red
Crosse Knight in the realm of Despair where the temptation
was searching enough to have created a possibly disastrous
result. Guyon does not seem personally responsible as the Red
Crosse Knight had seemed after he was led astray when his
belief in Una had been destroyed; he had never lost his trust in
the Palmer—'Firme in thy faith, whom daunger never fro me
drew' was the first thing he said when he regained consciousness. On the other hand, if the temptation did not carry all the
weight it carried for the Red Crosse Knight it was an under-
mining experience. Guyon had to witness all that Mammon
displayed to him in the mysterious darkness of the Underworld,
he saw what no man had ever seen before, he had to endure the
explanatory comments of Mammon as they went through his
world, and he had to avoid making mistakes. Guyon had always
been a success morally and he had constantly to face the possibilities that this time his intelligence or will might fail him.
Whether his triumph through his experience was sufficient to
earn him so great a blessing as the care of an angel, a message to
the Palmer, and the rescue by Arthur is debatable. Seen in contrast with the problems of the Red Crosse Knight it may
require fuller explanation.

The explanation, I am inclined to think, lies in Spenser's belief that human nature cannot achieve total success without help from others. There is an implicit need for love or for friendship or for salvation in the scenes where the hero has to manage to find a path through great suffering or great danger. In the Red Crosse Knight's situation Arthur first and then Una supplied his need in his darkest moment. In neither case was it deserved. For Guyon too there was need for salvation. His fainting illustrates the insufficiency of human virtue in itself. He has gone heroically through the wicked world of Mammon but that had made demands upon him that he did not consciously recognise. The swoon is not a punishment for success but a revelation of its limitations. The introduction of Arthur in this Book and in the others is made to show that human beings always need help from each other.

The Palmer, after the departure of the Angel, examines Guyon and finds some sign of life. But danger in the form of Pyrochles and Cymochles is approaching accompanied by Atin. These two knights express themselves offensively and crudely when they see the Palmer. They assume that Guyon is dead and since they cannot avenge themselves upon him they can only steal his armour. The Palmer attempts to prevent what appears to him a blasphemous act. To them the Palmer is a 'dotard' and Guyon a 'dead dog' worthy to be entombed in birds of prey, the raven or the kite. Pyrochles and Cymochles at this stage of the plot are labelled as pagan knights who use oaths suitable to their beliefs, 'by Mahoune' and 'by Termagaunt'. This may have been a change of characterisation on the part of Spenser but it can equally well be a development needed by the religious context in which they now appear. The passage about the Angel, the divine voice which calls the Palmer, and the rescue by Arthur whose final requirement of Pyrochles is that he should become his true liegeman, are all consistent with a Christian pattern.[1]

Archimago, always on the spot when evil may spring up, joins them with the warning that Arthur, the destroyer of many Saracens, is on his way and exhorts them to prepare for battle.

[1] For this change of character, see W. B. C. Watkins *Shakespeare and Spenser*. Princeton, 1950, pp. 189-190.

Arthur greets the Palmer and enquires about the apparently dead knight beside him. His courtesy bears a conspicuous contrast to the unmannerly behaviour of Pyrochles and Cymochles and, having discovered the situation, he turns with equal courtesy to the two knights so as to appeal to their sympathy due the corpse of Guyon. He receives rude replies from both, followed by a violent attack from Pyrochles. The battle between the two Saracens and the one Christian breaks out.

This is the type of scene which probably gave more pleasure to the Elizabethan than it can to a modern reader because it involves a considerable amount of technical material both in the references to the armour worn by all three combatants and in the expertise displayed in its conduct. On the whole, battles between knights, as distinguished from those between a hero and a giant or a dragon, do not stimulate Spenser to any outstanding power. This battle, however, is exceptional in that Arthur has undertaken his customary important rôle of coming to the rescue of the central figure of the Book and has to fight against two barbarous characters for whom little liking is now felt. Moreover, the many descriptive details introduced in its progress and the frightening situation of Arthur facing one of the Pagans armed with Guyon's sevenfold shield and a sword which has been produced by Archimago provide an unusual degree of excitement. Arthur, we know, must win but how he will do so remains in suspense. Consequently, we concentrate more fully upon the process of the fight than we might otherwise have done. Archimago had rightly informed Pyrochles that the sword he has brought, 'Morddore' is not a reliable weapon to use against its owner, but Pyrochles had no respect for the alleged enchantment attached to its making and too much pride in his own swordsmanship to take any notice of such foolish legends. He is as insulting to Archimago as he has been to the Palmer. Apart from the sword, the Saracen has another advantage during the combat because Arthur, recognising the image of his Faerie Queene upon Guyon's shield, hesitates to smite a man bearing it.

At the end of the combat Guyon recovers his senses and rejoices to find the Palmer at his side. He expresses his gratitude

to Arthur for his timely aid and together they travel to their
next destination. This is the House of Temperance, and Spenser
has an opportunity of defining the quality of Guyon's virtue
the same way as he had in Book I when the Cave of Despair was
followed by the account of the House of Holiness.

It is probably not unreasonable to suggest that the powerfully
imaginative scenes such as those with Despair and with Mammon can never be succeeded by anything equally strong in
emotional tone. There is a relaxation in each of the descriptions
which follow. This is due principally to the absence of concentration in the extended accounts of the two Houses and their
occupants. It is due also to lack of action. Admittedly, Arthur
and Guyon are required to fight against the enemies of the
House before they are admitted, but after that the scene is presented at length and the allegorical figures primarily make contact with the reasoning faculty, not at all with the feelings.
There is little to stimulate Spenser's poetic skill and the total
effect is dull. What is not dull, of course, is the attack made
upon the House by its enemies. They are 'ragged, rude, deformed', armed with weapons which are crude versions of the
proper equipment of the knights:

> Some with unweldy clubs, some with long speares,
> Some rusty knives, some staves in fire warmd.
> Sterne was their looke, like wild amazed steares,
> Staring with hollow eyes, and stiffe upstanding heares.
>
> II. ix. 13

Although they create an appearance of reality, Arthur and
Guyon soon discover that they are unreal. Fighting against
them, both

> Broke their rude troupes, and orders did confound,
> Hewing and slashing at their idle shades;
> For though they bodies seeme, yet substance from them fades.
>
> II. ix. 15

These creatures, like their weapons, are a new example of
distortion. Their unreality had been anticipated by the man
who talked to the knights when they asked for admission and
told them in an ambiguous confused style:

> Here may ye not have entraunce, though we would:
> We would and would againe, if that we could.

This is an impression of nightmare.

Guyon and Arthur now enter and are welcomed by Alma and her train. The House of Temperance into which they are now admitted provides a study of Elizabethan psychology. This is its limitation and the limitation of Spenserian allegory.

For treating the mind and the feelings, he turns to personification: Alma is Anima, the soul, her train of fair ladies represent states of mind, happy or sad as the case may be. Guyon and Arthur each become linked with one who is in effect an expression of his own constitutional make-up. Arthur's lady admits her pensiveness and sadness of outlook but she refutes his objection to it on the grounds that he shares the same sense of values. She is Prays-desire, 'That by well doing sought to honour to aspire'. Guyon talks to a shyly blushing lady who looks down and is too bashful to talk to him. Alma explains to him:

> She is the fountaine of your modestee;
> You shamefast are, but *Shamefastnesse* it selfe is shee.

This allegorical method has the advantage here of illuminating the two heroes whose characters have nowhere been explicitly set out. Hall objected to Spenser's characterisation on the grounds that his people were 'misty morall Types'.[1] This is often true and is more evident in Book II than in any of the other Books; the two figures give them if not more lifelikeness at least more intelligibility.

Alma's House also contains three personifications which are interesting in that they illustrate Spenser's attitude to mental conditions:

> The first of them could things to come foresee:
> The next could of things present best advize;
> The third things past could keepe in memoree.
>
> II. ix. 49

The figures and their rooms are fully described so that it is possible to identify them. It would not be particularly profitable to spend much time on them and they can be classified and left aside as *Phantastes* (imagination), Judgment, and Memory.

---

[1] Joseph Hall, 'His Defiance to Envie'. *The Collected Poems*, ed. A. Davenport. Liverpool, 1949.

Elizabethan psychology is a theory all of its own. The chief merit in this account is what it tells us of Spenser's own outlook —his streak of melancholy in the make-up of *Phantastes*, for instance, his respect for law and for wit in the section on Judgment, and finally his feeling for history in the room of Memory.

A few separate items also need some remark. First, it must be noticed how deliberately Alma is contrasted with Philotime. Her manner is charming and she shews herself 'both wise and liberall'. She is a real person, not a fake that Philotime was discovered to be. She takes them all through her house interpreting the difficulties the two knights find in their contact with the ladies they cannot understand. Secondly, when Spenser describes *Phantastes* he is writing about the material of creative art. Consequently, he decorates *Phantastes's* room with paintings of 'infinite shapes of things dispersed thin', some of which are unknown and have never been formulated by man, others which are familiar and wander about without purpose or direction. He fills the room with 'flies' which symbolise all the uncontrolled notions which may be the basis of fruitful ideas but are largely

> Devices, dreames, opinions unsound,
> Shewes, visions, sooth-sayes and prophesies;
> And all that fained is, as leasings, tales, and lies.

II. ix. 51

None of this is very clear but it is, I think, an attempt on Spenser's part to indicate what the creative process involves. It is comparable with Yeats's poems on the same topic; *Byzantium*, for instance, which is better organised but seems to aim at a similar object. In personifying *Phantastes*, apart from his melancholy, he gives him 'sharpe staring eyes, That mad or foolish seemd'. Clearly for Spenser, as for Shakespeare, the lunatic is very close to the poet.

Thirdly, stanza 22 in the first part of the account of the human body is remarkably difficult. It is an attempt to unite body and soul in terms which are largely geometrical. Upon this Sir Kenelm Digby makes an interesting comment. He argues that it is very unlike Spenser's allegorical technique.[1] It

---

[1] Sir Kenelm Digby. *Observations on the 22nd stanza of the Faerie Queene*, 1644.

is evidently the Author's intention 'to describe the bodie of a man inform'd with a rationall soul, and in prosecution of that designe he sets down particularly the severall parts of the one and of the other. He comprehends the generall description of them both, as (being joyned together to frame a compleat Man) they make one perfect compound.' He then analyses the stanza line by line and demonstrates the nature of the obscurity resulting from Spenser's attempt to combine two types of allegory into one form. Admittedly Digby has perceived the root of the failure. His conception of the operation of Spenser's allegory is very sound. He maintains that during its progress 'he doth himself declare his own conceptions in such sort as they are obvious to any ordinarie capacitie' but in this exceptional stanza he merely glances at 'the profoundest notions that any Science can deliver us' and leaves 'his Readers to wander up and down in much obscuritie, and to come within much danger of erring at his Intention in these lines.'

Looking back upon Book II, one can recognise the truth of Digby's conception of the art of reading Spenser. Concentration and response to meaning expressed in poetry are what is needed; an expectation of intellectual complication is not, and it is only when the allegory fails that the reader feels forced to search for it. *The Faerie Queene* asks for what Dr E. M. W. Tillyard wisely called 'tact', and Canto IX is a visible instance of its necessity. Without it, readers make too much fuss over what the Canto contains. One cannot take an allegorical version of the human body too seriously, nor can one neglect the passages where Spenser is treating his ideas as important. *The Purple Island* by Phineas Fletcher is the outstanding example of the fatal tactless application of the type of allegory Spenser had begun.

Canto X is rarely read by even the most devoted of Spenser's admirers. It emerges directly from Canto IX through the personification of *Memory*, 'an old oldman' physically feeble but still preserving a genuine vigour of mind, and it is to his library, crammed with documents and histories that Arthur and Guyon are conducted. Each asks permission to read a book interesting to him, with the result that Arthur studies *Briton moniments*, a study of the growth of Britain, and Guyon *Antiquitie of Faerie lond*, a study of its mythology. Each discovers from his choice his own ancestry and both are led to the celebration of the Queen and her kingdom which are the climaxes of their two stories. Yet the books offer information of a kind not particularly enlivening to the ordinary reader.[1]

Following Arthur's volume we come across passages which are typical examples of Elizabethan historiography, associated with *The Mirror for Magistrates* in its account of the rise and fall of princes. Each ought, however, to leave the reader with the same impression as it left with Arthur, a sense of the greatness of his country:

> How brutish is it not to understand,
> How much to her we owe, that all us gave,
> That gave unto us all, what ever good we have.
>
> II. x. 69

For Guyon, the mythographical volume is equally impressive. It deals with the advance of the crown of Faerie land ending with the accession of 'fairest *Tanaquill*' or *Gloriana*. Guyon read it with eagerness because he is by origin one of the Faerie world and so he discovers his origin just as Arthur discovered his; and he is rewarded by a brilliant account of the Queen for whom he has gone forth on his quest.

Spenser introduces the House of Temperance with certain authorial comments which are designed to prepare the reader for the moral ideas embodied in its theme. At the beginning of Canto IX he describes the admirable contribution to strength and handsomeness made by the observation of the due government of the body and outlines the deplorable effects upon those who ignore the rules:

> It growes a Monster, and incontinent
> Doth loose his dignitie and native grace.

Canto XI begins with the same topic and stronger emphasis upon the power of reason in controlling the flesh, for this Canto turns upon the lusts which attack each of the five senses whom Arthur has to fight alone since Guyon has gone away in pursuit of his own quest.

This episode is one of those that stands out for its originality.

---

[1] The interest and significance of the chronicles has been defended by Harry Berger, Jr., *The Allegorical Temper*, pp. 89-114.

It is strange, even for Spenser, both in its central figure, Maleger, and in the details of Arthur's fight with him. One feels that in one aspect it follows rightly upon the patriotism Arthur has experienced at the end of his study of the history of Britain of which he will become a part. It also follows upon the attacks upon the five senses which the House of Alma finds difficulty in repulsing. But it is their captain who is the most significant adversary. This is the sole occasion in which the hero is completely mystified. Not even Morddore can help him, and his most skilful strokes produce none of the expected results. At one moment he has to be rescued by Timias, on the same principle in which we have already seen the failure of a great soldier to manage his life alone when Guyon faints after his time in the Cave of Mammon. Here Spenser says explicitly what was implied in Guyon's rescue that not even Arthur is proof against a lack of sure independence:

> So greatest and most glorious thing in ground
> May often need the helpe of weaker hand;
> So feeble is mans state, and life unsound,
> That in assurance it may never stand,
> Till it dissolved be from earthly band.

II. xi. 30

Spenser generalises upon the whole nature of humanity out of this situation and his generalisation creates the certainty of the dubious state of man. Nothing is sure, he says, until man ceases to be what he is, a mixture of body and spirit.

Before the fight with Maleger, Spenser spends some time describing his supporting troops. These have been divided into twelve groups, of which the first seven are only slightly treated (they appear to represent the seven deadly sins) and the remaining five are more fully represented and can be exactly identified. They express the vices which attack the five senses. All are corrupt, ugly and deformed, antimasques of the House of Alma. Spenser gives them animal heads which point to the nature of their distortion, he labels each to indicate which sense is being attacked, and generalises upon the evils they embody. It is not hard to deduce the reasons for the choice of animals for each possesses certain qualities actually or traditionally related

F

to the creatures Spenser includes. He clearly enjoys the accurate analogies which this kind of allegory offers him and transfers the concrete images he has found into generalised expressions of the concept they stand for and also into a condemnation of their singularly repellent form. Thus in the stanza upon Hearing he adds the moral idea that it includes

> Slaunderous reproches, and fowle infamies,
> Leasings, backbytings, and vaine-glorious crakes,
> Bad counsels, prayses, and false flatteries.

II. xi. 10

and the comment that these animal-headed beasts are

> Deformed creatures, in straunge difference.

This prelude to Arthur's venture out of the House of Alma in her defence illustrates an aspect of Spenser's use of allegory which is primarily fanciful. The reader is provided with sufficient clues to understand the meaning of each detail and he can appreciate the author's power of relating factual information to moral ideas. He has met it before in Book II and in Book I. He may well agree with Coleridge's judgment that 'the dullest and most defective parts of Spenser are those in which we are compelled to think of his agents as allegories'.[1] They are parts which do not banish our interest altogether but they tend to slow up our responses. The description of the five attacks on the senses is not markedly sensuous; it is analytical and appeals to a rather superficial element of the mind. Its principal excuse depends upon its preparation for what is to come, for it provides the foundation of the characterisation of Maleger.

Spenser is imaginatively at home in his treatment of this mysterious figure. He brings to it all the subtlety of his narrative and descriptive skill. Speed is visibly present in the movement of the stanza as it reflects the mobility of the chief of the army of sensual vices. Contrasted with their torpid presentation, Maleger creates an effect of surging energy. He enters riding upon a tiger, swift and fierce, moving like the wind, a beast which goes so fast that it defeats the capacity of the eye to follow it and is scarcely seen to step upon the ground. He cannot be caught and eludes every attempt of Arthur's magnificent

---

[1] Coleridge. *Miscellaneous Criticism*, ed. J. M. Raysor, p. 31.

horse to overtake him. Even the sight of him is frightening. Spenser's imagery and description bring terror in their train. They suggest death:

> of such subtile substance and unsound
> That like a ghost he seem'd, whose grave-clothes were unbound.

He carries with him a magnifying power of fear. Excessively lean and pale despite his large broad shoulders, he induces the image of 'a rake' in his meagre body and of 'a dryed rook' in his wrinkled skin. He is dressed in what might be a shroud, in 'canvas thin', and he wears a skull for a helmet. These ideas are rushed upon the reader who absorbs them as best he can, breathless from their impact.

Spenser's style is not normally ideal for creating bodiless figures, but here he has done so. The rapidity of the lines partly accounts for this impression and its success is increased by the details of the portrayal. Milton could achieve a vision of Death more briefly in the single phrase, 'if shape it might be called that shape had none', but Spenser has attained a similar result in a longer form. The longer form gives scope for extended expositions of his meaning. To Ruskin, Maleger stands for the 'captain of the lusts of the flesh', an explanation enunciated in the narrative. Child defines him as 'badly diseased' which is what his name indicates. Osgood agrees with this definition, using the phrase 'sick unto death', and dismisses various other interpretations—'Passions, Sensuality, Death, Deadly Sin'—supporting his and Child's version by alluding to the two hags who accompany Maleger—'Impatience (low resistance) and Impotence (weakness)'.[1] The truth is that all these meanings combine because Maleger is conceived not solely in terms of allegory, as were the monsters in his army, but in terms of symbol which cannot be pressed into one single translation. The figure is memorable in his uniqueness and no solitary meaning can bind him.

Spenser bases his characterisation partly upon a dramatic sense and partly upon a use of imagery. Maleger fights in retreat like a Parthian. He turned his face

> Unto his Tygres taile, and shot at him apace.
> Apace he shot, and yet he fled apace.

---

[1] See *Variorum*, Book II, p. 343, for a full discussion by C. G. Osgood upon the different meanings suggested.

These tactics take Arthur by surprise so that even his military skill, designed for careful delay until the arrows should have been exhausted, fails because Impatience and Impotence collect them again to hand over to their master. Arthur then tries turning attention to the two hags but this move is fatal for it involves a combat of three against one. When his Squire comes to his aid, he is shamed into a revival of energy. Yet all that he attempts to achieve never produces the effect it ought. Each time he is sure that the field is now his own, he encounters a fresher, stronger enemy. This unforeseen result brings the force of drama into the story and creates greater excitement. Everything appears to Arthur, and to the reader, more and more inexplicable. The reactions are co-operated into the action for Spenser avoids any authorial statement but simply expresses natural responses through the mind of Arthur. Why does everything fail, even his own sword, against this horrible death-like figure? No answers seem to hold. Arthur is portrayed as mentally paralysed by Maleger's physical lack of sensibility:

> Ne wist he, what to think of that same sight,
> Ne what to say, ne what to doe at all.

He pursues various theories—magical illusion, perhaps, or an unburied ghost, or a false spirit, or fiend from hell? In the situation before him he encounters a series of paradoxes:

> Flesh without bloud, a person without spright,
> Wounds without hurt, a bodie without might,
> That could doe harme, yet could not harmed bee,
> That could not die, yet seem'd a mortall wight,
> That was most strong in most infirmitee;
> Like did he never heare, like did he never see.

II. xi. 40

Elsewhere comments have been provided upon the narrative by the Palmer, Mammon, and Guyon, but now they are presented in the form of internal reflection of the kind that belongs more commonly to the novel. This is the single occasion in Book II when what is going on in the mind of the hero is defined and it occurs where intelligence is asked from the central character. Naturally the character is Arthur.

Spenser formulates the problem that any experienced knight

and any reader familiar with other battles in the poem considers beyond the power of reason. The speed with which the
conflict began ceases when Arthur stops to meditate; and his
further effort when he casts his sword away and tries to crush
the life out of his enemy merely extends his state of bewilder-
ment. This time he believes Maleger is dead; the event records
his action in casting the body down as triumphantly as the fall
of the Dragon at the climax of Book I was repeatedly recorded,
yet the corpse springs up to fight as furiously as before. Spenser
uses the narrative techniques—surprise, suspense, repetition—
which have been so successful in the past, and the story gains
tremendous emotional forcefulness from them. We become so
completely absorbed that the action is as mystifying to us as it
is to the protagonist. Spenser anticipates the reader's queries as
the tale progresses, identifying them with those of Arthur and
working up to climax when he casts down the supposed carcase

> That backe againe it did aloft rebound
> And gave against his mother earth a gronefull sownd.

It is this fact which provides Arthur with the solution, that
Maleger is the son of Earth and gains his undying life from contact with her. He devises a resolute counterstroke, not to commit him into 'grave terrestriall', but to transport him to a
standing lake three furlongs away.

This is, of course, the legend of Hercules and Antaeus, and
one detail in Maleger's appearance serves to remind classically-
learned readers of this fable, the skeletonic helmet;[1] but Spenser
has dramatised his version so brilliantly that such information is
forgotten in the complete absorption into the action. Typically,
he has also included imagery, which emphasises his concept of
Maleger's nature, and other similes, which give a many-sided
character to the story. Thus the return to consciousness of
Arthur after his collapse, like 'one awakt out of long slombring
shade', is described in a stanza-long simile which builds up the
stature of the hero and enlarges the scale of the conflict; for it
is only then that Arthur is shown to be seriously puzzled by
the resurgence of his adversary. Many images are original in

---

[1] Antaeus was a giant who boasted that he would built a temple out of
the skulls of his adversaries. He was the son of Terra and Neptune.

selection. The bear victimised by dogs and the habits of the fal-
con find their obvious place, but when Spenser chooses a stone
for Arthur's attack he chooses an object which is unexpected
and which enforces the sense of the strangeness of Maleger:

> Thereby there lay
> An huge great stone, which stood upon one end,
> And had not bene removed many a day;
> Some land-marke seem'd to be, or signe of sundry way.
>
> II. xi. 35

This is the normal world of peace which makes Arthur's adversary seem all the more abnormal. It is a detail which looks
forward to the plain perfection of the concluding line to the
Canto. For when the hero returns to the house so weak that he
cannot even mount his horse, Alma sees that he is released from
his arms and laid on a sumptuous bed:

> And all the while his wounds were dressing, by him stayd.

It is the right note to strike for the last sight of Arthur in this
Book. Great poets can always teach others of their kind how to
reach a quiet end. One is reminded of the conclusion of *Paradise
Regained*:

> hee unobserv'd
> Home to his Mothers house private return'd.

iv

We have been waiting for the Bower of Bliss for a long time.
The Book had opened with a scene of its devastating effect upon
one who succumbed to its power and it has been recognised
throughout as the object of Guyon's whole quest, the place
where his merits would ultimately be tested. It is not forgotten
in the course of the other adventures in the Book; traces of its
influence upon other characters, particularly upon Cymochles,
have been seen and the glimpses we have of it in the early stages
of the narrative are all pointers towards the delights radiating
from it. Naturally the reader wants to see it directly, and independently of the eyes of those who are acclimatised to it.

At last Guyon sets out from the House of Temperance, but
even then procrastination intervenes so that the Maleger tale
may be recounted. This incident, significant for its own sake,
is also an anticipation of what Guyon is to encounter both during

his voyage and in the Bower of Bliss itself. Structurally, it is a postponement which increases expectation and suspense since from the moment when Guyon and the Palmer rowed away with the wind and weather favourably inclined we have been eager for the continuation of this journey and find the battle of Arthur something of an interruption. The battle, of course, justifies itself but Spenser, as his manner is, has begun with what will become the climax of the narrative and has then left the beginning hanging in the minds of the reader. Provided one can trust the narrator this, after all, is an imaginative way of conducting a story; one day the trail will be picked up and meanwhile there are many other matters to be attended to.

The sea journey proves to be an Elizabethan tale of intense interest. It proves also to be a reminder of earlier tales, particularly of the *Odyssey* round which much allegorical material had grown. And in many of its details it becomes a reminder of experiences Guyon had sustained in the earlier parts of his story and also an anticipation of what he will encounter in the Bower of Bliss when he reaches it. For these reasons this voyage stands out as one of the most distinctive facets of Book II. On one level it possesses the excitement of the sea explorations known to historians and to readers of Hakluyt, and Spenser has contrived to shed upon it the mysteriousness of journeys into the unknown which hovers over the narratives of Hakluyt. The goal *is* known in the present situation but what it will mean to Guyon and the Palmer who have not seen it has yet to be discovered. They have been instructed to destroy it once they have had a comprehensive view of it. But the reader is curious about the response they will make and even uncertain of what it is really like beyond the fleeting impressions it has made upon him. In effect, the answer to these doubts is partly supplied by the nature of the voyage which tells a good deal about what the Bower of Bliss truly is.

During the journey the thread of the narrative is kept going by Spenser's description of the Boatman's rowing and the Palmer's steering. The solid reality of a sea voyage remains constant all the time in the seamanship of the Boatman and his direct instructions to the Palmer. He knows the hazards of his profession, what are the dangers in each stage of the voyage, what sailors' gossip has reported—'That is the Gulfe of Greedi-ness they say'—and at what moment he has to employ all his strength to bring the boat safely through.[1] Spenser nowhere resists an opportunity to describe the powerful movement of the oars in terms that are beautiful as well as informative:

> So forth they rowed, and that *Ferryman*
> With his stiffe oares did brush the sea so strong,
> That the hoare waters from his frigot ran,
> And the light bubbles daunced all along,
> Whiles the salt brine out of the billowes sprong.

There is time for that, just as there will be time in Book III for a beautiful description of Cymoent gliding over the sea in her dolphin-drawn chariot. But the Boatman has to employ all his skill to keep his oars stiff and stretch 'his brawnie armes, and all his bodie straine' to avoid the treachery of the sea's violence. His awareness of the traps beside their path is so extensive that he can use it both to advise the Palmer upon his piloting and to correct Guyon's notion that they are reaching land by pointing out to him that these are only the *Wandring Islands*. He is also able to warn Guyon against the mermaids they are going to pass who will probably appeal to his susceptibilities by their 'false melodies'. He possesses a sailor's caution on such matters.

---

[1] Part of the practical skill and factual knowledge displayed by the Boatman are probably based on Spenser's experience of voyages round the Kerry coast. Miss Pauline Henley (*Spenser in Ireland*, 1928, pp. 113-114) has traced the passage from the Kenmare river to Smerwick so as to relate it to Lord Grey's expedition against the Spaniards in Smerwick harbour. She identifies each of the hazards encountered by the three voyagers with topo-graphical details: the Gulf of Greediness with Ballinskelligs Bay, the 'hideous rock of Magnes stone' with the Skelligs Rock, 'Vile Reproche' with Little Skellig, the Wandering Islands with the Blaskets, the violent ocean where the mighty sea monsters lurked with the Atlantic, and the calm haven of the mermaids with the peaceful entrance to Smerwick harbour. She suggests that Spenser must have heard the dangers discussed by Admiral Winter and by the sailors. Other investigators have attempted to identify the wrecked ship laden with precious merchandise, but the most plausible theory, that of Sir Humphrey Gilbert's *Delight*, is recorded too late by Hakluyt for Book II (Lois Whitney, 'Spenser's Use of the Literature of Travel in *The Faerie Queene*, Modern Philology, 19, 1921, pp. 145-162). Spenser may also have read the *Legend of St Brendan*, probably in *The Golden Legend*. The apprehension of actuality in the whole of this scene suggests that it was not so much reading as first-hand information gathered in conversation with those who had journeyed over the seas round Ireland.

The Palmer profits too from his knowledge but he has plenty of ability of his own when faced by some of the hazards of the sea. When he has carried out his practical assignment and kept the ship clear of the *Gulfe of Greediness* and the *Rocke of vile Reproch*, he turns to his own preoccupations, and draws a moral against those who desired extremities of wealth or pleasure. For their excess resulted in damage to themselves since they

> Did afterwards make shipwracke violent
> Both of their life, and fame for ever fowly blent.

He rebukes Phaedria who attempts to draw them near the dangerous shore and he can banish with his wand the sea-monsters sent by Acrasia, just as he can banish the land beasts which greet them when they reach the harbour. More than that, he speaks firmly to Guyon when he is attracted by the solitary maiden lamenting on an island and wishes to rescue her. The Palmer points out that she is deceitful and intends only to ruin him despite his knightly purpose of succour. The mermaids are equally deceptive: the five of them are, according to Upton, representative of the pleasures of the five senses. They recall in a different and more enticing form the five groups against which Arthur fought outside the house of Alma. They live in a delightful place:

> it was a still
> And calmy bay, on th'one side sheltered
> With the brode shadow of an hoarie hill,
> On th'other side an high rocke toured still
> That twixt them both a pleasaunt port they made,
> And did like an halfe Theatre fulfill.

> II. xii. 30

These mermaids were sirens and what song they sang Spenser's poetry utters in lingering sounds. It was the song of idleness and peaceful melodiousness, striking the same kind of note and some of the tone of Despair, and it awakened a sensuous response in Guyon. Spenser creates a lyrical effect by linking their song to the music made by the sea and the wind:

> With that the rolling sea resounding soft,
> In his big base them fitly answered,

F *

And on the rocke the waves breaking aloft,
A solemne Meane unto them measured,
The whiles sweet *Zephirus* lowd whisteled
His treble, a straunge kinde of harmony;

II. xii. 33

Spenser is employing the technical terms of the composers of Elizabethan 'ayres' and at the same time is introducing a vocabulary euphonious in itself. The stanza here becomes a singing form relying upon diction and rhythm for its 'straunge kinde of harmony'.

If it can create these gentle tuneful impressions it can also roar, as could Bottom: 'like any sucking dove'. When the monsters of the ocean, the 'bright Scolopendraes arm'd with silver scales' and the 'mighty *monoceroses* with immeasured tayles', which enchanted Keats, begin to appear, and Spenser makes a long, fantastic list of them as all 'dreadfull portraicts of deformitee', the sea creates an appropriate setting:

The waves come rolling, and the billowes rore
Outragiously, as they enraged were,
Or wrathfull *Neptune* did them drive before
His whirling charet, for exceeding feare:
For not one puffe of wind there did appeare.

II. xii. 22

The sea is always unexpected in its ways, and the travellers are constantly open to terror or to delight according to what it chooses to do. There are further surprises, for they come next into a fog where:

all things one, and one as nothing was.
And this great Universe seemd one confused mas.

In the darkness it is impossible for them to trace their direction. Spenser comments succinctly

Worse is the daunger hidden then descride,

and outlines what the unseen danger consists in, birds of death flocking round the boat, and flapping their wings in the faces of the voyagers. This is the landscape of the mind where horror and mystery live. There the journey reaches its culmination, not even the enchanted monsters were as fearsome as these 'fatal birds' which represent the surrounding evils of the island

upon which Acrasia has set her Bower of Bliss. Spenser makes a
list of these invisible creatures which fill the sails with fear, but
the Boatman rows steadily on and the Palmer steers 'stiffly' until
they come to a clear beach and see the land they are searching
for.

Looking back over the journey, we become conscious of the
order in which its hazards have been experienced. First, there
were the physical dangers which represent the moral extremes
into which man may fall; then follow subtle visions of destruction, the nightmare of the sea-monsters, the sirens and the
mermaid who appeal with seduction, not fear, and the spiritual
darkness represented in the fog and in the fatal birds which
lurk in it. All this has been anticipatory to the Bower of Bliss
and the Palmer is justified when, settling into his didactic rôle
once more, he observes that here on land is the place 'where all
our perils grow'. One might reflect upon how many perils had
already grown on the way, but these were only warnings of the
more dangerous temptations which will henceforth call upon
the Knight's capacity for resistance.

Guyon has had predecessors, more than he knows, as well
some whose succumbing he has already witnessed during his
quest—Mordant and Cymochles have become preys to the
allurements of the place and its wily occupant. In fact, their
arrival is heralded by Acrasia's numerous victims who have
been transformed into monsters and hail their presence with
bestial roars. They were once human beings and the Palmer
drives them away with the wand he had used to banish the
fictitious beasts of the ocean. It is no longer the magic wand of
romance tales, but has taken on a greater power. It is alluded
to as a 'mighty staffe', made of the same wood as was employed in the creation of Mercury's rod. A long simile connects
it with the Caduceus and associates it with the action of
Mercury when he descended to Hades and ruled the furies and
the Stygian creatures below. The analogy has the effect of
enlarging the purposes for which the Palmer uses it. These
roaring monsters have been turned into creatures of the Underworld, they will finally be restored to their original forms, but
the hellish activity of Acrasia's witchcraft has been indicated
in this simile even before Guyon and the Palmer have entered

the gardens of the Bower of Bliss. Spenser has prepared the judgment that must be made both in the whole action of the Book and in the sense of urgency of the journey to the site of the Bower before we come to it. The arrival has all the effect of drama.

The Bower of Bliss has attracted much enthusiastic commentary based upon its power of enchantment, and many of its admirers have torn it out of its context in Book II and have dwelt largely upon the poetic quality so inescapable in it. For several readers, perhaps the majority, it has appeared in itself too beautiful to deserve Guyon's roughness of response, his readiness to attack the courteous gestures of those who welcome him on its outskirts, and his willingness to destroy the whole Bower once he has finished his exploratory path through it and has captured its creator.

This opinion inevitably ignores what Acrasia had stood for throughout the Book. Spenser, of course, is forced to make Acrasia's setting alluring in order to create the temptation to which so many characters have succumbed strong enough to be convincing; he has also to make it subtly, if not conspicuously, evil to warrant its destruction. Admittedly, the unprepared mind will find little in the scene itself to suggest the wickedness associated with it. But the voyage has created an impact by which a reader becomes alert and ready for the worst. Some sharing of the Palmer's outlook does the rest. Guyon's virtue is not impregnable—that has been shown in his reaction to the lure of the mermaid and the sirens—and although there is no fear that he will not successfully carry out his quest there still lingers a suspicion that he may find it harder to achieve than he found the conquest of Mammon in Canto VII. There he was able to answer the offerings of wealth with a vision of the golden age and the days when

> with how small allowance
> Untroubled Nature doth herself suffise.

Now, in the Bower of Bliss he is required to see Nature incapable of sufficing herself and needing to be enhanced by the elaborations of art. He is inevitably tempted in a way he was not in the Cave of Mammon. There had been plenty of warnings

during the voyage where he had encountered various forms of
evil, but the evil he has now to identify and destroy is more
subtle, more attractive, and to someone of Guyon's calibre
more deceiving since it incorporates natural beauty increased
by the power of art. It was, in contrast with the world Guyon
had referred to in his debate with Mammon:

> A place pickt out by choice of best alive,
> That natures worke by art can imitate:
> In which what ever in this worldly state
> Is sweet, and pleasing unto living sense,
> Or that may dayntiest fantasie aggrate,
> Was poured forth with plentifull dispence,
> And made there to abound with lavish affluence.
>
> II. xii. 42

Round this place was set a fence intended to keep the visitors
inside, and the beasts, which Guyon and the Palmer had seen
on their landing, outside. But the fence was 'weake and thin'
because there was no serious fear of attack and even the entrance
gate had been built of light material because it had been
designed for pleasure and not for defence or war. The important
comment upon the description of the place in which the Bower
of Bliss is sited lies in the explanation of its failure to provide any
protective measures:

> Nought feard their force, that fortilage to win,
> But wisedomes powre, and temperaunces might,
> By which the mightiest things efforced bin.
>
> II. xii. 43

Here is the moment when the strength of the defences is to be
tested by what Spenser regards as their greatest danger; the
Knight of Temperance and the wise Palmer are ready to enter
the world of Acrasia and to win 'that fortilage'.

The approaches to the Bower, its gate and its fountain display the surpassing attraction of visual art, and the Bower
itself offers a wide-ranging appeal to all physical senses and
intensifies the power of the natural scene. Spenser observes that
everything that is pleasing to 'living sense' and whatever can
be created by imagination are set forth there. It seems that
these two together express the meaning of the phrase:

That natures worke by art can imitate.

Whether 'that' depends upon 'place' or 'best alive' is immaterial. The point is that nature is present overwhelmingly but its productions are multiplied in quality and quantity by contributions of art. The two are balanced in the images which follow, and although there is greater emphasis on the works of art in the description of the gate and the fountain, nature comes to its own in the image of the Bower itself.

The relation between nature and art in this particular scene has been discussed by C. S. Lewis in an influential chapter in *The Allegory of Love*. It is his view that the Bower of Bliss ought to be distinguished from the Garden of Adonis in Book III as an example of art contrasted with nature. 'He (Spenser) understands Nature as Aristotle did—the "nature" of anything being its unimpeded growth from within to perfection, neither checked by accident nor sophisticated by art. To this "nature" his allegiance never falters ... and when Nature personified enters his poem she turns out to be the greatest of his shining ones. In some respects, indeed, she symbolises God Himself.' Art, on the other hand, creates a world dominated by 'artifice, sterility, death'. 'The similarity between them is just that similarity which exists between the two gardens in Jean de Meun; the similarity of the real to the pretended and of the archetype to the imitation. *Diabolus simius Dei*.'[1]

Many objections can be raised against this distinction. Spenser elsewhere in *The Faerie Queene* demonstrates the power of art to take over at the stage where nature left off. Outside the Temple of Venus in Book IV, for example:

> For all that nature by her mother wit
> Could frame in earth, and forme of substance base,
> Was there, and all that nature did omit,
> Art playing second natures part, supplyed it.

> IV. x. 21

Here it seems plain that art is not doing anything different from what nature had done. She plays the rôle of 'second nature' which seems to imply an extension of nature's function. In *Paradise Regained*, Milton who frequently remembered the

[1] *The Allegory of Love*, pp. 330-336.

thought and phraseology of Spenser throughout his poetry,
describes the grove which Christ found early in the morning
after his first temptation in terms which are consistent with this
opinion. It is a natural scene with some contribution from
human activity:

> . . . Cottage, Herd, or Sheep-cote none he saw,
> Only in a bottom saw a pleasant Grove,
> With chaunt of tuneful Birds resounding loud;
> Thither he bent his way, determin'd there
> To rest at noon, and entr'd soon the shade
> High rooft and walks beneath, and alleys brown
> That open'd in the midst a woody Scene,
> Natures own work it seem'd (Nature taught Art)
> And to a Superstitious eye the haunt
> Of Wood-Gods and Wood-Nymphs; . . .
>
> II. 288-298

We hear no more of the appearance of this Grove except that it
was used at once by Satan as a setting for the first stage of his
second temptation, that of the kingdoms of the world, and
provided an ideal background for the creation of an imaginary
feast. Milton then abandons his principle that Nature has
taught Art because the feast offers an appeal of infinite
splendour directed to all the human senses. It is made up of
richness of food and wine drawn from every part of the world,
decorated by the presence of mythological and legendary
figures derived from the romances, and associated with the
appeal of music and with exquisite Arabian scents. Art here has
become something else, an expression of a physical temptation
which is hemmed round by all that might attract sensuously
and imaginatively the choice of Satan's victim. In the context
it is evil, and might be used to support C. S. Lewis's contrast
between art and nature. Christ dismisses the feast as 'pompous
Delicacies', and it is swept away in the talons of harpies. One
remembers that in *Paradise Lost* the world in which Adam and
Eve are placed does not suffer from the designs of Art. The Art
condemned consisted of 'Beds and curious Knots' (the Elizabethan garden in fact) but the position of the trees, hillocks,
and rivers suggests shapeliness of another kind. Sir Thomas
Browne in *Religio Medici* refers to nature as 'the art of God', and

Paradise is Milton's expression of this concept. Sir Thomas Browne carries his definition beyond Milton's Paradise for in his view 'all things are artificial' since God uses Nature as his instrument in bringing about the Art of his created world. By Art, Browne means, in effect, the coherent ordering of God's Providence which may include pattern and design or may simply be the teleological character of created things.

For the Elizabethans, art fulfilled the function described by Sir Thomas Browne and disposed a formal excellence upon natural material. 'Sensuous vividness,' as Miss Tuve has pointed out, 'goes beyond precision and accuracy alone to achieve what Quintilian says amplification requires, "the gift of signifying more than we say" (IX. ii. 3).'[1] Art consequently consisted in concentrating upon the significance of the images and not in confining itself to copying their external appearances. Hence the rôle of the emblematic image in Spenser's poetry. In it, as in the poetry of Sidney and Drayton, the 'moral' is more important than the visual description which only contributes to it. 'No study is more fruitful as a clarification of the relation of "picture" to "poem" than careful observation of the interplay between statement and image throughout a fairly long passage in any of the greater poets. Spenser's judgments of when overt statement is necessary in an image are extremely subtle, and his degrees of explicitness are consciously and most delicately varied.'[2] It is this conception that has to be kept in mind when following the overland journey to Acrasia's Bower. This is divided into two sections, each of which prepares Guyon for the evil embodied in her person. First, there is the gate illustrating the story of Jason and Medea guarded by a figure seated in the porch who is 'Pleasures porter'. Secondly, there is the fountain in which two living girls are bathing, guarded by a 'comely dame'. Both these guardians are dressed in loose inadequate garments and both offer drinks to the incoming visitors.

The gate is described in detail as a work of art. But its subject is that which would have soon been recognised by the Elizabethan reader as a warning. The story of Jason and Medea is a

R. Tuve, *Elizabethan and Metaphysical Imagery*, 1947, p. 40.
[2] *ibid.*, p. 58.

study of 'voluptatum desiderium',[1] and Spenser underlines the
emblematic meaning by adding generalised comment to his
pictorial representation. The gate is made of ivory and reflects
the themes of magic, gold, love and treachery in the tale. These
are summed up in the first descriptive stanza ending with the
voyage of the *Argo* which:

> First through the *Euxine* seas bore all the flowr of *Greece*.

Spenser then develops its themes in a more detailed treatment
of it as a work of art with the Elizabethan admiration for the
skill with which an image can resemble a true thing. Its art is
the art of transforming a mobile subject into rigid material.
The ivory is inseparable from the waves through which the
Argo is speeding; the waves turn into the ivory:

> Ye might have seene the frothy billowes fry
> Under the ship, as thorough them she went,
> That seemd the waves were into yvory,
> Or yvory into the waves were sent;

II. xii. 45

Here the verb 'fry' gives much more exactitude to the image of
the movement of the water than the expected 'fly' would have
achieved. This is a piece of sensuous vividness where the pictorial impact is mingled with the medium through which the
boat travels. The rest of the stanza combines further description
with generalised statement:

> And other where the snowy substance sprent
> With vermell, like the boyes bloud therein shed,
> A piteous spectacle did represent,
> And otherwhiles with gold besprinkled;
> It seemd th'enchaunted flame, which did *Creusa* wed.

Here is the emotional response to the murder of Absyrtes, and
to the flaming robe which Medea designed for her rival.

The keeper of the gate is strongly distinguished from the true
Genius, 'good *Agdistes*', for he carries out none of the virtuous
activities of the figure whose name he bears. The true *Genius*,
Spenser defines as a power which looks after human interests
and is fundamentally man's moral sense protecting him from

[1] H. G. Lotspeich, *Classical Mythology in the Poetry of Edmund Spenser*,
pp. 21-22. See *Variorum, The Faerie Queene*, Book II, p. 351.

personal mistakes. The false *Genius*, whom the occupants of Acrasia's garden so label, is exactly the opposite:

> The foe of life, that good envyes to all,
> That secretly doth us procure to fall
> Through guilefull semblaunts, which he makes us see.

He produces a distorted vision of the world. The violence of Guyon's response to him depends upon this contrast. He throws down the bowl in which the, apparently consecrated, wine is profferred to him and breaks the staff with which this false Genius has created clever deceptive appearances. Thus free of this idolatrous temptation Guyon and the Palmer can go forward to their goal.

The fineness of Spenser's visual senses stands out at this stage of the journey and the specific description of the appearance of the gate and its guarding figure suggests that there may be a visible as well as a literary source for them. Its outstanding effect partly depends upon the Spenserian movement from exact precision to the more general stretch of landscape which acts as a link between the gate and the more dangerous fountain which is to follow. Spenser's use of foils is constantly apparent in his more heightened passages, and the 'large and spacious plaine' which now creates a scene of natural beauty comparable with the familiar classical landscapes or with Eden 'if ought with Eden mote compaire', is introduced to create a further type of physical temptation. Miss Tuve suggests that there may have been in Spenser's memory some actual image of Jason in ivory and some real mazer which he could have seen. Her argument is convincing and one which would be useful also in relation to the tapestries in Books III and V. It is 'one reason for his extraordinary clarity of literary and visual sources—a combination which I think could be pointed out far oftener if we knew as much about his artistic interests—and took as much cognisance of them—as we do of his literary sources.'[1] This suggestion starts a hare which any reader must wish to chase. What of those tantalising phrases from E.K. in *The Shepheardes Calender*, what of the comments in the Proems to each Book of *The*

[1] R. Tuve. 'Spenser and Mediaeval Mazers; with a note on Jason in Ivory.' *Studies in Philology*, 34, 1937, pp. 138-147.

Faerie Queene, and what of the recognisably emblematic figures
like Furor in Book II and all the sea monsters derived from
Gesner and from who knows what sculptured ceilings or frescoes
in Elizabethan homes? There is, as yet, no answer to such
questions but they do at least pose themselves and direct critical
interest towards the style of description of certain items in
Spenser's treatment of visible material.

The stretch of landscape is here consistent with previous discussions of the relation between art and nature and begins with
an example of the activity of each within its own sphere. Art, it
seems, triumphs at first, for the grassy ground was

> Mantled with greene, and goodly beautifide
> With all the ornaments of *Floraes* pride,
> Wherewith her mother Art, as halfe in scorne
> Of niggard Nature, like a pompous bride
> Did decke her, and too lavishly adorne,
> When forth from virgin bowre she comes in th' early morne.
>
> II. xii. 3

'Niggard', 'pompous', 'too lavishly' are all words detrimental
to appreciation and the effect is fortified by the gate at the end
of the meadow which was made of vines which were wound in
'wanton wreathings intricate' so that it resembled, but was not,
in fact, a solid gate like its predecessor. One is reminded of
George Herbert's phrases for sin which were so frequently
expressed in imagery that was 'curved' and 'trammelled'. Here,
in the Porch, stands a personified figure, of *Excesse*, reaching for
the grapes to squeeze into a bowl. Spenser builds up this
personification partly by emphasising her setting: the grapes
were like jewels, hyacinths, rubies and emeralds with some
made of gold 'lurking' (as Cymochles lurked in Acrasia's
Bower) among the rest and inducing a cloying appearance; and
partly by direct description: she was comely but dressed in loose
unwomanly attire, a contrast with the trim garment of Medina,
but all too like the untidy fashion of the false *Genius*. In some
ways this scene creates an atmosphere that is more tempting.
At least, Guyon has to bridle his will and proceed looking
neither to right nor left. The usual offering of a drink from the
guardian's bowl is met with an equally violent response. Guyon
throws it to the ground, breaks it to pieces so that the wine

'stained all the land'.[1] Yet once past this danger he meets a worse. The degree of its appeal can be measured by its effect upon Guyon: for the first time he begins to weaken and has to be called to order by the Palmer. Beyond the Porch they come upon a 'Paradise', that characteristic feature in Spenser's scenery. Art's earlier triumph over nature is not carried further; the two here beautify each other. It is not this which attracts Guyon, nor the lavish splendour of the fountain in the centre where the many channels are filled with statues of naked boys and covered by a trail of golden ivy (an emblem of lust) which dipped its 'lascivious arms' down into the water. All this brings the art of sexual attraction in poetry as far as one might expect it to go if Acrasia's Bower is to remain the culmination, but one final allurement is left for Guyon's susceptibility—the two naked girls bathing in the pool below the fountain. They are alive and shameless. It is now that the Palmer has to recall Guyon to his proper duty. They are on the edge of their goal.

All that the long journey embodying Guyon's quest has signified must now be concluded in the vision of Acrasia with the last of her lovers. We know how many good and bad characters (Mordant and Cymochles) have been bewitched by her, we have learnt the range of her defences during the sea voyage and the range of her sensuality on the land journey. What else can Spenser add to make her the object of Guyon's unrelenting capture, and to destroy her surroundings without restoration? He discovered the answer, as only a poet could, by discovering means to surpass the physical, sensual character of the two scenes presented on the way to the Bower with a subtler movement of the verse. Anticlimax which might have resulted is avoided and Spenser creates an unsuspected richness in scene and person.

---

[1] An interpretation of this scene has been suggested by N. S. Brooke, 'C. S. Lewis and Spenser: Nature, Art, and the Bower of Bliss', *The Cambridge Journal*, II, 7, 1949, pp. 420-434. He identifies the three stages of the journey after the entrance as representing three aspects of the human body, the Liver (tempted by *Excesse*), the Heart (tempted by the two bathing girls) and the Brain (tempted in Acrasia's Bower where the Body succumbs to the passions and the Brain does not rule as it should). This is a perceptive analysis which illuminates details of the journey. *Excesse's* drink 'stained all the land' because it is absorbed by the body.

'It seems to me that poetry has two outstanding characteristics. One is that it is indefinable. The other is that it is
essentially unmistakable.'[1] This remark may be obvious but it
reaches out towards the impression which distinguishes the
scene in which Acrasia appears from its predecessors. Both epithets can be directed to the nature of the poetry when the witch
hovers over her willing victim, by now satisfied and asleep.
The unmistakable feature of Spenser's poetry depends chiefly
upon his use of his stanza form and it is in such a section that its
individual quality essentially lies. Its most striking merit relies
on its determination to avoid open statement, to leave the
nature of the melodious sound which haunts the atmosphere as
a mystery. It cannot be described nor placed exactly. Only a
great poet is willing to refrain from trying to do so. It was, he
says,

> Such as attonce might not on living ground,
> Save in this Paradise, be heard elsewhere:

II. xii. 70

Moreover, the hearer could not ascertain what kind of music it
was, since it grew out of the harmony of all kinds of musical
sounds. Spenser combines them in one line:

> Birdes, voyces, instruments, windes, waters, all agree.

II. xii. 70

He then finds words for the music towards which each makes
its own contribution: the birds 'attempred' their notes to the
voice, the 'angelical voices' correspond to the instruments, the
'instruments' meet the cadence of the waters, the 'waters' varied
their strength to that of the wind, and

> The gentle warbling wind low answered to all.

II. xii. 71

This stanza draws together the nature of audible effect by
analysis and by the scheme of assonance so that parts combine
to create a harmonious consort.

Yet it preserves the suggested mystery by qualifying references to its origin. The music 'seemed heard to bee', while on
the bed of rose-leaves Acrasia reposes enjoying the presence of

[1] G. M. Young, 'Magic and Mudlakes' in *Daylight and Champagne*, 1948,
pp. 170-171.

her new lover. In this situation delight bears with it the awareness of mutability; a sense of transience runs through the song
that is chanted as the destroyers descend upon the two lovers.
'Gather the Rose of love, whilest yet is time', is the old trouba-
dour note, the contemporary Elizabethan refrain, and the
eternal cry through all literary generations. It gains irony in
that it is here regarded as a 'horrible enchantment' where an
honourable knight, Sir Verdant, has enchained himself and
where Acrasia, too, shows a consciousness of the brevity of the
joys she will share with him. Her attitude, hanging above her
sleeping lover, is that of a professional and beautiful mistress.
The physical reminiscence of sexual pleasure is conveyed in the
description of her 'snowy brest', which enhances the attraction
of her person.

The poetry is indefinable as well as unmistakable. The reader
becomes conscious of its quality, and, while recognising the
condemnation of the description, must respond to the magic in
it. He could attach that magic to the imagery but would have
to agree that the imagery contrives to suggest far more than its
context requires. Both the reference to the spider's web and
that to the starlight upon the water contain greater emotional
force than their introduction needs:

> More subtile web *Arachne* cannot spin,
> Nor the fine nets, which oft we woven see
> Of scorched deaw, do not in th'aire more lightly flee.

and:

> And her faire eyes sweet smyling in delight,
> Moystened their fierie beames, with which she thrild
> Fraile harts, yet quenched not; like starry light
> Which sparckling on the silent waves, does seeme more bright.

Each occurs in a stanza which possesses a falling cadence and,
granted the beauty of the words and associations in the two
images, we are driven to conclude that the 'indefinable' nature
of the poetry ultimately lies in the rhythm. Here must be the
secret of Spenser's power when all else is set aside.

The end of the Canto and of the Book is precisely what is
expected. The witch is secured in the Palmer's net, Sir Verdant
reforms his ways, and the wild beasts become human beings

again. The distortion which has afflicted them is not easily shaken off: some are ashamed, some angry, and one only rebelled against losing his bestial form. For Guyon there is an opportunity to end as he began, as a moral figure, prepared to deplore the weakness of mankind. And it is Spenser's voice we remember at the end, accepting the unnatural character of man at his worst, and ready to find a better prospect in the next Canto:

Let *Grill* be *Grill*, and have his hoggish mind,
But let us hence depart, whilest wether serves and wind.

Chapter VI

BOOK III. SOLITUDE AND SEPARATION

BOOKS III and IV are designed very differently from their two predecessors. Officially the topic of III is 'Chastity', that of IV is 'Friendship' which means, in effect, the relationships between individual characters. Spenser finds here an opportunity for greater variety of content and the exercise of a wider range of imagination. Books I and II required some channelling of his ideas and his powers. He treats Holiness as a discovery, but limited to certain specific activities of humanity; to morality, illusion, and knowledge of religious truth. He treats Temperance as a quality definable and maintainable, although the definitions become vaguer on the voyage to the Bower of Bliss for there the sea is beginning to create the manifold impact it is to make in Book III. But Chastity and Friendship are interpreted in a way that is more inclusive. Book III is focussed upon the making and conduct of the relationships between people through love; Book IV upon the sustaining of such relationships, hence the prominence of Concord and Discord and the conclusions in marriage. Their themes demand the presence of many different kinds of character and a general diversity of setting. In both Books the life of the sea and the life of the forest are introduced, each representing some particular type of meaning. Strict formulae break down, as Spenser discovered in the *Fowre Hymnes*, because he wanted freedom of imagination. His object was to widen the scope of the allegory so as to include all that man experiences as a human being in relation to others of his kind.

Book III, which is closely joined to Book IV in plot and technique, is the Book in which Spenser's alleged desire to 'overgo Ariosto' is most plainly seen. He suspends the progress of the story so as to allow a fresh one to begin just as was Ariosto's habit. He introduces most Cantos with generalised comment on the nature of its material, adding some kind of apology where the event appears to need it. Moreover, the Book lacks a central focus for its narrative. Admittedly it begins and ends with the story of Britomart; but into the centre are pushed the Ariostan adventures of Florimell. Neither story reaches its end in Book III, each develops during Book IV and reaches its conclusion in Book V, where Justice attains its right of winding up unfinished personal relationships.

Book III is characterised by the presence of a number of long passages, each good of its kind, but all markedly varied in substance and feeling. These are not subordinated to one narrative purpose as in Book I, nor to one principal topic as in Book II. Recognisably in Book II the incident of Trompart and Braggadocchio belongs to something different and the presence of Belphoebe there is designed as a contrast with the recurrent concept of Acrasia. Yet unity is given to the whole by the central theme which controls the material and directs the nature of the episodes in relation to the essential topic. The Cave of Mammon, Arthur's fight with Maleger, and Guyon's voyage to the Bower of Bliss spring from a deeper level of imagination, yet the three episodes are directed by the evolution of the Book as the experience of a single knight in the demonstration of Temperance. But in Book III we have two distinct narratives each coloured by its own individual impressions. The incidents in the two separate narratives are not drawn together in any type of structural unity. Britomart is the chief figure, outstanding in significance and character, and Spenser has emphasised her importance by putting her in touch with all the other lesser characters. The Book opens with her fight against Guyon, an episode in which Guyon behaves in a manner apparently out of key with the temperate figure who has commanded the tone of the previous Book. Now he asks Arthur to allow him to attack an unknown knight whom they meet; in the fierce duel which follows Guyon is knocked off his horse, and responds with angry determination to continue with his sword. The Palmer, whose knowledge tells him that Britomart's spear possesses an enchanted magic force, combines with Arthur to pacify him so that the two make peace, 'through goodly temperance and affection chaste'. The allegorical meaning in this scene can be interpreted from two aspects: perhaps Guyon is still having to learn how and when his reason can best control his emotions, or perhaps Spenser wishes to demonstrate that Chastity is a higher virtue than Temperance and sacrifices Guyon to this end. There is decided narrative merit in this episode, apart from its allegorical interest, in that Arthur calms Guyon with singular tact by attributing his failure not to incompetence but to the swerving of his horse. Here the literal nature of the situation is distinctly brought out.[1]

Spenser has in his scene linked Book II with Book III by putting their heroes together in the first episode, just as he is to recall Book I in the next scene by enabling Britomart to rescue the Red Crosse Knight outside Malecasta's castle. It is Britomart who fights with Marinell as part of his destiny, she who spends the night in Malbecco's house, thus meeting Satyrane, the Squire of Dames, and Paridell who are all kept outside until Malbecco is forced to admit them. Florimell crosses her path at the beginning, and Timias is with Arthur when she is attacked by Guyon. All these figures have, or have had, stories of their own which are related in *theme* to that of Britomart. In Canto v the isolated Marinell episode and the isolated Florimell episode are shown to have in common the basic character of love; and, later, the love of Timias for Belphoebe harmonises with the ideal which Britomart represents. Moreover, Florimell in her refusal of salvation from any knight who tries to help her, stands as an extreme reflection of the Chastity at the core of the Book, just as Paridell and Hellenore and the false Florimell are versions of its opposite.

Britomart remains central to what Book III is about, but her story does not govern its sequence as the Red Crosse Knight and Guyon governed theirs. Instead (as has been pointed out in Chapter II, p. 43), Spenser went out of his way in the Letter to Raleigh to insist that there are 'other adventures intermedled rather as Accidents then intendments' such as the 'love of Britomart, the overthrow of Marinell, the misery of Florimell,

---

[1] The third and more convincing explanation is that this Guyon is not the Guyon of Book II. This Guyon, though accompanied by the Palmer, is riding his horse, although it had been stolen in Book II, and in Canto VIII. Braggadocchio arrives still in possession of it and it is not officially returned until Book V. This has been considered in Chapter II which is concerned with the textual peculiarities in the narrative of *The Faerie Queene* as a whole, pp. 46-52.

the virtuousness of Belphoebe and the lasciviousness of Hellenore'. It is this freedom of substance which gives Book III its
spirit and its integrity.

Leaving aside for the moment the allegorical significance of
each episode, the reader rapidly becomes absorbed in the unexpected variety of the stories he meets. After the duel between
Guyon and Britomart, a number of unforeseen events come into
play. Florimell crosses the path of the knights, and her mysterious flight provokes a separation between them all. Arthur and
Guyon pursue her, Timias follows the rough forester from whom
she is escaping, and Britomart, little interested in the situation
of an unfortunate, if beautiful, girl, waits for their return and
then continues her own journey independently. The adventures
of each of these figures (apart from that of Guyon who vanishes
from the scene) are treated separately as stories which Spenser
finds attractive in themselves. He has consequently succeeded
in incorporating into Book III a collection of tales which are
characteristically Elizabethan and which obviously appealed to
readers of his time. Some come from romances, some from folk-
lore, some from Chaucer, and some from Ariosto. Spenser and
his readers were familiar with the origins of the tales; but the
degree of the closeness of each to its source varies with the use
to which Spenser puts it.

The first occurrence of a strongly romantic episode appears
in Britomart's adventure after her parting with the other
knights. She reaches a castle in which she finds a knight defend-
ing himself against six enemies. This is an occasion where a hero
is called upon to assist a man who is being unfairly attacked.
This man proves to be the Red Crosse Knight who is required
to sacrifice his loyalty to his own lady and become the servant
of Malecasta, the owner of the castle. The six knights who are
attacking him possess italianate names bearing sexual associations (Gardante, Parlante, Jocante, Basciante, Bacchante and
Noctante); they belong to the world of the courts of love but
their nomenclature connects them particularly closely with
Malecasta's ill-omened castle with its tapestries portraying the
love of Venus and Adonis. Britomart, learning the motives of
the attackers and the fidelity of their victim who will never
abandon his lady, the 'errant damsel' (i.e. Una), maintains

that love cannot be sacrificed at their demand. We are reminded of the *Merchant's Tale* by the distinction of love from lust. Here is one type of narrative in Book III, where the Chaucerian influence is greatly evident. It is also present in the episode of the magic mirror which comes from the unfinished *Squire's Tale*, in the fabliau told by the Squire of Dames, and in the story of Malbecco and Hellenore. It is equally apparent in Book IV. In both Books there is a less obvious, but equally recognisable, sense of the Chaucerian model in charge of the tempo of events. The ability to write briefly can scarcely be regarded as one of Spenser's merits, but in these two Books and in Book V there are signs that the narrative art of his predecessor can always bear fruit when occasion allows. Thus Britomart's triumph over the six knights provokes the briefest of moral conclusions when the last two yield without fighting:

> Ah (said she then) now may ye all see plaine
> That truth is strong, and trew love most of might,
> That for his trusty servaunts doth so strongly fight.

Thus, too, in Book IV Belphoebe finds the minimum comment when she comes upon Timias kissing Amoret:

> Is this the faith, she said, and said no more,
> But turnd her face, and fled away for evermore.

Both these examples are instances of Spenser's sense of the advantage of brevity in the use of speech related to comparatively full description of action. That he could also introduce brief generalisations to sum up emotional responses in narratives becomes apparent in these Books. Scudamour, as we recollect, in the blacksmith's hut has a long wretched night, kept awake by the labours of the smith (Care) and by the dreams that interrupt his sleep, for:

> The things that day most minds, at night doe most appeare.

This is an instance of Spenser's often profound psychological perception of the mental states of his characters but it is expressed in terms of a short comment rather than in a fully expanded exposition.

To return to the variety of the stories occurring in Books III and IV, it is noticeable that Spenser has clearly discovered ways of telling a dramatic tale so as to bring out its dramatic nature. This is partly a matter of timing, and here, more often than in Books I and II, he can achieve this result because the demands of allegory are outweighed by the demands of story as story. We cannot, of course, ignore the presence of allegory, but the shift in these Books from one type of allegory to another leaves Spenser free to imply the change by concentrating upon the plot and action in the tales themselves. The introduction to each Canto points to the interpretation embodied within the narrative leaving it free to grow of its own accord. Britomart's search for Artegall begins in a long inserted explanation which emerges out of her enquiry about him from the Red Crosse Knight as they are departing from Malecasta's castle. She had discovered that Artegall is the man she is to marry by her sight of his picture in the mirror given to her father, King Ryence. Her determination to find him had led her to visit Merlin, the enchanter who had presented the mirror to King Ryence, and from his answer she decided to travel through the land of the Faeries disguised as an Amazon.

The source of this story is a mixture of medieval legend, hedged about with romance detail, and Renaissance poetry. Spenser described all that the mirror could do for King Ryence and linked its power with that of the Egyptian tower built by Ptolemy for his love, Phao. It has other associations not mentioned by Spenser some of which must have been known to Elizabethan readers. Warton refers to the mirror in Chaucer's *Squire's Tale* which was presented to Cambuscan as a means of information regarding his friendships and the safety of kings and kingdoms. He also associates it with the globe shown to Vasco da Gama in Camoens's *Lusiad* which represented the system of the world and its future history, and with the mirror in Drayton's *Heroical Epistles* where Surrey is recorded as having seen Geraldine lying on a sick-bed. Similar images, derived from medieval romances, are used by Boiardo and Ariosto.[1]

The retrospective account of Britomart's visit to Merlin occupies two complete Cantos (ii and iii) and gives Spenser an opportunity to develop his presentation of the character of

[1] See for all these sources *The Faerie Queene*, Book III, *Variorum* edition, 1934, pp. 216-217.

Britomart and to place her in a historical setting. Weight is given to this account by the importance of Merlin. Spenser describes how he hides in an underground cave for fear of the Lady of the Lake, and he adds a naturalistic presentation of the region where the cave is sited. This is, he suggests, a place the reader might wish to visit as a sightseer, but only if he avoids entering the cave itself for it is haunted by evil spirits. By the river Barry, among the Dynevour hills, Merlin conducts his magical operations, and it is here that Britomart and Glauce come, cautiously preserving their anonymity. They are promptly identified, and Merlin embarks upon a vision of Britomart's future, just as he had done for Bradamante (*Orlando Furioso*, III, 17-48). Spenser, like Ariosto, is more interested in the personality and the future history of his heroine than in the moral theme embodied by her. Britomart's sense of emotional affliction has been set out at length and her efforts to cure herself of these unexplained feelings described with considerable wit. A visit to church brings little assistance. She and Glauce goes:

> With great devotion, and with litle zeale:
> For the faire Damzell from the holy herse
> Her love-sicke heart to other thoughts did steale;
> And that old Dame said many an idle verse,
> Out of her daughters hart fond fancies to reverse.
>
> III. ii. 48

Witchcraft is the alternative next suggested by Glauce and she performs an elaborate ritual to banish all dangerous sentiments from Britomart's mind. Spenser describes her complicated rite with due respect to its technique but without any of the poetic effects with which Campion could endow a magic spell. In fact, his account has a distinctly satirical tone, suitable as a comment upon Glauce's limited outlook and the uselessness of her design. These were, after all, only 'idle charms' incapable of banishing the love now so firmly fixed in Britomart's mind.

The visit to Merlin begins a new Canto, opening with an exordium to love. Characteristically, Spenser distinguishes it from lust, and insists upon the need for its restoration to the God who inspired men to deeds of heroism and upon its attachment to the art of Clio who can bring the power of poetry to express the glory of Britomart's future. These stanzas introduce an epic style in their appeal to the Muse and are designed to raise the level of the poem to its due importance. They include a reference to Queen Elizabeth whose ancestor Britomart is, and follow the praise of her in the opening stanzas in Canto II. There Elizabeth was cited as a precedent for the wisdom displayed in the conduct of the Book's heroine. Spenser's own voice is constantly heard in the opening part of Book III. His description of heroic women strikes a note of wonder in Canto II, and in the Proem an apologia is offered for the presentation of the Queen in 'coloured shows' throughout *The Faerie Queene*. In it she is to be seen in 'mirrors more than one'. She has been Raleigh's Cynthia, and now is Spenser's Gloriana and his Belphoebe. An aspect of her will be reflected in Britomart in that Britomart is a figure of historical significance. Her chastity is imaged as a virtue associated with a noble marriage. Out of Britomart's union with Artegall will emerge the greatness of a kingdom.

In the interview with Merlin Spenser accompanies prophecy with patriotism as he had in the rendering of Arthur, and in the monuments of Britain in Book II. This rhetorical passage comes out of long-remembered poetic belief, and for Spenser it was an idea that conveyed the excellence of the Tudor dynasty. It stimulates in Merlin's mind a quality of Virgilian grandeur:

> Renowmed Kings, and sacred Emperours,
>   Thy fruitfull Ofspring, shall from thee descend;
> Brave Captaines, and most mighty warriours,
>   That shall their conquests through all lands extend,
>   And their decayed Kingdomes shall amend:
> The feeble Britons, broken with long warre,
>   They shall upreare, and mightily defend
> Against their forrein foe, that comes from farre,
> Till universall peace compose all civill iarre.
>
>   III. iii. 23

In reply to the tentative enquiry from Britomart he outlines the reason for her vision in the magic mirror:

> It was not, *Britomart*, thy wandring eye,
> Glauncing unwares in charmed looking glas,
> But the streight course of heavenly destiny,
> Led with eternall providence, that has
> Guided thy glaunce, to bring his will to pas.
>
> III. iii. 23-24

Merlin goes on to promise the proudest knight that has been known and foretells his reappearance from the Faerie world to acquire the throne that is his right, through the assistance of Britomart. Their life would be involved in warfare for the sake of the children who would be born to them. He continues to describe the history of their descendants fighting for their country against the Saxons until all seemed lost:

> Then woe, and woe, and everlasting woe,
> Be to the Briton babe, that shalbe borne,
> To live in thraldome to his fathers foe;
> Late king, now captive, late lord, now forlorne,
> The worlds reproch, the cruell victors scorne . . .
>
> III. iii. 42

Merlin's powers of lamentation, very different from the joyful prophecies with which his history had begun, move Britomart deeply and she asks whether any conclusion can be reached after these disasters. Merlin promises a union between the British and Saxon tribes, out of which will emerge internal peace and ultimately the rule of a 'royal virgin' whose government will direct successfully a struggle against the nearest threatening country, the Netherlands. 'But yet the end is not . . .' Merlin says, leaving the future in the hands of the spirits who have empowered his foresight. Britomart follows what she has learnt from Merlin's vision. She acquires a set of armour possessed by the defeated Saxon Queen, Angela, and a spear of magic properties which enables her to defeat Guyon, the six knights and, later, Marinell.

These two Cantos are sources of information about Britomart. They establish her central significance in Book III by setting her in a royal context and by endowing her with the qualities of a living human being. Spenser's style varies from the grandeur that befits the royalty of his subject to an informal naturalism which can transform Britomart into a young woman in love. It is she who, 'as maydens use to done', looked into the mirror to see whom fortune would allot to her as a husband; she who asked about the appearance of Artegall from the Red Crosse Knight, and derived pleasure from the glowing praises she heard:

> For pleasing words are like to Magick art,
> That doth the charmed snake in slomber lay:
> Such secret ease felt gentle *Britomart*.

III. ii. 15

(a Spenserian view of the power of poetry); and it was she who would not remove her armour in Malecasta's castle, preferring to remain thus protected from the admiration of the knights she had defeated. As the narrative proceeds, Britomart becomes more and more recognisable as an individual person. She is solitary and always cherishes her knowledge of the knight who is one day to be hers. Consequently, like Arthur, she meditates upon the separation she has yet to endure and the joy that will come when it is over. What keeps her alive in the reader's experience is the personal reaction she shows on every occasion. Her dignity and innocence stand out in the evening in Malecasta's castle where she regards her hostess's lightness of attitude as shaming to her sex but is willing to give her credit for the honesty of the passion towards herself she expresses. It is only when Malecasta creeps into her bed that she springs for her sword, fights Gardante who wounds her in the resultant uproar, and abandons the lascivious household when its nature is impressed upon her. This is a person who arouses respect among those who encounter her.

Britomart is a figure whose fate has been allotted to her by destiny and her stature is the measure of her promised future. Yet she preserves a natural humanity in her journeys through the Faerie world. Marinell's offensive attack angers her, in the house of Busyrane she moves from room to room with natural curiosity, and after her lover has left her on his quest, she waits, looking through the window that faces to the west and rages at Talus when he comes to tell her the news of Artegall's capture by Radigund. Her rescue is accomplished with a courtesy

G

towards him, looking away from the sight of his shameful victimisation. Una, seeing the Red Crosse Knight released from Orgoglio's prison, had wept over his appearance and greeted him warmly in full consciousness of his frail condition,

> But welcome now my Lord, in wele or woe,
> Whose presence I have lackt too long a day;
>
> I. viii. 43

But Britomart has her own judgment to make:

> Ah my deare Lord, what sight is this (quoth she)
> What May-game hath misfortune made of you?
> Where is that dreadfull manly looke? . . .
>
> V. vii. 40

Artegall is not the man she thought him, a heroic courageous proud soldier. Finally peace is made between them and while Artegall is recovering from his wounds Britomart rules in Radigund's place. She reforms her government, releases the knights from their thraldom, subjects the women to them, and enables the men to become magistrates in the city, requiring them to swear fealty. In all this she is carrying out the principles of true Justice which her lover had represented throughout his own Book until he lost them in his contact with Radigund. In these circumstances Britomart displays the quality her destiny requires of her, and emphasises with due humility the merits for which her future husband will afterwards stand.

After her parting from the Red Crosse Knight Britomart proceeds on her way alone, meditating upon what he has told her about Artegall. He has become for her a lover, 'wise, warlike, personable, courteous, and kind', and she allows her imagination to wander over all that he may contribute to her life. Her solitude creates in her mind a sense of grief, and when she reaches the sea she begins to formulate her thoughts into a lament. This is the first of many which occur in Book III, lamentations in which the solitary speaker transforms the stanza into a form of lyric. Britomart expresses her emotions in emblematic terms, in which a familiar set of analogies are developed. Sorrow is the sea upon which her feeble ship is tossed; love provides its pilot, fortune its boatswain, but neither can direct its movement efficiently, for both are blind and are forced to sail against wind and tide, without the assistance of any stars. The emblem draws to its inevitable moral in an appeal to Neptune who could bring the boat into a safe harbour. Spenser makes use here of a commonplace formula which is traceable to books of rhetoric, to Petrarch and several Elizabethan sonnets, and to Whitney's emblems.[1] It creates little emotional effect because it depends too obviously upon well-worn analogies. Arthur's invocation to Night in subsequent stanzas in the same Canto carries something of the same limitation, but here there is more scope for feeling and fewer superficial parallels. Admittedly, Arthur enumerates the evils which are committed in darkness and lists them with double epithets, empty adjectives, and those abstract nouns which are so attractive to Spenser:

> Light-shonning theft, and traiterous intent,
> Abhorred bloudshed, and vile felony,
> Shameful deceipt, and daunger imminent;
> Fowle horror, and eke hellish dreriment.

III. iii. 58

We have met these before, in the Cave of Mammon, and shall meet them again, but a contrasting exaltation of day is added to balance the evil activity of night:

> For day discovers all dishonest wayes
> And sheweth each thing, as it is indeed.

The idea of truth, of each thing 'as it is indeed', is set up against the power of darkness and gives a new vitality to the stanzas so that its clichés become less tedious.

It is the solitude of the single characters which occasions laments of this type, and looking further through Book III we realise how frequently they occur. Those of Britomart and of Arthur in Canto IV possess slight poetic merit; all they do is to hold up the narrative while the feelings of the thinker are

---

[1] Puttenham uses it as an example of the rhetorical device of allegory: 'Allegoria is when we do speake in sence translative and wrested from the owne signification, nevertheless applied to another not altogether contrary, but having much conveniencie with it as before we said of the metaphore: as for example if we should call the common wealth, a shipe; the Prince a Pilot, the Counsellors mariners, the stormes warres, the calme and (haven) peace, this is spoken all in allegorie.' *The Arte of English Poesie*, p. 186-7.

expressed. In the later examples, the stanza form is patterned to create a lyrical character in the soliloquy. One example of this patterning occurs in the reflection of Timias in Canto v, stanzas 45-47. Timias has realised that he loves Belphoebe who has succoured him after he had been wounded by three foresters. She cures him physically, but emotionally he has been stricken by a passion which he knows will not be accepted by her. His reflection is repetitive in manner, a formal monodic 'rebuke to the lover'. It is based upon a recurrent phrase 'dye rather dye' followed by a concluding clause—'dye rather, dye, than ever love disloyally' or 'dye rather, dye than ever from her service swerve'. Timias sways between the conviction that he cannot expound his feeling to Belphoebe and the belief that love is justified in its acceptance by God from all creatures. The passage exemplifies self-argument by the character involved and is given a lyrical turn by its recurring phrases.

Another example which may well be introduced in this context is the soliloquy of Scudamour. This is overheard by Britomart, who attempts to encourage him and find out the cause of his grief. It takes the form of a lament, each stanza being linked to its successor by repetition. This gives the impression of a lyrical handling of the material, but it is basically an exposition of the source of Scudamour's sorrow. In the first lament, Scudamour, unconscious of Britomart's presence, utters an outcry against heavenly injustice, culminating in:

> What booteth then the good and righteous deed,
> If goodnesse find no grace, nor righteousnesse no meed?
>
> III. xi. 9

The succeeding stanza switches the question into a statement:

> If good find grace, and righteousnesse reward,
> Why then is *Amoret* in caytive band, . . .

Spenser repeats this scheme in several stanzas and then moves to another more fully expository set where the evil actions of Busyrane are expanded and Scudamour repeats the lamentation at the opening and close of his speech. Here, as elsewhere in Book III, soliloquies provide the means of transforming the isolation and solitude of a character into a mode of lyrical expression.

ii

After Britomart's emblematic set piece there begins the central part of the action. Marinell, attached to the sea by his name, his origin, and his ownership of the *Rich Strond* upon which Britomart stands meditating, gallops up to banish her from his property. Undeterred, she fights him and leaves him wounded upon the shore. This episode stands out both for the beauty of its language and for its relation to the other narratives of Book III.

Marinell is the son of Cymoent, a sea-nymph, the daughter of Nereus. Here for the first time there enters into Book III the mythology which occupies so large a share of it. Cymoent has demanded from Nereus the riches of the sea for her son; consequently for him there is provided all the wealth from treasure ships that have been destroyed. The shore is heaped with 'the spoyle of all the world' as Britomart observes as she rides over it after her victory over Marinell. They were at her disposal but she despised them all, and continued along her way. But Marinell has been wounded and the news is brought to Cymoent as she gathers daffodils by the water. She drives over the sea in her chariot drawn by dolphins, mourns the apparent death of her son, condemns Proteus who had falsely prophesied that a woman would bring great danger to him, and, informed by one of her nymphs that Marinell was wounded but not dead, transports him to her bower where Tryphon can cure him.

This summary gives small estimate of the character of this scene. In style and thought it is outstandingly beautiful. One notices first that the sea 'voluntary brings' its wealth to Marinell and that his battle with Britomart is characterised by an image which transforms him into a sacrificial victim:

> Like as the sacred Oxe, that carelesse stands,
>   With gilden hornes and flowry girlonds crownd,
>   Proud of his dying honor and deare bands,
>   Whiles th'altars fume with frankincense arownd,
>   All suddenly with mortall stroke astownd,

> Doth groveling fall, and with his streeming gore
> Distaines the pillours, and the holy grownd,
> And the faire flowres, that decked him afore;
> So fell proud *Marinell* upon the pretious shore.
>
> III. iv. 17

Imagery is frequently employed by Spenser as a structural device. Here it is intended to define the nature of one character. It performs a similar part in connection with Florimell who, like Marinell, is the victim of evil chance. Florimell is described in images which emphasise her helplessness against the powers which she considers are hostile. She is compared with a dove:

> Like as a fearefull Dove, which through the raine,
> Of the wide aire her way does cut amaine,
> Having farre off espyde a Tassell gent,
> Which after her his nimble wings doth straine,
> Doubleth her haste for feare to be for-hent,
> And with her pineons cleaves the liquid firmament.
>
> III. iv. 49

with a hind 'of her owne feet affeard', and with a bird in a tempest. The imagery is used consistently in key with what the character stands for, and becomes in Book III a means of unification to draw together the ideas associated with a particular figure or a particular action in connection with the figure. In this Book Marinell and Florimell are closely connected, as two figures who are frightened of human beings. For Marinell a prophecy has warned him of his danger from a woman, for Florimell there is the terror of all men except Marinell who will not accept the love she feels for him.

The description of Cymoent's journey in search of Marinell is imaginatively evocative in a fashion which is in tune with the mythological setting of Cymoent and her nymphs. The language is essentially poetical, recalling the associations of Greek lists of names in the *Odyssey* and their links with the Olympian hierarchy. Neptune, seeing the voyage of the water chariot, kept the movement of the waves gentle, and even the monsters which had proved so hostile to Guyon on his journey were now quiet:

> And all the griesly Monsters of the See
> Stood gaping at their gate, and wondred them to see.
>
> III. iv. 32

They were primitive but not violent and provide the appropriate perspective for the calm, beautiful voyage of the nymphs:

> A teme of Dolphins raunged in aray,
>   Drew the smooth charet of sad *Cymoent*:
> They were all taught by *Triton*, to obay
>   To the long raynes, at her commaundement:
> As swifte as swallowes, on the waves they went,
>   That their broad flaggie finnes no fome did reare,
> Ne bubbling roundell they behind them sent;
>   The rest of other fishes drawen weare,
> Which with their finny oars the swelling sea did sheare.
>
> III. iv. 33

This description is markedly sonorous: the speed of the dolphins, their unruffled movement, and their orderly harmony are conveyed through the sound of the verse. It is free from any roughness, such as was created by the vigorous rowing of Guyon's ferryman. This is a mythological journey in which the dolphins keep in the water when they reach the shore so that their fins should not be bruised by the stones on the beach. Spenser rhythmically defines the sliding motion of Cymoent's barque and relies upon abstractions to tone down the sharpness of any single word. So he discovers a Miltonic phrase 'with their finny oars the swelling sea did sheare' to bring the particular details into a generalised picture. The alliteration of the sixth and seventh lines plays down the individual quality of each separate word so that they are thought of in terms of sound rather than of pictorial impact.

Cymoent's lament, when she thinks Marinell is dead, expresses an intensity of feeling which relies upon melancholy unanswerable questions:

> O what availes it of immortal seed
>   To beene ybred and never borne to die?
> Farre better I it deeme to die with speed,
>   Then waste in woe and wailefull miserie.
>
> III. iv. 38

And it relies too upon a broken line, presumably deliberate, when Cymoent insists upon her hope that she might have been present at Marinell's death-bed and closed his eyes:

> Sith other offices for mother meet
> They would not graunt.
> Yet maulgre them farewell, my sweetest sweet.

Pathos is embodied in these simple woeful speeches, and in the way the nymphs disarm Marinell,

> spredding on the ground
> Their watchet mantles frindgd with silver round.

This exquisite passage gives to these slight figures a rarity belonging to the unearthly world from which they have come. *Liagore*, 'lilly handed' in the Greek phrase, is the nymph who discovers that Marinell is not dead and they carry him to Cymoent's bower which is deep in the bottom of the sea. It is built out of billows and vaulted within

> like to the sky
> In which the Gods do dwell eternally.

This scene brings charm to the Book and it gives Marinell a quality which cannot be neglected. He remains remote, but in some way important. Positive weight is added by Florimell whose love for him is conveyed after this description. Yet we are left with one difficulty. It is Britomart, the heroine of the Book, who has wounded him and she is evidently a more significant character than Marinell. One answer has been offered by Padelford:

> Marinell is the enemy of chastity because, giving himself completely to the acquisition of riches, he refuses to admit the claims of love. . . . His conduct is neither natural nor chivalric. Quite properly, then, Britomart assails and conquers Marinell.
>
> Incidentally this episode furnishes an opportunity to the poet, through the behaviour of Cymoent and her sister nymphs, to present the grief of these fanciful children of nature against a background of marine beauty.[1]

Some query may be raised about this interpretation. In the first

[1] F. M. Padelford. 'The Allegory of Chastity in *The Faerie Queene*,' *Variorum*, Book III, p. 325.

place, Marinell does not give himself completely to the acquisition of riches. The sea brought its wealth to him voluntarily, and the splendour of the *Rich Strond* endows Marinell with its own merits. Secondly, he does not refuse to admit the claims of love; or, if he does, his refusal is based upon a legendary story of the dangers that would befall him if he accepted its claims. Thirdly, the setting is never to Spenser a background or a digression but is quite essential to the meaning. The value of Marinell is inseparable from the scene in which he is placed.

The imaginative quality of the image of the Ox, and of Cymoent's journey over the sea undoubtedly contribute something to the estimate which Spenser intends us to make of Marinell. Yet he has been defeated by Britomart. That this makes him 'an enemy to Chastity' is not proved. It appears from a study of the battles between the various knights in *The Faerie Queene*, particularly in Books III and IV, that Spenser has not necessarily established an absolute scale between the different figures. So often it is a matter of degree. Britomart is plainly more important and valuable than Marinell; she is more active, more alive, and altogether more positive than he; but Marinell, none the less possesses qualities which Spenser admires and does not attach to Britomart. The mythological beauty of the story in which Marinell appears has inspired a poetic skill which is far from that associated with Britomart. On Spenser's scale, Britomart's scorn of the riches tossed up by the sea is creditable to her; but her independence of any of the sea-born beauty connected with Marinell sets her in another context altogether, and the two cannot satisfactorily be measured against each other. In the Book as a whole the personal strength of Britomart emerges firmly and the two succeeding Books will increase that strength, yet Marinell cannot reasonably be dismissed in the terms Padelford has chosen. For it is he who eventually succumbs to the misery of the imprisoned Florimell and prevails upon Cymoent to obtain her release from Proteus.

Spenser certainly has a scale of values in which humanity matters more than mythology, and for that reason Britomart will triumph. But in the long run it proves to be more a scale of shades and degrees than of good and bad. This is a problem which hardly emerges in Books I and II for there is little

G *

mythological material in them, but once Books III and IV are
reached it becomes a serious issue. Spenser in these Books has
lavished an extensive range of poetic art upon the non-human
figures. The effect is to give them a remoteness from human
experience, yet they are not so remote as to be cut off from all
that humanity suffers. Cymoent feels as a mother naturally feels
about her son for all the distant beauty of her nature and surroundings. And Marinell has an entrée into her sea-plumbed
world as well as a life of his own upon the shore. He must be
defeated by Britomart, not because his chastity is falsely
grounded, but because he is only partially human. All the
beauty which Spenser sheds upon him as 'a sea nymphs son'
will not counterbalance the truthfulness of the human record of
such a person as Britomart. This is an issue which will be at
stake through many of the mythological episodes in Books III
and IV, for instance in the story of Chrysogone and the birth of
Belphoebe and Amoret, and in the story of the Garden of
Adonis. Spenser has to discover links which may, or may not,
attach these events to the world of humanity. In the case of
Marinell and Cymoent, it remains apparent that the emotional
force and descriptive beauty of the treatment of the theme still
leave the figures remote from human nature. They belong to the
sea and share its strangeness and its fruitlessness. Aesthetic
vitality was never enough in itself to satisfy the demands of
Spenser's preoccupations.

The Marinell plot is abandoned after he has been drawn
away to Cymoent's bower, and will be revived only at the end
of Book IV. Meanwhile the rest of the Canto, and the subsequent Canto follow the Ariostan plan of recalling the activities
of the other characters who had been riding with Britomart. Her
journey is briefly recalled, Timias's pursuit of the forester and
Arthur's attempt to catch Florimell are brought to mind, and
Arthur's invocation to Night concludes Canto IV. Characteristically, Spenser then directs the reader's attention towards the
exalting operation of love within the mind. The two introductory stanzas in Canto v rely upon rhetorical and lyrical
repetition of phrase to indicate the meaning of the episodes that
will occur within the narrative that is to come. Love, for a
heroic character, will do all that is valuable. The feelings of

Arthur are duly analysed, the faith of Florimell is also established through the words of her Dwarf, and the second episode
which deals with the adventures of Timias is also anticipated.

One of the distinctive features in Books III and IV depends
upon the methods of Ariosto who prefers not to label characters
until they have made an impact upon the course of the narrative. Thus Florimell, although named in the introductory lines
preceding Cantos I and IV, remains a mysterious, unexplained
figure fleeing from a villainous rough-looking forester. It is only
in Canto V that she enters the story with any degree of completeness. Then she is associated with Marinell whose death she
has learnt about and whom she has set out to seek.[1]

Another feature peculiar to Books III and IV is the device of
setting a single knight into conflict with several others at once.
Britomart had rescued Red Crosse from the six attackers outside Malecasta's castle, and Timias in his pursuit of the forester
becomes a prey to him and his two brothers. Timias is the
gallant squire, whose absence Arthur is constantly regretting,
but he is forced to fight against three savage men whose weapons
are typical of the world in which they live—a boar spear for one
forester, a dart for the second, and a forest bill for the third. The
scene is closely localised, and the bad aspect of the forest is
reflected in the use the brothers make of it. The forester eludes
Timias because his 'knowledge of those woods where he did
dwell' enables him to escape, and with his brothers he sets an
ambush for Timias in a narrow ford which they know he must
cross. Flooding makes the ford more dangerous and Timias and
his horse have great difficulty in passing it.

This Book ranges surprisingly from high to low. The atmosphere of the struggle Timias has to face is that of an agricultural society, as the weapons indicate. Spenser's precision of
vocabulary is illustrated here, and again in the treatment of

---

[1] This is one of the confusions in the plot of Book III since Florimell was
seen in flight by Britomart before the duel with Marinell had taken place.
A similar difficulty occurs in Canto VII when Sir Palladine, a maiden
knight, is seen pursuing Argante, but is never heard of again and was perhaps intended to play the part of Britomart. Book IV also has a confusion in
the narrative of the fight between the knights. Some revisions were made in
Book III when it was reprinted with IV to VI, but Sir Palladine is preserved, perhaps to be employed in the destruction of Argante and Ollyphant.

Florimell's journey through the forest. She reaches a cottage inhabited by a witch, a dwelling

> built of sticks and reedes,
> In homely wize, and wald with sods around.

Florimell finds it squalid, yet her innocence and naturalness create a crude feeling of admiration in even this unlikely old woman. Adoration of beauty is one of the topics which recur in Book III and Spenser evokes it in connection with every ideal heroine in it. The witch's son responds like his mother, but more dangerously. Florimell, playing for time, accepts the country offerings he brings her—wild apples, birds trained to sing her praises and tame squirrels, but escapes as soon as she can. Her departure leads her to an equally natural scene, the seashore with a fisherman asleep in his boat. Florimell thinks the ordinariness of the places she comes to brings promises of safety: the smoke from the cottage chimney, the sight of the fisherman's nets drying on the beach, appear harmless, yet the witch sends a hyena to chase her and the fisherman wakes up in his boat and attempts to rape her, thus driving her to seek further refuge from the passing figure of Proteus. Spenser's allegorical form provides him with a freedom by which he can combine observed details of daily life with startlingly improbable events. The hyena is alleged to devour women's flesh; nevertheless, savage as it is, it can be tamed by Satyrane who discovers it eating Florimell's palfrey and ties it up with her girdle. Escape from the fisherman drives her only into the clutches of Proteus who will take her below the sea.

It is therefore suitable that Timias after being gravely wounded by the three foresters should be restored by an otherworldly figure. Belphoebe is not a new character to readers of Book II since she appeared there briefly as an embodiment of honour, which Braggadocchio who met her had never encountered. It was difficult to agree with Professor Berger's note that she was a 'conspicuous irrelevance' there, but she is certainly even less susceptible to this term in Book III. Here she is an essential part of its action and its meaning. Spenser says outright that her coming was caused by heavenly providence which brought 'comfort to him that comfortless now lay'. Timias

regards her as an angel or a goddess sent down for his help.
She sets about his healing and her pragmatic treatment is
described in detail, so that it banishes the memory of the im-
practical lamentations of Cymoent. With skills unknown to the
water-nymphs, she collects herbs, crushes them, applies them to
the wound and ties it up with her scarf to keep it warm. This
therapeutic activity is given the appearance of exactitude by
the names of the herbs: 'divine Tobacco, or Panachaea, or
Polygony'. Moreover the patient's horse is not forgotten. Upon
it Belphoebe's nymphs carry him to the glade in the forest where
she lives. Here Spenser portrays the good aspect of the woods;
in it is a valley surrounded by trees, adorned with a stream and
brightened with the songs of birds. Here Belphoebe has built
her abode, and here she cures Timias.

This Book is preoccupied with personal relationships and as
soon as the cure is effected Timias becomes overpowered by his
love for his rescuer. This is also the Book in praise of love and
chastity, and in it Spenser's high esteem of those virtues is expressed in fully developed images. Towards the end of the Canto
he exalts their splendour in the juxtaposition of virginity with a
rose. Belphoebe beautifully protects her virginity in terms
which are metaphorical:

> That dainty Rose, the daughter of her Morne,
>   More deare then life she tendered, whose flowre
>   The girlond of her honour did adorne:
>   Ne suffred she the Middayes scorching powre
>   Ne the sharp Northerne wind thereon to showre,
>   But lapped up her silken leaves most chaire,
>   When so the froward skye began to lowre:
>   But soone as calmed was the Christall aire,
> She did it fayre dispred and let it florish faire.

> III. v. 51

This is followed first by a religious comment attributing the
origin of the rose to Eden, where God had first planted it, and
then by an appeal to beautiful women to preserve their
chastity. Then the character of Belphoebe slides into a praise
of Queen Elizabeth who has already been identified with her
in the Proem. Spenser does not point the parallel explicitly but
makes the direction of his thought evident by referring to 'the

highest staire of th'honorable stage of womanhead' and to the presence of 'stedfast chastity' which strives with 'grace and goodly modesty' for a place in her 'Heroic mind'.

Book III provides several occasions when Spenser chooses to speak in his own voice, a tendency which may be attributable to his loneliness as a poet isolated in Ireland. There are times when he enters the poem in a personal way, not disguised as Colin Clout nor through the faculty of imagery. By such preservations of contact with the reader Spenser achieves a bridge between the remoteness of his material and the normality of human responses to it. He can also continue the narrative design of the poem simultaneously with elaborations of its theme.

The account of the birth and upbringing of Belphoebe and her sister Amoret extends the mythological content already introduced in the Marinell episode. Spenser's marvellous sense of the world of the classical gods is joined with a realistic interpretation of their activity upon the earth. Joy is expressed by them at the birth of Belphoebe:

> *Jove* laught on *Venus* from his soveraigne see,
> And *Phoebus* with faire beames did her adorne,
> And all the *Graces* rockt her cradle being borne.
>
> III. vi. 2

This dancing rhythm sweeps through the story of the conception and birth of these children. Their mother, Chrysogone, who was made pregnant by the beams of the sun and brought them forth without knowledge

> Who in her sleepe (a wondrous thing to say)
> Unwares had borne two babes, as faire as springing day.

> Unwares she them conceiv'd, unwares she bore:
> She bore withouten paine, that she conceived
> Withouten pleasure.
>
> III. vi. 26-27

For Spenser, this belief in the generative power of the Sun was fascinating; the image of the creation of living things through its influence upon the inundation of the Nile occurs here as it had in Book I (i. 21), and as a popular concept of Elizabethan biology, it gives credibility to the impersonal purity of Belphoebe's origin. The story continues within the scheme of the gods' participation in it. Venus, coming to earth in search of the errant Cupid, examines the society of the Court, city and country and finally tries Phoebe and her nymphs. Here the element of realism which Spenser can bring to the presence of the gods on earth takes charge. Venus, suspecting that Cupid may be hidden with Phoebe describes his charms and

> So saying every Nymph full narrowly she eyde.

This proves too much for Phoebe who spitefully suggests that Venus's relationship with Mars may produce a better solution, and vows with an oath to appropriate to her standing ('by Stygian lake') that she will punish Cupid if he appears in her reach. However, a friendly mood leads them to search together and in so doing they find Chrysogone. Each adopts one of the babies—Phoebe to bring up Belphoebe 'in perfect Maydenhed' and Venus to rear Amoret 'in goodly womanhed'.

It is to the Garden of Adonis that Venus carries Amoret. Adonis has been mentioned in the tapestry adorning Malecasta's castle, but here he is portrayed as the centre of the mythical Garden. Spenser now reaches the most significant part of Book III. The paeon of chastity leads him to a philosophical discourse upon the idea of love. Critics have suggested various Neo-Platonic, Lucretian, or Ovidian sources for the thought embodied in Spenser's theories, but it appears more probable that he was drawing upon generally accepted popular conceptions and no precise sources can helpfully be used. The Garden, as one commentator has said, 'is intended only as the meeting place of form and substance';[1] it is set out in a vision, symbolical in its expression rather than narrowly allegorical. Symbols suggest always that more is beyond the actual statements used and any interpretations are liable to become prosaically didactic unless the full imaginative effect of the visionary style is allowed for. The external nature of creation is contained in this Garden: everything which enters the world and everything which returns from it has its being here. These come and go through the discretion of the *Genius* who directs all the material which lives under his sway. All created things, not

[1] Brents Stirling, 'The Philosophy of Spenser's Garden of Adonis'. *Variorum* edition of *The Faerie Queene*, Book III, pp. 347-352.

merely human but the occupants of the earth and the ocean are ranged in ordered groups so that in Spenser's view nature appears to be a perfect organisation until its contents are banished for a time into the everyday world.

The substance of the material in the Garden comes from chaos which is in itself shapeless and horrible, but exists as the source of eternal matter. The character of all the living things which come out of it derives from the form with which they are endowed. Consequently

> That substance is eterne, and bideth so,
> Ne when the life decayes, and forme does fade,
> Doth it consume, and into nothing go,
> But chaunged is, and often altred to and fro.

> III. vi. 37

Through this conception Spenser emphasises the goodness of physical phenomena and the transcience of the forms which they adopt. The Garden, in itself, contains perfect bodies which grow independently of their own accord, happy in relation with each other, and ready to be despatched into the outer world whenever fate ordains. Yet in this apparent perfection the power of Time intervenes and it can destroy the bodies in the Garden. They are not immortal because even here, in its unsullied harmony,

> All things decay in time, and to their end do draw.

It is this factor which makes it difficult to regard Spenser's thought as plausibly philosophical. At least he seems to be defining the ultimate source of created things as good and eternal, and yet making them subject to mortality even before their entry into the world.

The sole exception to this paradoxical situation is Adonis himself. For within the Garden is a mount where the seasons are perpetual, issuing in spring and autumn together, and forming a Paradise where Venus lives her earthly life, and her lover, revived after his death from the boar, remains to create satisfaction for her and life for all the creatures in the Garden. The Boar is imprisoned under the mount, the certain proof of the security of their love. As for the danger from Time, Adonis is no longer a victim to it.

All be he subject to mortalitie,
Yet is eterne in mutabilitie,
And by succession made perpetuall,
Transformed oft, and chaunged diverslie;
For him the Father of all formes they call;
Therefore needs mote he live, that living gives to all.

As the 'father of all formes' Adonis is fulfilling the functions of the sun as it was described in the story of Chrysogone; and he is unique in his safety from death. Others will decay in time, and Venus mourn their loss; or they will be sent out into the external world, receiving forms appropriate to their life there. But Adonis remains in the Garden, no longer susceptible to death as humanity understands it; he lives for ever in different guises, and remains 'eterne in mutabilitie', subject to change but not to destruction.

This part of Book III can best be called 'visionary' since it demands the kind of interpretation which applies only to poetry, the poetry which occurs in single paragraphs or lines, but rarely in the extended scale set out here. It is far from the didactic mode adopted by certain sections of the allegory. The phrase 'eterne in mutabilitie' is expounded in the two Cantos in the surviving fragment of the Book on Constancy in which Mutabilitie challenges the rights of the Gods to rule over the world since they are subject to change. In both places Spenser demonstrates his capacity to deal with abstract ideas and to transform generalisations into moving poetry. He can create out of them a vision, and it is that, rather than a philosophical exposition, which gives power to this particular section in Book III.

iii

Canto VI sums up the thought running through the mythological incidents in the preceding narratives and it stabilises the scattered topics in the events which are to follow. These possess one factor in common: they all deal with attempts to minimise or destroy the power of love and reduce it to objects of mockery or to vilify it. The value of Canto VI lies in its constructive static nature which enables it to remain in the reader's mind as a standard against which the weakness or wickedness of the content of the stories which succeed it may be measured. Nonetheless, there *are* three figures who contribute rightly to the idea of love—Florimell, unable to find Marinell to whom she remains faithful, Britomart still in search of Artegall, and Scudamour who has lost his beloved Amoret. Against these are developed the destroyers, Proteus offering the inevitable blandishments of a seducer, Paridell interested only in the seduction of Hellenore, and Busyrane who has seized Amoret from the arms of her husband Scudamour.

The last sight we have of Florimell is in her contact with Proteus, whose approaches she, true to the laws of her own nature, firmly rejects. Swept down to his ocean retreat she continues her rejections until he imprisons her in a dungeon surrounded by stormy waves and alarming water beasts. Yet she is not forgotten by the knights of Maidenhead who have been shown her girdle and have heard from Satyrane of the bloodstained hyena. And she is replaced by an imitation of her made by the witch to whom the hyena returns with part of her girdle. The false Florimell is clothed in garments of the true one and is vivified by a fiend, drawn from Satan's company in hell. She delights the witch's rough son who had been wooing her true predecessor, and willingly goes off with Braggadocchio when he takes possession of her. In effect, Florimell's appearance remains in the narrative, but not her chaste reality. As Spenser insists, his course is often arrested but 'never is astray' (VI. xii. 1). So he keeps the reader mindful of the actual Florimell who was essential to the concept of chastity, by inserting her opposite into the narrative. Moreover Proteus, carrying on the mythological subjects for a further period, is also consistent with the notion of evil in the whole poem. He tries numerous disguises, including one of a knight, in order to attract his captive, but like those of Archimago and Guile in Book V his transformations merely demonstrate the wickedness of his nature.

Meanwhile other episodes have taken place while Florimell has been suffering on the sea. These reduce the plane upon which subsequent actions occur. Satyrane, after his conflict with the hyena, fights against a giantess who comes galloping across his path bearing a young squire upon her saddle. Like the foresters, she is equipped with a weapon suitable to her savage nature, a 'huge great yron mace', throws down her captured squire, snatches up Satyrane in his place and throws him down when she sees the Knight who is following her about to catch her up. She speeds away unencumbered and Satyrane learns her history from the squire. It is an unpleasing story. She is Argante, twin to Ollyphant, both representing physically and mentally all that the other twins are not. They are lustful, incestuous, and bestial, and carry off young men to a secret isle where their disgusting habits may be satisfied. Plainly they are introduced into the plot as a self-damaging means of highlighting the integrity of the good characters. The Knight who pursues Argante is named Sir Palladine, an Amazon, who is probably an early version of Britomart. A less crude contrast with the portrayal of chastity is supplied by the Squire of Dames, whom Satyrane has rescued. He describes, in a Chaucerian fabliau, his search for chaste women who will refuse his bawdy temptations. A typically Spenserian anecdote records his failure in the discovery of only three, a prostitute unwilling to provide her services for the small sum he can offer, a nun suspicious of his trustworthiness, and a simple country girl who prefers chastity for its own sake. In the narrative of the Squire of Dames, the Book reaches a witty social situation focussed upon human beings, and, apart from the magical activity of the witch in creating the false Florimell, continues on that level in the remaining Cantos.

Comedy pervades the account of Braggadocchio's loss of the false Florimell to an unidentified knight, and the long episode of Malbecco and Hellenore. Here several knights are involved, Satyrane, the Squire of Dames, Paridell, and Britomart, who has not been seen since her fight with Marinell. Again the theme concentrates upon lust, not love, and is developed in conditions nearer the experience of daily life than were the romance episodes attached to Florimell. The allegorical aspect of the main plot has been discussed in Chapter III, but since there is much else that contributes to the total impact of his narrative in relation to Book III something more must be said of it.

First of all, it recalls Britomart to the central action. Her physical splendour, once she has removed her armour, makes a deep impression upon the other knights, and her status is conveyed in a simile which compares her with Minerva. When the conversation after dinner turns upon the fall of Troy, she is drawn into it by Paridell's claiming descent from Paris. He deplores the war which destroyed a great kingdom although he remembers that the escape of Aeneas guaranteed the growth of a second Troy in the foundation of Rome. This provides an opening for Britomart who can describe the third city which is to be, 'Troynovant' upon the Thames. Paridell supports her memories of what Merlin had told her of her descendants, by his reminiscence of another branch of the Trojan line which should spring in a distant land. As readers, we may look back to Book II where Arthur, reading the Chronicles of Britain, reaches the account of 'Troynovant' to be built by Lud who gave his name to a gate in the town (i.e. Ludgate). This conversation between Paridell and Britomart, however, gives more life to the historical introduction acquired by Arthur because it occurs in a natural social occasion and because it draws upon the earlier adventure of the heroine of the Book. It also supplies the dimension within which Paridell's seduction of Hellenore will follow.

Secondly, the study of the relationship between Paridell and Hellenore strikes a satirical note in the narrative. It is recounted with a verve rarely achieved by Spenser, in a way more reminiscent of *Mother Hubberds Tale* than any part of *The Faerie Queene*. Where else in this serious Book are found sharpness of wit combined with speed of narrative? The influence of Ariosto is conspicuously present in the love scenes between Paridell and Hellenore and in the apology with which the narrative begins, although it is typical of Spenser to raise the incident to a higher level by drawing a parallel between the fall of Hellenore and the fall of the angels from heaven. This is a characteristic instance of Spenser's tendency to elevate a scene which appears in some degree different from the general tone of the Book.

The conduct of Paridell expresses the practice of a man fully experienced in the techniques of secret seduction. Malbecco's half-blindness is symbolical of his character and Paridell takes advantage of the fact that his position at the table prevents his gestures to Hellenore from being visible to his host. He conveys his desire to her in a message written in a spilt glass of wine:

> Which well she red out of the learned line,
> A sacrament prophane in mistery of wine.

There is judgment in the irony of 'learned' with its ambiguous reference to the skills that are being applied, and even stronger judgment in the blasphemy of the word 'sacrament'. Hellenore replies by upsetting the glass offered as a pledge; and the success of the flirtation is summarised in the proverbial neatness of the phrase about putting the ape in Malbecco's cape. It continues through the dramatisation of the allurements Paridell adopts to maintain his ends. Vigour and vitality cover the wiliness of his methods: all the amusements and the triviality of courtly social life are offered, songs, love-lays, dances, riddles, games, against which Hellenore has no desire nor capacity to put up any defence. The warning comment enters in Spenser's own voice generalising upon the falsity of Cupid who is not blind but can see all that goes on and can find mirth in the beguilements which are taking place. The narrative creates all that is needed for their departure in a sinister phrase:

> Darke was the Evening, fit for lovers stealth.
>
> III. x. 12

Within this atmosphere the marriage is destroyed. Hellenore 'this second Hellene' makes away with Malbecco's wealth and sets fire to his room, leaving him to decide whether his love was greater towards her or towards his wealth. The balance between his two devotions is brilliantly presented, a tug of war set out in the construction of the stanza:

> Ay when to him she cryde, to her he turnd,
>   And left the fire; love money overcame:
> But when he marked how his money burnd,
>   He left his wife; money did love disclame:
>
> III y 15

His ultimate decision lies in a miser's faith, in favour of the 'God of his desire'; and Hellenore, who had joyfully run into her lover's arms, while at the same time crying for rescue, flees with him.

The narrative switches to Malbecco's search for his errant
wife, a fruitless attempt because:

> his woman was too wise,
> Ever to come into his clouch againe,
> And he too simple ever to surprise
> The jolly *Paridell*, for all his paine.
>
> III. x. 20

From one point of view some sympathy is felt for Malbecco.
For all his miserliness, or the meanness of his outlook upon
humanity, he had a genuine devotion to his wife, and, of
course, the discreditable rôle of Paridell transfers feeling towards
him, however worthless his standards may have been. The rest
of the action develops Malbecco's adventures, his meeting with
Braggadocchio and Trompart (a farcical occasion in which the
Boaster undertakes to fight Paridell but is prevented by some
difficulty with the girth of his stolen horse (Guyon's) when the
occasion arises), his meeting with Paridell whose attitude is
characteristically casual to the woman he has betrayed and
now deserted, his fear that the unprotected Hellenore may have
been destroyed in the forest, and his despairing comment 'Then
all the world is lost, and we in vaine have toyld'. His 'pale eyes'
and his impotence both register against him, but he has partly
become the victim of circumstances. His discovery of Hellenore
among the satyrs, her refusal to return home with him, his enforced observation of the sexual activity of the satyr with which
she was sleeping, and his realisation

> That not for nought his wife them loved so well
>
> III. x. 48

combine to condemn the lasciviousness of Hellenore with some
feeling for Malbecco's distress. The story of Malbecco and
Hellenore is obviously a moral tale, and its ending with the
total corruption of Hellenore among the bestial satyrs and the
transformation of Malbecco into a savage bird who 'forgot he
was a man and Gealosie is hight', gains heightened impact from
its context in a Book where the perfection of love had been so
fully expounded.

iv

Book III concludes with the great achievement of Britomart undertaken for the sake of Scudamour and Amoret. Scudamour had married Amoret but she had been dragged away from him during the wedding ceremonies by the sorcerer, Busyrane. Scudamour's laments have already been referred to, but Britomart can do little to console him. He outlines Amoret's suffering to Britomart in a closely observed scene when he begins to speak, 'leaning on his elbow', and there is a suggestion of the beginning of a friendship between the mourner and his comforter. They set out together for Busyrane's House and Britomart discovers what prevents Scudamour from rescuing his wife. A wall of fire rises in front of the house in which she is imprisoned. Britomart tries, unsuccessfully at first, to enter it. She retires and hesitates, reflecting upon the danger of her situation. It would be, if she tried again, foolhardy:

> as th'Earthes children, the which made
> Battell against the Gods. So we a God invade.

A similar event occurs in *Gerusalemme Liberata* when Tancred attempts to enter an enchanted forest but is prevented by flames. Both Tancred and Britomart are forced into a temporary halt but both by sheer determination get through. Britomart's cautious hesitation is shown to be a due respect for the hierarchic nature of the enemy, but there being no alternative she protects herself with her shield and forces the fire to yield before her drawn sword. Presumably Britomart's chastity, as well as her courage, enables her to do what Scudamour fails to achieve for he is again turned back by the flames.

Once inside Busyrane's House, Britomart begins to explore it. It is decorated throughout its first room with tapestry. Spenser has various methods of portraying works of art, and the continuous and consistent method everywhere is the insistence that Art should truthfully report the actual appearance of its subject. This is the recurring attitude in the description of the tapestries. Yet another method, and one which is not, necessarily, contradictory to the first, lies in the emphasis upon a pre-eminent theme running through the pictures in the tapestries. In Busyrane's House their subjects are the amorous exploits of Jove and

of the minor gods as well. Everywhere the imagery of fire
threads its way recalling the flames through which Britomart
has had to make her entrance. Fire occurs directly in the
descriptions, or in the brightness of the gold woven into the
tapestry. Gold is used in the weave, avoiding conspicuousness
and shining secretly to provide richness of texture. Spenser
indicates this quality in a simile; the gold is

> Like a discolourd Snake, whose hidden snares
> Through the greene gras his long bright burnisht backe declares.

In a magnificent employment of the terminal alexandrine, this
line relies upon an alliterative vocabulary to draw out its length.
Pope, of course, bettered it in *An Essay on Criticism* by turning the
long line into a scornful relative clause, its condemnation
depending upon the force of the deprecatory verb 'drag':

> A *needless Alexandrine* ends the Song,
> That like a wounded Snake, drags its slow length along.

Yet Spenser's snake is vivid and brightly coloured, and it creates
a credible impression of what a snake looks like in its natural
habitat. Ireland, despite St. Patrick, can still show adders in the
grass of its mountain slopes, and it is likely that Spenser
observed them in Kilcolman. Their precise appearance is not
as important as their significance. Spenser regularly introduces
snakes in connection with something especially sinister. A snake
is mentioned in relation to Duessa, it occurs as an emblem for
Envy in Book I, Canto IV, 31, and in Canto IX, 28, as a simile
for the temptation of Despair who comes 'creeping close as
snake in hidden weedes', and in Book II in similes representing
the sensuality of Cymochles (v. 34) and the physical appearance
of Maleger (xi. 22). Malbecco's hatred of himself and sense of
abandonment from womankind become to him an inescapable
thought, 'that as a snake, still lurked in his wounded mind'.
Guile chose a snake for one of his disguises and it was the last
shape he attempted to return to before he was killed by Artegall
and Arthur. The only kind word for them occurs in this Book
(see p. 193). From all this, we might conclude, like Caroline
Spurgeon, that 'Spenser did not like snakes', but this is not a
biographical but a critical topic. It is the use he makes of them

all through *The Faerie Queene* that chiefly matters. It is worth noting that no reference to them occurs in Book VI, an omission which measures the normality and comparative freedom of this Book from the wickedness which had preoccupied Spenser in all the rest. The cannibals and the Blatant Beast cannot be ignored in it, but the tone of the whole Book is more placid and more positively natural than that of the others.

The treatment of the snakes in Book III indicates some power of observation by Spenser, and the rest of the Canto concerned with Britomart's response to the tapestries in Busyrane's house develops that particular aspect in Spenser's outlook. There are many other examples that one would wish to link with exactness of perception; for example, how *Europa's* heart 'did lively seem to tremble' as she was drawn through the sea by Jove disguised as a Bull, how *Leda* 'twixt her eyelids closely spyde' the on-coming rush towards her of the Swan, how the shepherds called to Ganymede to take firmer hold as they saw him flying on the back of the Eagle into which Jove had transformed himself. Are all these evidences of Spenser's sense of realistic detail in psycho-logical or natural occurrences, or can they be attributed to something less realistic and closer to an idea or emblematic concept? One would prefer, with many critics of the eighteenth and nineteenth centuries, to give Spenser the credit of a vivid perception of the external world, and of course he clearly did possess that gift, but so often the examples which present them-selves prove to be examples of ideas and to a much lesser degree examples of observation. Every long descriptive passage in *The Faerie Queene* tends to be primarily conceptual and only second-arily graphical. The description of the tapestry in the House of Busyrane is held together by the thread of an idea, the idea of passion formulated in fire. Jove's disguises were adopted 'to slake his scalding smart' and some were, in fact, disguises of flames. The forms in which he appeared to *Danae*, as a golden shower, to *Semele* and to *Aegina* as a fire, express a burning emotion. In other stanzas the concept of fire is sufficiently existent to keep the image constantly in mind, not only in the disguises of Jove but in those of Phoebus, of Neptune, and of Mars. Neptune, driving over the ocean in his chariot, brought the fiery passion to the water in the fury of his sea horses:

That made the sparckling waves to smoke agayne,
And flame with gold, but the white fomy creame,
Did shine with silver, and shoot forth his beame.

III. xi. 41

Images of this kind, suggest how dangerous Busyrane's enchantments are, and the golden statue of Cupid which domi-
nates the room unites the topics in all the tapestries. The dedication attached to it, *Unto the Victor of the Gods this bee*, inspires an
inclination in the people of the house to adore him and commit
'fowle idolatree'. Moreover Spenser's parenthetic exhortation
indicates further the nature of this Cupid, equipped as he is
with arrows of gold or 'sad lead':

(Ah man beware, how thou those darts behold)

III. xi. 48

Britomart's eyes are dazzled by the brightness of the blindfolded
figure, and the repeated phrase, *Be bold*, leaves her wondering
about the meaning of what she is seeing. In Malecasta's castle,
which was also decorated with tapestries illustrating the passion
of Venus and Adonis, she had no difficulty in assessing what
Malecasta represented, but here she cannot interpret the significance of the dedication and the mottoes. Their evil is ineluct-
able, but beyond knowing that they amount to a warning she
can go no further. Spenser is using an innocent and good character as a medium to make an evaluation of the scene.

It is in the second room that Britomart looks more deeply
into the sorcery of Busyrane. The tapestry in the previous room
appeared comparatively harmless contrasted with what she sees
here. The golden walls are crammed with monstrous figures,
'as they living were', expressions of misplaced passion, trophies
of its victims bearing broken swords and battered garlands, all
illustrations of the destructive powers of false love. It is here
that the Masque finds its setting. Britomart becomes conscious
of the silence and absence of any ordinary talkative life in these
rooms. Spenser frequently uses silence to indicate the strangeness of a situation: the enigmatic quiet which surrounds the
magic trees which Red Crosse and Duessa reach after the fight
with Sans-foy, the soundless grief of the abashed sea monsters
after the wounding of Marinell, 'the still and calmy bay', which

Guyon reaches on his voyage, all create an impression of mystery. Here Britomart finds something ominous in the silence and in the sheer emptiness of the rooms she had entered. The final blazon, *Be not too bold*, above the iron door at the farther end of the room, adds a further warning: it is through this door that the Masque of Cupid will come.

Night is the centre of evil in Book III, and although it was customary to conduct masques in the evening as well as during the day, Britomart's witness of the Masque of Cupid in the night amplifies its danger. It is preceded by the sound of a trumpet, by thunder and lightning, and a violent blast of wind which brings with it poisonous smoke. This storm lasts for two hours and culminates in an even fiercer blast of wind which forces open the iron door and heralds the appearance of a Prologue to the show which is to follow. It seems to Britomart that the Prologue, whose name she discovers is Ease, is calling for attention to the procession by his gestures. A crowd of minstrels follow him and there is an accompaniment of alluring music. After this, the file of masquers enters, all personifications, none necessarily bad in themselves but sinister as they are paired off. These figures arise from legendary incidents in the *Romance of the Rose*, or other stories, *Amadis of Gaul* and *Arthur of Little Britain*.[1] The origins of this material have been tracked down by research into the sources employed by Spenser who describes each personification in detail, showing that their garments are projections of their nature. The objects they carry are emblematic of what they represent. The first in the procession is Fancy dressed in a style typical of his character:

> His garment neither was of silke nor say,
>> But painted plumes, in goodly order dight,
>> Like as the sunburnt *Indians* do aray
>> Their tawny bodies, in their proudest plight.
>> As those same plumes, so seemed he vaine and light,
>> That by his gate might easily appeare,
>> For still he far'd as dauncing in delight,
>> And in his hand a windy fan did beare,
>> That in the idle aire he mov'd still here and there.

III. xii. 8

---

[1] See the study upon the Masque of Cupid in the *Variorum* edition, pp. 353-366.

Hazlitt commenting upon the figures in the Masque says of Spenser: 'He is the painter of abstractions, and describes them with dazzling minuteness'. This is precisely the effect of this particular description; the abstraction is that of emptiness of mind, and the slightness of mentality is embodied in the airy thinness of the plumes which provided Fancy's attire, in the frivolous dancing movement, and in the fan he was carrying. This personification is primarily an embodiment of a concept; the only vivid detail is contained in the simile of the Indians, sunburnt but dressing their tawny bodies in feathers, yet this is not enough to switch the passage from the idea upon which it is focussed. All the other stanzas are founded upon figures fully described in terms of dress and emblematic imprese. For instance, Desyre, Fancy's son, accompanies him, wearing a crooked 'embrodered Bonet' and blowing sparks in his hands which burst forth in flames. Doubt and Daunger[1] accompany each other, carrying a net and a rusty blade, Feare and Hope follow, Feare fully armed and frightened of the sound of his armour, Hope bearing the deceptive imprese of 'an holy water Sprinckle dip't in deowe'. These personifications instance disasters resulting from mistaken love. The emblems they carry criticise their nature: for instance there come Dissemblance, wearing false hair and twisting two threads of silk in her hand, and Suspect glaring at her and peeping through a lattice window for protection, Griefe bearing a pair of pincers and Fury with a firebrand, Displeasure with 'an angry Waspe' and Pleasance with 'an hony-lady Bee'. Many of these figures are traceable to emblem books or to Natalis Comes but Spenser's way of displaying them with 'dazzling minuteness' demonstrates his capacity to seize a moment of visual intensity. Each is compressed into a single stanza and the effect created is one of accumulated horror.

The personifications appear in sequence because Spenser is adopting the Masque form, and it is a form which suits his methods of description. The Seven Deadly Sins in Book I and the twelve months in Book VII follow the same orderly sequence with the description of each item stanza by stanza. Dr

---

[1] Chaucer in *The Prologue to the Canterbury Tales* uses it as an instance of power, haughtiness, difficult in matters of love.

Gottfried criticises Spenser's composition for its failure to see a complete picture. It consists in a 'series of separate groups or single figures, and Spenser's eye does not embrace the movement of the whole; he sees them one by one, as if they were passing by outside a narrow door'.[1] This is true about a number of pictures in *The Faerie Queene*, perhaps about the most impressive of them, but it does not allow for Spenser's presentations of action, particularly in scenes when a single, powerful figure bursts in upon other static character or characters. For example, when Orgoglio descends upon Duessa and the Red Crosse Knight, or when Pyrochles and Cymochles rush upon the Palmer and the unconscious Guyon, the narrative takes account of all the characters concerned, and it is the whole not separate sections that the eye is focussed upon. Dr Gottfried also argues that 'Spenser subordinates the pictorial element to the moral allegory',[2] and, consequently, there is a limited range of colours, particularly, for example, in the attire of Faith, Hope and Charity in the House of Holiness. Upon this point there will be no very strong disagreement. The ideas in the Masque are weightier than the aesthetic quality of the descriptions, yet such an image as that of the sunburnt *Indians* keeps an original picture clearly in view. It is not so much colour as literal perception which gives Spenser's descriptions their individuality: the embrodered bonnet of *Desyre* which 'sat awry' and the 'discolour'd cote' of *Doubt*, who had at his back 'a brode Capuccio' and 'sleeves dependant *Albanese*-wyse' give distinctiveness to the personifications.

This procession is followed by *Despight* and *Cruelty* who lead Amoret in a condition of extreme torment. She has rejected the lustful importunity of Busyrane and now is forced into the Masque of Cupid, her heart drawn out of her breast and laid in a silver basin with death visible upon her face. She is followed by Cupid, seated upon a lion, who insists that the bandage should be removed from his eyes so that he can enjoy the cruelty of his reign. To enlarge his empire there follows a new set of figures, which exemplify the pains of love gone astray,

---

[1] Gottfried. 'The Pictorial Element in Spenser's Poetry', *E.L.H.*, 1952, p. 211.

[2] *ibid.*, p. 210.

repentance, shame, strife, anger, inconstancy, false disloyalty and many others, free from full description, only slightly defined by the presence of an epithet. The whole procession walks three times round the room and then disappears into the room from which it has first set out.

Britomart cannot follow it through the iron door and has to wait until the next night when she expects it to return. This time, when the door of the forbidden room opens, Britomart is bold, goes in only to find the Masque figures all vanished and Amoret chained to a pillar with Busyrane writing his charms in her blood. Britomart, in the power of her chastity, can destroy the sorcerer, but it is Amoret who dissuades her, explaining that if he were killed she would remain spellbound for ever. Britomart therefore offers him life if he will restore Amoret to her own being. The enchanter, aware of Britomart's sword hanging over him, fulfils the order. The spells have to be recited backwards until their magic fails. Spenser's liking for ritual gives this scheme plausibility. The House rattles and Amoret's tortures disappear—the pillar falls, the chain drops off her and the wound in her heart is healed. Britomart ties her captive up in the chain and leads Amoret back through the rooms, from which the splendour is wholly banished.

The meaning of this narrative is open to some discussion both in relation to the Book as a whole and to the character of Amoret in particular. The personifications in the Masque gain considerable force because what they represent has occurred in other characters or scenes. We have seen Desire in Malecasta and in Paridell, Pleasure, as good in the Garden of Adonis, Hope, as good in Timias, Suspect and Cruelty in Malbecco. In this respect the scene in the House of Busyrane binds together the various episodes in the preceding parts of the narrative. But it is uncertain whether all, good or bad, are reflected in the person of Amoret. Morally, the allegory represents the corruptions which can enter into and destroy even genuine love, which one may suppose Amoret possesses for Scudamour. Psychologically, it is concerned with the state of mind into which human beings can fall if their sense of true love is damaged or lost. Hence the validity of Amoret's appeal to Britomart to make the 'enchanter' undo the spells he has set upon her. Release is only

possible, psychologically or morally, by going back along the
same road and having each failure corrected or cured. Busyrane's desire for Amoret's heart is cancelled by stages, with first
the chain dropping from her, then the pillar breaking into
pieces, then the knife coming out of her heart of its own accord,
and finally the wound being closed up. What caused Amoret's
becoming the prey of the sorcerer is difficult to discover. In
Book IV she becomes the victim of another wicked creature,
Lust, who keeps her imprisoned in a cave until she is rescued by
Belphoebe. It is natural, therefore, to conclude that she is
susceptible to some kind of sexual evil and has no defence
against it. It may well be that the figures in the Masque of Cupid
are interpretable as projections of Amoret's mind, and that it is
weakness within which promotes them. This is not an interpretation which is particularly acceptable—it belongs more to
the post-Freudian world than to the time of Spenser. Yet
granted what we know of Amoret and Scudamour it has some
element of plausibility. And granted what we know of Spenser's
use of allegory it has even more. Despair is plainly a projection
of the Red Crosse Knight's mind, just as Acrasia is of Guyon's.
Yet these two Knights are heroes and able to look after themselves, with a little help from their ideal counterparts, whereas
Amoret is inevitably a helpless victim. It is Britomart who is
the heroine in the scene with Busyrane and she is capable of
holding her sword over his head although his magical phrases
fill her mind with horror and alarm. Her chastity is sufficient in
itself; Amoret's clearly was not.

In the cancelled stanzas which were introduced to be the
conclusion of Book III, Amoret's capacity for passion meets that
of Scudamour. In his embrace she:

> overcommen quight
> Of huge affection did in pleasure melt,
> And in sweete ravishment pourd out her spright:
> No word they spake, nor earthly thing they felt,
> But like two senceles stocks in long embracement dwelt.

That Amoret is capable of strong physical response to the desire
of her husband is obvious. That she could reach the state of
mind indicated in the House of Busyrane is possible. What we

have witnessed there is the other side of the coin. It is regrettable that those five stanzas which illuminate so much about Amoret had to be cancelled to allow Book IV to begin, and to allow another union altogether between Scudamour and Amoret.

Chapter VII

BOOK IV. UNITY AND RECONCILIATION

BOOK IV marks the beginning of the second instalment of *The Faerie Queene* but it is in fact a sequel to Book III, diverging even more widely than it from the designs carried out in the first two Books. It thus lends a further argument to the belief that Spenser regarded his allegorical structure as a device capable of whatever modifications the theme in hand required. Strictly its subject is Friendship and in Spenser's large view this means unity or concord, that harmonious relationship which binds humanity together. Here, for the only occasion in the poem there is no central hero and no quest: the title page provides two heroes, Cambell and 'Telamond', but their story occupies only a small share of the Book and after the fifth Canto they are seen no more. Their characters are not drawn on a great scale, nor, which is more to the point in *The Faerie Queene*, do they go through experiences more intense than those of other figures in the Book. Instead, the narratives begun in Book III are continued or concluded with a few other independent episodes relevant to the theme added to the plot.

It may be said in justification for this departure from precedent that Friendship is not a virtue which can be vested in a single hero; one knight cannot go wandering through the world exercising a virtue which by its very nature requires two. Hence the solitary figure in flight exemplified by Florimell and the other figures lamenting a condition of solitude such as Britomart by the seashore, Arthur in the night, and Scudamour in the forest, are replaced by a pair or group of characters. Some of the depth of feeling which Spenser was able to elicit from their experiences has now vanished and we find in its stead an atmosphere of social situations, knights meeting and exchanging news, agreeing or quarrelling as opportunity arises. This is not, of course, all that happens in Book IV, for Spenser's conception of Friendship, being as multiple as his conceptions of every other virtue, requires other kinds of expression. There enter personifications, characteristic of the earlier Books: *Ate* appears as a source of discord among the knights and *Cambina* operates as her antitype, the maker of harmony. A monster, *Lust*, and a Giant, *Corflambo*, act as destroyers of marriage, while all the sea-gods and river nymphs balance them as witnesses to the marriage of Thames and Medway. There enter, too, characters from Book III to continue the love-stories opened there. Timias and Belphoebe, Scudamour and Amoret pursue their relationships, Britomart at last meets Artegall, and Florimell is rescued from Proteus by Marinell's discovery of her love for him. A self-contained new episode, the story of Amyas and Aemylia, interposed with that of Placidas and Poeana, illustrates a successful achievement of unity. And at the core of these formulations there stands the great image of concord in the Temple of *Venus*, analogous to the Garden of Adonis in Book III. Friendship by the end of Book IV has ceased to be simply a social accident and has become a moral concept portrayed philosophically and pictorially as had been the central themes in the previous Books.

If Book III was dominated by the idea of separation, the key to Book IV is to be found in the complementary idea of unity. It is in this sense that the two Books may be seen to go together, the one continues the other not only by carrying on or finishing its narratives but also by completing its thought. The idea of unity underlies the early scenes in which various knights are divided in discord and restored to amity of differing degrees of worth and permanence; it also directs the plots of the love-stories enabling them to develop towards the union or reunion of separated characters; and, more independently of narrative, it is celebrated lyrically in the procession of the rivers and expounded philosophically in the scene at the Temple of *Venus*, where Scudamour finds his bride. A single hero and a single quest were obviously encumbrances to themes like these, nor did Spenser find any solution in the scheme of introducing two heroes instead of one. Cambell and Triamond[1] belong to the same stratum of the Book as the miscellaneous knights and are

---

[1] 'Telamond' appears on the title of Book IV but Spenser had decided in the process of writing to change his name to the third of the brothers, Priamond, Diamond, and Triamond.

abandoned with them when the idea of Friendship moves from the everyday social world to a profounder level. Spenser has here introduced a radical, and perhaps damaging, change in his structure. The lack of an outstanding central hero means the lack of that point of focus which, however far Spenser may move from it in the course of the narrative, is still the thread which the reader keeps in his mind. It is not difficult to accept a prolonged interlude when the principal hero's place is taken by another; this occurs in Book III with Britomart and in Book VI with Calidore; but it is much harder to follow a narrative in which there is no single person, or even a pair, in whom the theme of the Book is concentrated.

In its design Book IV is closely affiliated with Book III. In each there is employed an induction to every Canto as part of its structural scheme, and in Book IV this takes the form of a reflective contemplation upon the virtue of Friendship. Supplemented by brief generalisations made during the development of the narrative, these have the effect of building up a theoretical view of the theme. The events consequently become a little remote and read more like illustrations to a manual upon Friendship than narratives in their own right. This impression is strengthened by the mechanical way in which each Canto is terminated. The author has not sufficient space to continue his story but must wait for 'another tide' before he can proceed. This seafaring metaphor is used frequently and results in drawing attention to the activity of the narrator and in distracting concern from the story itself. Spenser had used the chance of introducing his own voice at the opening of a new stage in the narrative in Book III, when, for example, he recounts the birth of Belphoebe and Amoret at the opening of Canto vi, and sometimes at the close of a Canto when he is going to move on to a story which had been suspended for some time, as in the case of Florimell at the end of Canto vi which had been occupied with the descriptions of the Garden of Adonis. In Book IV, however, the termination of each Canto is a regular, flat statement which is more conspicuous owing to the arbitrariness of the division of the material into Cantos. There is a constant overflow of events from one Canto into the centre of the next. The story of Cambell and Triamond begins in the middle of

Canto II, the tournament in which Cambell and Triamond take part, ends in the middle of Canto V, the tale of Timias and Belphoebe runs from the second part of Canto VII to half way through Canto VIII, and the restoration of Aemylia to Amyas begins there and concludes in the middle of Canto IX. In Cantos x, XI and XII the more logical disposition of single episodes into separate Cantos is resumed.

No other Book treats its narrative in quite this fashion; in them the story itself governs the distribution into Cantos, and interruptions, which are rare, are occasioned only by internal requirements, as for instance when we leave the Red Crosse Knight in Orgoglio's dungeon in the centre of Canto VII, and go with the Dwarf in search of Una. The abrupt divisions in Book IV are characteristic of the method of Ariosto; but Ariosto turns his breaks into a deliberate device for heightening the suspense: his heroines are abandoned in circumstances of the utmost danger while another equally alarming story is carried to another crisis. This principle Spenser grasped well enough to put into practice in Book III in the Florimell plot, but in Book IV it is either not introduced or not used successfully. Ariosto would have described Amoret's capture by *Lust* and her rescue in two separate stages (as he does in the episode of Isabella from which this story is derived) but not in Spenser's way in one Canto with Timias's defection and banishment by Belphoebe attached to it.

The effect of this method of combining the narrative gives Book IV an air of having been put together in a somewhat haphazard fashion. It may well be, as Mrs J. W. Bennett suggested, that Spenser was using materials designed for another purpose. If he has, in fact, employed his material in a design for which it was not naturally suited, he has, nevertheless, given some coherence to his Book by his generalisations about the content of each Canto and by preventing any episode from appearing irrelevant. The best that can be done in reading this Book is to grasp the consistency of its theme in its completeness and to ignore details which appear inexplicably unsatisfactory.[1]

---

[1] The outstanding problems occur in Canto IX which hardly hangs together as a piece of narrative. Mrs Bennett pointed out how closely the characters imitate the actions of those in Ariosto, Britomart behaving like Marfisa, *Ate* like Gabrina, Scudamour like Zerbino, Amoret like Isabella,

In the opening scenes a number of short episodes are presented. First, Britomart and Amoret reach a castle in which it
was the custom to exclude knights who had no ladies with
them, an anecdote based upon Ariosto. One of these lays claim
to Amoret, thus provoking Britomart to her defence. She fights
and defeats him, and then revealing her sex as an Amazon,
obtains admission for the knight as well as for Amoret whom
she had protected. This was a fortunate event since it assures
Amoret that she need no longer fear the intentions of her companion and can conduct happy discussions about her love for
Scudamour with a woman who is also separated from the
object of her desire.

Next appear Paridell with Duessa and Blandamour with *Ate*.
Their association strikes a note of unreflecting consonance,
which is soon dissolved by *Ate* who finds means of planting seeds
of discord between them and also between Scudamour and
Britomart, who join them. *Ate*, like Duessa, seems beautiful but
her appearance is wholly misleading. Spenser describes her true
nature in terms of caricature and gives considerable space to her
dwelling which, like those of Mammon in Book II and Guile in
Book V, is close to the gate of Hell. All sources of discord and
the names of the cities, legendary persons, and historical characters who had been damaged by her power are gathered in
her house. Spenser exemplifies among them Babylon, Thebes,
Rome, Jerusalem and Troy, with the emblem of the cause of the
Trojan war, the apple over which the goddesses quarrelled,
hanging high above it. The nature of *Ate* is defined by the
character of her dwelling:

> Yet many waies to enter may be found,
> But none to issue forth when one is in:
> For discord harder is to end then to begin.
>
> IV. i. 20

The friendship between Paridell and Blandamour is only

---

and the false Florimell choosing at the Tournament the treacherous
coward, Braggadocchio, just as Doralice preferred Mandricardo. Whether
or not one goes all the way with Mrs Bennett and accepts her chronological
assessment of the growth of the poem, some element of replanning is undoubtedly present. See Chapter II, pp. 46-52.

temporary and they soon enter into the spirit of *Ate's* outlook. Spenser does not deny that a superficial form of friendship can be valuable and he explores the grounds upon which it is based and the conditions in which it can be maintained. The level on which the allegory proceeds in this section is that of ordinary social life; the characterisation and incidents are kept in tune with that. Paridell's peevish competitiveness and Blandamour's natural quarrelsomeness and fickleness are brought out in their speech, as colloquial as Spenser's medium will allow, and in their behaviour. Both are ready to fight each other without provocation, and each forces the other to fight on his behalf when Britomart and Scudamour appears in turn as the enemy.

Duessa consoles Scudamour for the appearance of falsity in Amoret when Spenser recalls the phrase used by Britomart in her support of the Red Crosse Knight's determination to remain faithful to Una. It came from Chaucer, the *Franklin's Tale*, and has been quoted above on p. 13, note 1.

Duessa echoes the passage in her own language:

> For Love is free, and led with selfe delight,
> Ne will enforced be with maisterdome or might.
>
> IV. i. 46

Ate adds her own fictitious evidence and reduces Scudamour to a state of uncontrolled fury. Meanwhile Paridell and Blandamour patch up their friendship in a way that lacks any element of permanence.

> Yet all was forg'd and spred with golden foyle,
> That under it hidde hate and hollow guyle.
> Ne certes can that friendship long endure,
> How ever gay and goodly be the style,
> That doth ill cause or evill end enure:
> For vertue is the band that bindeth harts most sure.
>
> IV. ii. 29

The two knights whom they meet at this point are exemplars of the friendship based upon virtue, linked not only by common interests and occupations but also by ties of marriage and selfless affection. They are the nominal heroes of the Book, Cambell and Triamond, the story of whose first enmity and its resolution is told in a passage of retrospective narrative, and whom we see acting in a fashion directly opposite to that of Paridell and Blandamour.

Triamond is the third of the three sons of Agape, a fairy, who had prevailed upon the Furies to grant that the life of each should be absorbed on his death by his surviving brother. When, therefore, all three came to fight for Canacee, the heroine of Chaucer's unfinished *Squire's Tale*, the power of Priamond slid into Diamond, the next contender, and that of Diamond into Triamond. Canacee had given her brother, Cambell, a ring which would preserve his life. The narrative describes fully the battle between Cambell and each of the three brothers. Spenser keeps the action interesting and relies extensively upon imagery to distinguish duels between Cambell and each of his opponents. Priamond, skilled in the use of shield and spear, reels back under Cambell's blows like an old oak in a storm and is rapidly defeated. Diamond fights with an axe bringing even greater violence to his attacks until, heaving his weapon too strongly, he loses his balance and falls to his death as does a vulture when it descends too far in attacking a heron. Only Triamond remains, while Cambell, through the merit of his ring, is as strong as ever. The final battle is even more ferocious than the others and relies upon a concentration of verbs to give pressure to the movement of the warriors. A pause is provided by a stanza-long simile describing the effect of the tidal bore upon the Shannon which returns more powerfully to the ocean as it goes back along the course of the river. Finally, each appears to have slain the other and the spectators rise, leaving the seemingly dead contestants upon the field. However, Triamond gains another life from his dead brother and Cambell recovers from the stroke which had momentarily stunned him and both begin to fight again.

Spenser succeeds in turning this joust to his own ends, partly by his use of the underlying magical spells for each warrior and partly by the similes which individualise the style of each duel. What concludes the whole struggle is the arrival of Cambina, Triamond's sister, bearing in one hand a rod of peace resembling Mercury's caduceus of two intertwined serpents crowned with an olive branch, and in the other a cup of *nepenthe*. This was the drink which Jove granted to heroes whom he intended to place among the gods. Its virtue lay in its ability to create love and forgetfulness of evil deeds. Cambina, having failed to persuade the two to cease from fighting, strikes them with her wand and gives them a draught from her cup. They then become friends for life, and the joust concludes with expressions of joy from all who had witnessed it. Cambell takes Cambina for his bride and Triamond marries Canacee.

After this episode, Cambell and Triamond become models of all that true friends ought to be. At the tournament organised by Satyrane for the right to obtain Florimell's girdle, each champions the other even to the extent of wearing his armour to 'purchas honour on his friends behalve' (Canto IV, 27). The point of this exchange is made by Spenser to illustrate the Aristotelian doctrine that genuine friendship requires the desire to advance another's well-being and even to yield the performance of a noble action in preference to undertaking it oneself if there is credit to be won.[1] Consequently after fighting at the tournament in each other's armour Cambell and Triamond offer the prize to one another:

> Each labouring t'advance the others gest
> And make his praise before his owne preferd:
> So that the doome was to another day differd.
>
> IV. iv. 36

Conceived as opposites of Paridell and Blandamour, Cambell and Triamond are nevertheless figures out of the same mould. They join these unknown knights peaceably and it is Cambell who prevails upon them to husband their pugnacious inclinations until the tournament begins, so that 'turning all to game' they ride together to the appointed meeting-place. This is the sociable aspect of friendship, and all the knights who come to take part demonstrate chivalric vigour and a due sense of honour. Many of them have never been seen before in *The Faerie Queene* and are not to be seen again; they are simply introduced to provide a large enough group of warriors to

---

[1] *Nicomachean Ethics*, VIII, viii, translated by J. A. K. Thomson.

establish the tournament upon a sufficiently grand scale. Against such a distinguished background, the familiar figures are able to show their prowess, or in the case of Braggadocchio their cowardice. In addition to the knights who have already appeared there comes one strange figure whom nobody knows. He is dressed in rough armour, his horse wears a harness of oak leaves, and his 'ragged shield' bears the motto *Salvagesse sans finesse*. His encounter with two well-known knights and with seven others marks outstanding ability in the art of jousting; Sir Satyrane's supporters are all put to flight. This strange figure is, in fact, Artegall and it is only at the end of the day when Britomart joins the tournament that he is defeated. Her enchanted spear thrusts him back 'over his horses taile above a stryde'. No other knight is successful afterwards in attempting to restore Artegall's reputation and Britomart is acclaimed the hero who had saved the fortunes of the 'Knights of Maidenhead'. To her also the 'Salvage Knight' was unknown and it is only after Artegall had united with Scudamour to attack her that she at last discovers his identity.

The whole of this tournament is characterised by imagery of fierce animals. It is as 'two bulls', or 'two wolves', or 'two boars' that the contestants carry on their joust. The vocabulary, too, is comparatively realistic: the knights conduct themselves 'cuffling close' and 'hurtling round' and the description of the fighting is summed up in proverbial phrases: 'to beare the bell' which is attached first to Satyrane's success in jousting and later to Amoret's beauty, and the classical allusion 'so nought be esteemed happie till the end' is applied to the sudden appearance of Britomart just when Artegall seems to have achieved success in his dismissal of all Satyrane's party. Spenser writes this section in a naturalistic style and it is only in the later parts where Concord is demonstrated that his language becomes less colloquial and the verse more consistently poetical.

After the tournament the award of Florimell's girdle comes to the fore. It was to be given to the fairest of the ladies present, who would then become the reward of the successful champion of three days' jousting. Spenser describes its history before it reached Florimell. Vulcan had made it as a 'cestus' for Venus to prove her matrimonial fidelity, and when she took Mars as her

H *

lover she removed it and left it with the Graces. They presented it to Florimell whom they had brought up. According to Spenser, it was a symbol of chastity as well as of fidelity, and Florimell among the exemplars of Chastity in Book III was distinguished by her possession of it. Tasso in *Gerusalemme Liberata* has another interpretation of it when he describes the belt Armida wore to attract Rinaldo. This was superior even to the cestus of Venus, but it is linked with immoral love. Armida, like Acrasia, is determined to destroy chivalry among the knights who come into contact with her. Spenser, however, emphasises its connection with feminine virtue. All the ladies on this occasion are beautiful but their beauty is over-shadowed by that of the false Florimell, and all the knights agree that she is fairer than any other. Those who had known the real Florimell are delighted to find that she is not dead, as Satyrane's discovery of her girdle beside the hyena de-vouring her palfrey had previously suggested, and yet they do not recall such extreme degree of beauty in her. She ap-pears to them to resemble an embodiment of a heavenly spirit rather than a human being. Spenser supports this reaction by a simile of a dishonest goldsmith who covers base metal with gilding so that it appears brighter than real gold; for 'so forged things do fairest shew' (IV. v. 15).

The simile anticipates the sequel when the false Florimell proves unable to clasp the girdle round her waist. This failure mystifies the men who had awarded her the prize, and when no other lady succeeds either, the Squire of Dames brings frivolity into the episode by leading the knights into ribald laughter. When ultimately Amoret is asked to put on the girdle it fits her perfectly, which arouses the jealousy of the false Florimell, who tries again with no better success. Yet she remains the winner of the prize for beauty, and is awarded to Britomart, the champion of the whole tournament. This award Britomart refuses, preferring the virtue of Amoret to the alleged wonder of the 'snowy Mayd' who cannot wear the badge of chastity. The level of the narrative is reduced to absurdity when all the other knights lay claim to the prize rejected by Britomart. This is the moment when *Ate* triumphs by creating discord among the men who have united in common agreement about feminine beauty. After considerable unknightly irritation, Satyrane suggests that Florimell should choose for herself. When she chooses Braggadocchio, whose cowardice they have all despised, they determine to find some other means of obtaining her. But Braggadocchio is too much pleased with his triumph to leave anything to chance and promptly rides away with his acquisition.

ii

The episodes of these Cantos are principally concerned with realistic activities and have been cast in allegorical phrasing. Yet even at this realistic level the allegory operates by means other than that of example. *Ate* accompanies the knights as both the cause and the symbol of the dissensions that arise from slight or ill-grounded friendship. Neither Cambell nor Triamond, devoted to Canacee and Cambina, wish to involve themselves in the squabble focussed upon the desire for the false Florimell, but *Ate* has plenty of material to act upon with the rest of the company. Personification is introduced to point the universal implications of human behaviour in the early part of Book IV, and it will provide the conceptual background for later relationships of a naturalistic kind in the amity embodied by Cambina between Placidas and Amyas on the one side, and in the discord between the knights who fight so confusedly in Canto IX.

From such a beginning, Book IV moves to studies of friendship which seem at first to overlap with the subjects of Book III. Certainly the first episode after the tournament, Scudamour's night in the cottage of Care, belongs thematically to much that was experienced by Arthur and Britomart when they lamented their solitude. But its causes and its nature are different. Arthur and Britomart believe that they will one day find the object of their desire. Their isolation is from an ideal not yet attained and seen only in a vision. It belongs to Book III, the Book of separation and search. Scudamour, on the other hand, is in the grip of despair: his ideal has proved an illusion. Amoret is false. We know that the accusation is wrong, that Amoret is the victim of

Ate and of that other personification, *Sclaunder*, and that his suffering is of his own making. Scudamour's experience belongs to Book IV, the Book where misconceptions are put right, where Timias's infidelity to Belphoebe is expiated, Amyas's temporary yielding to Poeana is absolved, and where Artegall discovers that his enemy is the woman whom he loves above all others, Britomart.

These narratives are concerned with Concord, not simply in distinction from the kinds of dissent shown in the earlier Cantos, but in a positive and permanent stage of harmony based upon fundamental agreements. Hence the emphasis that is placed upon forgiveness in these. This was not an issue raised at all in Book III, unless Malbecco's plea to Hellenore to return to him from her life with the satyrs may be so understood, but it becomes prominent in Book V, where the question of the proper fields of Justice and Mercy in public affairs is discussed. Book IV, treating of the virtue that lies between Chastity and Justice, between, that is, what concerns the individual alone and what concerns society as a whole, demonstrates the need for forgiveness in the conduct of personal relationships. This topic the story of Timias and Belphoebe openly and poignantly expresses, and the marriage between Placidas and the erring Poeana implies. Scudamour's suffering in the blacksmith's cottage, sleepless and jealous, is the consequence of a personal misconception; and it is in the light of other real or possible misconceptions that it is criticised: Poeana reforms, and Placidas, not unblemished himself, is prepared to accept her; Timias expiates his guilt in solitude and is restored to Belphoebe's favour. Scudamour, less guilty than either, is also less generous; his estimate of Amoret is on a par with that of the hag *Sclaunder* when she sees her with Arthur. He discovers his error only when he realises that Britomart is a woman, and his mistake has done no direct harm to Amoret. It was caused by the spirit of *Ate*, of discord, and he has paid for it by his experience of despair. His story is another variation upon the need for forgiveness in personal relations.

In these particular episodes Spenser is elaborating and exploring a theme that he had raised, like so many others, in the first Book of the poem. The Red Crosse Knight is similarly

deceived about Una's fidelity and chastity; but there his illusion
is dismissed by Spenser's direct statements about her dignity
and her virtue. The accusation is made to come from another
world altogether and to be as outrageous and irrelevant as is
Leontes's accusation of Hermione in *The Winter's Tale*. Each is
'a great king's daughter' about whom 'to prate and talk for life
and honour' is wholly unfitting. Amoret does not occupy such a
position. She has been the victim of Busyrane and she will be
captured by the monster, *Lust*. The situation is more complicated, and Scudamour's misconception appears consequently
more understandable. Nevertheless it is unfounded, although it
is Belphoebe who has to release her from her second captivity
just as it was Britomart who had to free her from Busyrane. Her
innocence does not speak for itself as Una's could. Indeed the
narrative casts doubt upon it repeatedly. Yet the final impression with which Spenser leaves us is that of virtue. Britomart
gives it weight in her determination to admire Amoret's character rather than follow the knights in their assessment of the
false Florimell. It was this mixed rendering which occasioned
Scudamour's account of how he won her rather than any introduction of their reunion neglected from the passage at the
conclusion of Book III, which was designed as the final episode
of her story in this Book.

Allegorically, the account of Scudamour's suffering in the
cottage of Care, Amoret's seizure by *Lust*, and the appearance
of *Corflambo*, depend upon figures which are symbolical rather
than naturalistic. Care's cottage seems at first a typical portrayal
of the Irish background comparable with the witch's dwelling
in Book III, or that of Abessa and Kirkrapine in Book I.
Mentioned in Chapter I, p. 26, the cottage is characteristic of a
scene which could have been glimpsed on an ordinary walk in
Spenser's environment. Yet Care is presented with special attention to the place in which he lives. Details soon make him more
and more remote from a recognisably blacksmith. He is
enormous, like a giant, works day and night upon the construction of iron wedges, and his occupation conveys unavoid-
able meaning:

> Those be unquiet thoughts, that carefull minds invade.
>
> IV. v. 35

His action keeps Scudamour awake:

> There lay Sir *Scudamour* long while expecting,
>> When gentle sleepe his heavie eyes would close;
>> Oft chaunging sides, and oft new place electing,
>> Where better seem'd he mote himselfe repose;
>> And oft in wrath he thence again uprose,
>> And oft in wrath he layd him downe againe.
>> But wheresoever he did himselfe dispose,
>> He by no meanes could wished ease obtaine:
> So every place seem'd painefull, and ech changing vaine.

IV. v. 40

As a study of human experience this brings an outstanding quality of perceptiveness. The ceaseless barking of the dogs, the crowing of the cock, and the 'loud shriking' of the owl add support to the noise of the hammers and the bellows, and yet more unrealistic are the strokes upon Scudamour's head by one of the blacksmith's hammers. Spenser sums it all up in one phrase:

> In such disquiet and hart-fretting payne,
>> He all that night, that too long night did passe.

IV. v. 45

The treatment of Scudamour's state of mind is remarkable for its mixture of naturalistic description of setting and psychological experience with intelligent use of emblematic and symbolic media. The whole section is made memorable through its skilful combination of the two styles.

The other two episodes which contain allegorical figures are less subtle than that of Care. *Lust*, the monster which seizes Amoret, is a crude embodiment of his name. He is truly a monster, hairy, wide-mouthed, with teeth like tusks, and huge ears longer than those of elephants.[1] He rapes the innocent

---

[1] The closest analogy that I have seen is a picture of a monster in the Middle French poem, *Yvain* (*Le Chevalier au Lion*), probably composed in 1170-1175. This was translated into Middle English and was published in Joseph Ritson's text *Ancient English Metrical Romances* in 1802. Certain lines are near to Spenser's detailed description of *Lust*, for instance:

> 'Unto his belt hang his hare'—and
> 'He had eres als ane olyfant'—and
> 'His browes war like litel buskes;
> And his tethe like bore tuskes'—and
> 'On his mace he gan him rest.'

women he catches and then devours them. His savage laughter is malevolent, and when Timias tries to rescue Amoret from him he uses her as a shield so that no stroke can be launched effectively against him. Timias inflicts one wound from which 'cole-black' blood pours. There is only one enemy he dreads— Belphoebe—and when she arrives he abandons Amoret and flees to his cave. There Belphoebe kills him and orders his victims to come out of the darkness into the safety of the day-light. The two who emerge are Aemylia, who will appear in the subsequent episode, and a repellent Hag who has been *Lust's* mate. The whole of this scene is reminiscent of that in which Ulysses and his crew become captive to Polyphemus, for *Lust* like Polyphemus rolled a stone in front of the cave's outlet to prevent escape from his clutches.

Two events follow the escape of Aemylia and Amoret from *Lust's* cave. First, when Belphoebe brings his victims to join Amoret where she has left her she finds Timias visibly consoling her and this results in her scornful dismissal of her erstwhile admirer. Second, when Aemylia is lamenting the fate of Amyas who has become the prisoner of *Corflambo*, and the need for his rescue is essential to the narrative of this Book. *Corflambo* represents the third allegorical figure after Care and *Lust*. He is a pagan giant who rides upon a dromedary and possesses the power of destroying his enemies by his eyes: his glance is that of a basilisk and with it he can ensnare beautiful women and heroic men. Little space, however, is given to him, for he is killed immediately by Arthur who is thus enabled to return Amyas, 'the Squire of low degree' to Aemylia. He is no more than one of Spenser's giants whose only purpose is to damage the innocent characters in the narrative. Arthur's appearance occurs in Canto VIII, according to Spenser's customary method, but he does not undertake any important activity in the Book. He is present, as any other knight could have been, to care for Aemylia and Amoret after their suffering in *Lust's* cave. In a brief interpolation all three spend the night in *Sclaunder's* cottage, who attacks them verbally and follows them uttering abuse on their departure in the morning. Spenser takes ad-vantage of her inhospitality to introduce a reference to the golden age where all had been perfect and glorious; his nostalgic description recalls that in Book II, Canto VII, and that in Ovid's *Metamorphoses*. It is characteristic of Spenser to introduce a counterbalance by introducing the ideal world of the past which he so much admired.

After the rapid removal of *Corflambo*, the narrative moves to the tale of Aemylia and the Squire of low degree, and of Poeana, *Corflambo's* daughter and her wooer, Placidas. This is a brief tale which belongs to the theme of friendship, for Placidas, almost indistinguishable in appearance from Amyas, changes places with him so that he can escape from *Corflambo's* prison. He has made a heroic gesture for the sake of friendship because he had no reason to think that he would gain anything from Poeana. However, this story ends fortunately, for Arthur, committed to his customary moral rôle, prevails upon Placidas to take her for his wife, and endows him with the property which had belonged to *Corflambo*. Poeana, having lost Amyas, decides that his substitute is equally desirable. There is little to choose between them in appearance, and morally Placidas has earned a higher stature by his self-sacrifice.

The ideas which underlie the allegory so far have their origin in Aristotle, and many of the aspects of friendship which Spenser treats are traceable to the *Nicomachean Ethics*. They may have reached Spenser through intermediate sources and they have been coloured by neo-platonism, but it is in Aristotle that most of the theoretical matter of Spenser's thought has been found. Nevertheless, the more one reads criticism which deals with sources and analogues the more clear it becomes that Spenser was borrowing his material from ideas that were widespread and generally acceptable to the Elizabethan view of life. Many of the notions about the nature of friendship can be traced to Cicero,[1] to Giraldi, Plutarch, Montaigne and to Aristotle. Moreover, the more one follows these analogies the more evident it becomes that Spenser was using this matter in his own way, and making out of it poetry which can be interpreted in a number of fashions. For example, as H. S. V. Jones points out, a milder form of Scudamour's suspicions is found in Belphoebe's estimate of Timias. In the case of both Scudamour and Timias there is shewn a contrast between that tranquillity

---

[1] *De Amicitia*, translated by John Harington, 1550.

of mind noted as one of the fruits of true friendship and the distress and anxiety which disturb associations not grounded on complete virtue. Scudamour in the home of Care is a companion picture to that of Timias living alone in the wilds. We can draw these parallels as we wish. One is forced to say that Belphoebe has *real* cause, Scudamour has none. He allows himself to believe ill of Amoret in the way that Aristotle says true friends never do. Friendship between the good is secure against calumny; hence *Sclaunder* and *Ate* on the one hand plausibly attack the appearance of virtue in different characters, whereas *Lust* and *Corflambo*, on the other, act ferociously against persons whose innocence should protect them.

Among the many discussions of Spenser's theory of friendship, there are several which arouse sound responses to the text as it stands. Charles G. Smith has assembled a mass of evidence to show that Spenser conceives of friendship as a harmonising principle of 'cosmic love operating in the realm of men to promote concord'. In one article he emphasises the rôle of Cambell and Triamond as 'the most important in the Book'.[1] Here the approach seems open to some doubt. It is difficult to accept this opinion in conjunction with the way in which the most important things in other books are presented. It is surely preferable to emphasise the significance of the philosophical houses—i.e. the expression of abstract ideas in concrete symbolical form—rather than the power of characters in the narrative of the Book. Another source for Spenser's conception of his subject is discussed by Professor Erskine,[2] who enlarges upon the debt of Spenser to Giraldi's *Tre Dialoghi della Vita Civile* which was translated by Lodowick Bryskett. This is the translation which claims to recount a conversation between Spenser and others in 1584-1589. Among the others was Dr Lang, Bishop of Armagh from 1584 till his death in 1589. It is unlikely that the conversation described by Bryskett ever took place since the whole dialogue, apart from some dramatic trimming, comes straight from Giraldi.

Aristotle, as the prime source, links friendship with love, and

---

[1] *E.L.H.*, 2. The set of five articles collected in *Spenser's Theory of Friendship*. Baltimore, 1936.
[2] Publication of the *Modern Languages Association*, xxx.

with justice as the bond which holds states as well as individuals together.[1] He distinguishes between true and false friendship, between what is absolute and founded upon virtue and what is accidental and arises from motives of pleasure and utility. Those which are accidental are liable to dissolve as soon as the cause ceases; they are most frequent in the young who are quick to make friends and quick to abandon them. 'Young men are amorous too; . . . hence they fall in love and soon afterwards fall out of love, changing from one condition to another many times in the same day.' The instability of such friendships is demonstrated in the relations between Paridell and Blandamour, and between these two and the ladies to whom they attach themselves. The permanence of the friendship between people who are good and alike in virtue, who wish the happiness of their friends for the friends' sake[2] is demonstrated likewise in the relation between Cambell and Triamond. Bad men are always in a state of discord[3] as is shown in the quarrels that spring up among the knights after the tournament; but good men try to promote concord as does Cambell between the knights, and Arthur in Canto IX. Aristotle also deals with friendship between brothers, the 'affection naturall' between Priamond, Diamond and Triamond; between equals, reflected in the devotion of the two 'squires of low degree' who are so alike as to be almost indistinguishable in appearance and character—even to their creator; and between people unequal in merit or power, as in the relation between Arthur and Timias which is faintly suggested or that between Amoret and her two protectors, Britomart and Arthur. Aristotle, moreover, begins his discussion by making the point that friendship is of various kinds and degrees, thus encouraging Spenser, who little needed the hint, to multiply his representations of it. Some of the general passages derived from Aristotle are not always clearly borne out in the subsequent narrative.

Arthur and Amoret come upon a troop of knights fighting. The combat is about the possession of the false Florimell, and one stanza outlines the tastes in love of the four knights thus

[1] J. A. K. Thomson. Translation of the *Nicomachean Ethics*, pp. 140-142.
[2] *ibid.*, p. 233.
[3] *ibid.*, p. 255.

connecting them with the introductory passage from Aristotle. The knights are the familiar figures of Paridell and Blandamour with an unknown pair Druon and Claribell who had also taken part in the tournament. Britomart and Scudamour stand aside watching them (stanza 22). After six stanzas of fighting between the four, the narrative appears to begin again with a fresh introduction of the arrival of Britomart and Scudamour who arrived here 'by fortune' (stanza 28). They then become engaged in the fight against all four and Arthur (having apparently shed Amoret) observes the mêlée from a distance and enters it to make peace among them (stanza 32). From this attempt emerges Scudamour's lament for the lost Amoret and Claribell's request to him to describe how he obtained her.

Obviously the narrative and the actions of the main characters are in a state of confusion. Scudamour speaks feelingly and yet in a few stanzas back Amoret has been present with Arthur. It may be that Spenser has put together two contradictory incidents to fill up the remaining half Canto so that the next event could have a complete Canto to itself. Or it may be, as Upton suggested, that the stanzas omitted at the end of Book III which described the reunion of Scudamour and Amoret ought to have been included here. Yet it is plain that Spenser preferred to leave the lovers still separated, and introduced a lament in the voice of Scudamour and an agreement that he should describe how he attained her before their marriage. This is Spenser's method of combining a double interest, for the theme of union is carried out but only retrospectively, the situation remaining as it had been at the beginning of the Book.

iii

The three subsequent Cantos share a common attitude. Canto x provides the philosophic core of the Book, comparable in intention with the House of Holiness in Book I, the House of Temperance in Book II, and the Garden of Adonis in Book III. It presents the Temple and Garden of Venus in which all the discords of the previous narratives are abandoned and only the image of amity remains to be set out. Canto xi is taken up with the marriage of Thames and Medway, a subject distant in its material from the human preoccupations which formed the focus of past events yet close enough in its theme to the idea governing the end of the Book. Its charm lies in its total change of tone within the consistency of outlook. Finally, Canto xii, linked with the procession of sea-deities, brings to a happy conclusion the story of Florimell and Marinell, preserving both the human and the mythological elements in the Book as a whole. These last Cantos splendidly complement the separation motifs of Book III and give weight to the idea of union which is the basis of Book IV, however varied its expression in the earlier parts had been.

Canto x is cast in an autobiographical form, for in it Scudamour at last describes his discovery of Amoret. He delights in telling this story since it cancels all the suffering through which he had gone in the past. She had been torn away from him by Busyrane and by *Lust,* events for which he had no explanation and could find no redress without the aid of Britomart and Belphoebe. It is in this Canto that he can insist upon his conviction of the permanence of her love for him; the suspicion and jealousy which he had experienced in the cottage of Care is now forgotten:

> So all that ever yet I have endured
> I count as naught, and tread downe under feet,
> Since of my love at length I rest assured,
> That to disloyalty she will not be allured.

Upon this note of joyful certainty he can begin to recount the struggle by which he obtained her.

His narrative is based upon the medieval conventions of the courts-of-love, opening characteristically in an address to an audience of knights and ladies. As we know, Scudamour is directing his story only to a handful of knights met in the forest and to Britomart who is scarcely an example of 'the ladies' the narrator has in mind. Nevertheless it provides a suitable setting for a story which depends upon the introduction of the familiar personifications of the Courts of Love world. Scudamour had heard of the adventure which he is now undertaking; the fame of the shield hanging outside the Castle and the Temple of *Venus* had spread widely among freshly qualified knights, and he, like others, thought this was the opportunity for him to gain honour and reputation. It was an adventure which required courage and enterprise since the castle was strongly defended and could only be entered by feats of swordsmanship and the power of outfacing whatever enemies were lurking inside. Spenser's description of the place is carefully localised. The Temple of *Venus* is established upon an island accessible by one bridge behind a castle. Scudamour had to fight against the twenty knights who lived in the castle, then seize the shield, and cross the bridge. The bridge is described in Spenser's most technical style:

> It was a bridge ybuilt in goodly wize,
> With curious Corbes and pendants graven faire,
> And arched all with porches, did arize
> On stately pillours, fram'd after the Doricke guize.
>
> IV. x. 6

Medieval as the context is, this bridge belongs to the newer, more advanced style of Elizabethan architecture. The shield of Love upon which Scudamour rapped to draw forth the knights is also Elizabethan in design, associated with the tournaments of the day, decorated with golden ribbons and the image of Cupid and his bow upon it.

Scudamour successfully defeats the knights and carries the shield to the end of the bridge. Spenser brings a childlike detail into the next stage of the journey when the victorious hero gains no response to his attempt to enter:

> I knockt, but no man answred me by name;
> I cald, but no man answred to my clame;
> Yet I persever'd still to knocke and call.
>
> IV. x. 11

The effect is mystifying and it is only when he sees inside the gate someone 'peeping through a crevis small' that he can force admission by showing the shield which the Porter recognises. The figures here are typically Spenserian and also those of the Courts of Love. Spenser's porters are always tuned to the setting in which they appear—*Ignaro* in Orgoglio's castle, *Zele* in the House of Alma, *Genius* in the Garden of Adonis—so here is *Doubt*, looking backward and forward, accompanied by *Delay* who does her best to hold Scudamour back. He, however, dismounts and walks firmly forward to pass through the *Gate of Good Desert* in spite of the terrifying appearance of the Giant, *Daunger*, who blocks the entrance. *Daunger* is another familiar figure in the conventional accounts of the Courts of Love, and Spenser has already introduced him in an earlier episode based upon the same formula. This was in the masque of Busyrane where he occurred in company with *Doubt*, and, although not in the form of a giant, he shared with him the alarming ugliness which creates fear in the mind of all who encounter him. Both, in fact, embody evils destructive to both friend and foe. In the masque *Daunger*, dressed roughly in a Bear's skin, carried emblematic signs of his nature, a net in one hand representing 'mischief' and a rustic blade for 'mishap' in the other. The Giant whom Scudamour faces is even more perilous for he has frightened off their path many successful knights who thus failed in the last stage of their quest. Scudamour, undaunted and strong in his trust of the shield he has won, attacks him with it and pushes his way through. Looking back, he sees how many horrors *Daunger* possesses to trap the unwary: 'hatred, murther, treason and despight' lurk behind him to ruin those who had not foreseen them. The terrors of his journey are now passed and before him lies the island where the Temple of *Venus* stands.

The description of the gardens and the Temple itself follows the normal Spenserian scheme. Its beauty depends upon the customary assumption that art contributes to supplement the power of nature. The world achieves complete perfection since every tree and every flower grows freely in it. As in other descriptions, Spenser combines the classical and religious ideals, the bliss of the Elysian fields and of paradise. His portrayal is collective and ecstatic:

> Fresh shadowes, fit to shroud from sunny ray;
> Faire lawnds, to take the sunne in season dew;
> Sweet springs, in which a thousand Nymphs did play;
> Soft rombling brookes, that gentle slomber drew;
> High reared mounts, the lands about to vew;
> Low looking dales, disloignd from common gaze;
> Delightfull bowres, to solace lovers trew;

False Labyrinthes, fond runners eyes to daze;
All which by nature made did nature selfe amaze.

IV. x. 24

The peace and orderliness here appeal both to the eye and to the sense of usefulness. Exceptionally there are no birds and little sound apart from the 'rombling brookes'. This is primarily the place in which pairs of lovers can happily delight in each other's company and wander free from any distress or suspicion. Spenser, however, does not confine it to the satisfaction of lovers; he also makes another setting away from it for true friends, heroes who have been bound to each other by heroic deeds. He is, in fact, offering a central image of the quality of friendship which had been defined during the progress of the Book. This is the philosophical reflection of the ideal towards which men like Cambell and Triamond or Amyas and Placidas have been aspiring. It is distinguished explicitly from that of the lovers who enjoy 'their spotless pleasures and sweet loves content'. Not only does Spenser provide another environment for the pairs of friends but he also illustrates the difference by quoting examples from biblical, classical and renaissance sources. Thus, beginning with Hercules and Hylas, Jonathan and David, the list proceeds through Greek legendary heroes to Titus and Gesippus and Damon and Pythias who have been recorded by Boccaccio, Surrey and Elyot. These last pairs had become stock examples of men who achieved perfect friendship. Their presence is typical of the sixteenth century and Spenser is employing a topical motif when he replaces the examples of famous lovers current in the courts-of-love poems with instances of famous heroes of present appeal who had united in friendship in their endeavours to achieve greatness. The stories of these figures were as well known as the stories of famous lovers, and Spenser alludes to them simply to establish the different nature of the relationship which they represent. Scudamour admires its satisfactory quality but he is still seeking the lady promised to him by the words engraved on the pillar from which he had withdrawn the shield.

His path leads him towards the Temple of *Venus* who is the model of beauty and of love. Typically, Spenser separates the wonder of this Temple from that of the two greatest Temples known in the past, both containing religious associations; one that of Diana of Ephesus, the focus of heathen worship and known to Christians from St Paul's reference to it in his phrase: 'Great is Diana of the Ephesians'; the other built by Solomon at Jerusalem which also carries Christian associations. Spenser has no hesitation in contrasting these unfavourably with the Temple of *Venus* partly because the combination of classical and biblical allusions caused no more trouble to him than the *well of life*, which he had praised in the episode of the Red Crosse Knight's fight with the Dragon, and partly because the love which *Venus* represents is love sent to human beings from God as well as love recorded by pagan poets. Before it is possible for him to go inside the Temple he has to pass another hazard, *Concord*, seated within the porch with her two armed sons Hatred and Love who stand beside her. Divine in origin, *Concord* is the power which holds the world together, preserving the courses of the heavens and the rightful places of the parts of the earth. Mother of Friendship and Peace, she ensures harmony between the nations and, metaphysically, she keeps the boundaries between the elements so that land and sea, fire and air, remain separate. Goddess-like, she is clothed in a robe enriched with golden thread and jewelled decoration and wears a Danish hood, a detail which appears to have sprung from Spenser's imagination. Her twin sons, born of two different fathers, are aspects of her rule. Hatred, described in a submerged personification, bites his lips and gnashes his 'yron tuskes' after *Concord's* insistence that he should hold the hand of Love. Yet he is weaker than his younger brother, and it is Love who defeats him in all points at issue. *Concord* is the principal figure in Scudamour's exploration of the outskirts of *Venus's* Temple and is, indeed, the personification of the ideal of friendship embodied in the whole of Book IV. She represents both the moral and metaphysical value towards which that Book has been reaching.

A more profound vision still awaits the reader in the interior of the Temple. Spenser lavishes the wealth of his descriptive genius upon the emotional and intellectual quality of this mysterious place. It possesses the fullness of a religious, or perhaps barbarous, context. In it are the overwhelming clouds of frankincense, the precious gifts offered from thousands of lovers, the hundred marble pillars, the hundred altars flaming with sacrificial fires, the hundred cauldrons intended for the expression of 'joy and amorous desire', all of which are cared for by white-robed priestesses. In the centre stands the statue of *Venus* made of an undefinable material which can be determined by a series of negatives, not precious stone, nor brass, nor gold, nor clay. Spenser can only find a repudiated simile: 'like to cristall glasse Yet glasse was not'. Likewise, the beauty of the statue can be established simply in terms of negative comparisons; this surpasses the statue made by Phidias with which a nameless youth fell in love. It is surrounded by a flock of cherubim, brothers of Cupid, which fly around it like little angels. It is covered with a veil to conceal the fact that it is hermaphrodite, capable of being both father and mother combined. The figure embodies *Venus Genatrix* and, although its description seems over-written, there sounds splendidly above it the anthem derived from Lucretius. This is the opening section of *De Natura Rerum*,[1] a magnificent invocation to *Venus*, which Spenser has translated freely but has endorsed it with a lyrical movement appropriate to its hymn-like nature. Repetition is used to speed the pace both in a single line as in 'Thee, goddesse, thee the winds, the clouds doe feare', and in two lines near the conclusion, and in the structure of the whole passage with its 'when' carried on from the first stanza to the 'Then . . .' 'And then' in the second, and 'Then' in the third. What gives particular vitality to the invocation is the preservation of the present tense either in the extensive form with 'doe' or in the brief direct phrase. The wide range of creatures from the flowers thrown forth from the Shelleyan 'daedale earth', to the birds, and then the beasts, brings a sense of the vigorous activity threading itself through the world. The lyric begins with a passionate invocation to *Venus* which points to her creative power and ends on an equally passionate note in which her quality of both sexes is emphasised:

[1] Some debts are owing to *Georgics* 2, 323, *Natalis Comes*, and to Chaucer, Prologue to the *Legend of Good Women*, and *Troilus and Criseyde* III, ii, but it is primarily to Lucretius that Spenser owes the hymn.

Great God of men and women, queene of th'ayre,
Mother of laughter, and welspring of blisse,
O graunt that of my love at last I may not misse.

IV. x. 47

The great anthem returns us to Scudamour and his search. Amoret he at last sees in the group at the feet of the goddess. Most of them constitute personified figures from Spenser's sources. Some he had introduced already, others are perhaps his own invention, *Womanhood*, in whose lap Amoret is sitting, and *Silence* which does not occur anywhere else, the rest are customary in the convention but perhaps are introduced by Spenser particularly to emphasise the humility and charm which had previously demonstrated in the character of Amoret herself, parted from her husband and yet still the wife whom he loves. It is left to Scudamour to lead Amoret away from her surroundings which he does with hesitation lest he should be treating sacrilegiously the Temple in which he had found her, but once more encouraged by his shield he can meet the rebuke made by *Womanhood* with a decisive answer:

Nay but it fitteth best,
For *Cupids* man with *Venus* mayd to hold,
For ill your goddesse services are drest
By virgins, and her sacrifices let to rest.

The joyfulness for which *Venus* had been praised now shines in her expression, and Scudamour knows that he may gently draw away his bride.

iv

The eleventh Canto is a considerable *tour de force* since it is occupied almost wholly with a description of a procession of sea-gods, rivers, and sea-nymphs. It opens with a few stanzas recalling the imprisonment of Florimell by Proteus and then proceeds to the celebration of the marriage of the Thames and the Medway witnessed by an aquatic procession. Although Spenser referred in a letter to Harvey dated April 2, 1580, to an 'Epithalamion Thamesis' it was probably not this work. The poem is now lost, and we have little knowledge of what it contained. Canto xi is partly based upon Camden's *Britannia*,

which was not published till 1596, and upon the second edition
of Holinshed which was printed in 1597. Osgood[1] points out
that the bride in the 'Epithalamion' may not have been the
Medway since this is mentioned in *The Shepheardes Calender* as the
younger brother of the Thames. Moreover, he points out that a
number of Irish rivers, with 'Mulla mine', are included as well
as three stanzas upon the great rivers of the world, nine upon
the sea-gods, and six upon sea-nymphs. It is best, therefore, to
consider Canto XI as part of Book IV, a relevant part since it is
concerned with the theme of union, essential to this Book.

The catalogue of the figures which attend the marriage of
Thames and Medway is distinguished by Spenser's remarkable
power of finding variety in content and his unfailing ear for
sonorousness of effect. He can introduce imaginative details
into the description so that the most important figures stand in
due proportion. The procession properly begins with *Neptune*,
the God of the Seas, and his Queen, *Amphitrite*. *Neptune* carries
his 'three-forkt mace' and wears his royal diadem under which
the briny water of his realm falls to the ground. *Amphitrite* is
equally close to the ocean, for it is she

> Whose yvorie shoulders were covered all,
> As with a robe, with her owne silver haire,
> And deckt with pearles, which th'Indian seas for her prepaire.

Before them goes *Triton*, blowing his trumpet which draws a
roaring sound from the rocks as he passes. This scene was never
to be forgotten, either by the author who improved upon it in
Colin Clouts Come Home Againe in the phrase 'Triton blowing loud
his wreathed horn' or by Wordsworth who ended his lament
that the 'world is too much with us' with the desire to 'hear old
Triton blow his wreathed horn'.

After *Neptune* and *Amphitrite* came the Sea-Gods. Those were
associated with familiar classical stories. The first mentioned is
Phorcys,

> the father of that fatall brood,
> By whom those old Heroes wonne such fame.

They included Medusa, whom Perseus slow, the Dragon of the
Hesperides which was one of the objects of the labours of

---

[1] C. G. Osgood, *Variorum*, pp. 241-242.

Hercules, and the Gorgons with Polyphemus among them. To the mention of 'that fatale brood' any Renaissance reader would naturally respond. In referring to other descendants of *Neptune*, Spenser provides some information, for instance, *Palemon*, who 'is sayler's frend', *Orion* 'that doth tempests still portend', and

> *Eurypulus*, that calmes the waters wroth;
> And faire *Euphoemus*, that upon them goth
> As on the ground, without dismay or dread:

These may have been familiar to Spenser's contemporaries; *Euphoemus* is tempting to mention because he was an Argonaut who could run as fast over the water as over dry land, without ever wetting his feet; an attractive legend even to ignorant readers of today. Among the descendants of *Neptune* there were many who had founded civilisations, those of Thebes, Phoenicia, Argos,

> And mightie *Albion*, father of the bold
> And warlike people, which the *Britaine* Islands hold.

Spenser recalls the legend that England and France were once one country and that *Albion* had been able to walk across what is now the Channel in order to fight against Hercules. Yet, following the model of Homer, he apologises for the limitation of his form which cannot measure the vastness of his material and is prepared to abandon a task of which the scale is beyond his powers:

> But what doe I their names seeke to reherse,
> Which all the world have with their issue fild?
> How can they all in this narrow verse
> Contayned be, and in small compasse hild?
> Let them record them, that are better skild,
> And know the moniments of passed times.
>
> IV. xi. 17

This humility may be characteristic of Spenser's outlook but it is also connected with the literary tradition to which he is attaching his catalogue of names. It enables him to move to topics which are more interesting to his readers and to himself. Nereus, for instance, is the last of the figures connected with the gods of the sea and he is mentioned because he was morally the most virtuous of them and the one best qualified to understand the language of the Gods. Through him Paris learned that the Trojan war and the destruction of Troy itself would result from his enticement of Helen, a topic widely adopted among Elizabethan poets and already used by Spenser in his narrative of Paridell and Hellenore.

The great rivers, first of the world, then of England and finally of Ireland provide Spenser with many opportunities for achieving imaginative effects. Line by line, what might have been no more than a dull catalogue becomes poetically exciting. Sometimes he draws upon the historical associations of a river, sometimes upon the linguistic interpretation of its name, sometimes upon a piece of general information which he had found fascinating; and always there is present the sonorous quality of name and epithet. In other parts of the poem certain particular rivers occur as similes and are consequently familiar as examples of Spenser's own personal feeling about them. For instance, *Nile* is 'fertile' because, as we have learnt in Book I, Canto I, 21, and Book III, Canto VI, 8, it was the source of newly created monstrous animals. *Pactolus* a golden river associated with Midas, had been the image to emphasise the quality of Britomart's golden hair. When they are not mentioned elsewhere, the great foreign rivers bring some poetic or historical character to the description. The Rhône becomes 'Long *Rhodanus* whose source springs from the skie', which is Spenser's way of reporting that it rises in the Alps and runs through the whole of France. 'Divine *Scamander*' is so called because it was a god and because it reminds readers of the *Iliad* that it was the river against which Achilles fought a battle and that the fighting was so heavy that it was 'purpled yet with blood of Greekes and Trojans, which therein did die'. The rivers of the world give Spenser an opportunity to vary his stanzas with unrepeated epithets. Here is one stanza which exemplifies what he can do with the names at his disposal:

> Great Ganges, and immortall Euphrates,
>> Deepe Indus, and Meander intricate,
>> Slow Peneus, and tempestuous Phasides,
>> Swift Rhene, and Alpheus still immaculate;
>> Ooraxes, feared for great *Cyrus* fate;

Tybris, renowmed for the Romaines fame,
Rich Oranochy, though but knowen late;
And that huge River, which doth beare his name
Of warlike Amazons, who do possesse the same.

IV. xi. 21

Some of these adjectives provide matters of fact which give greatness to the remote rivers: the Ganges *is* great, the Indus deep, and the Rhine certainly swift. Euphrates is called immortal because it was associated with the Garden of Eden. 'Intricate' is a natural interpretation of the movement of meandering; this kind of interpretation is used later in connection with the English 'Wyliborne', which Spenser explains, has a sly route and has earned its name from its wiliness, and with the 'Mole' which burrows underground. Alpheus is immaculate because legend maintains that it runs from Peloponnesus to Sicily without becoming salt. Of *Cyrus* readers of Herodotus would know that he crossed Ooraxes (or, more correctly, Araxes) but never recrossed it because he was killed in a battle on the other side. The Tiber must have been as familiar as the Rhine and the Rhône to Elizabethan travellers in Europe. The last two rivers refer to the voyages of Elizabethan seamen. Raleigh had sailed up the Orinoco, of which Spenser's version is 'Oranochy' and found *El Dorado* which lay between that river and the rivers guarded by the Amazons. Spenser may have heard about this South American exploration from Raleigh himself who published his account of it in the *Discoverie of Guiana* in 1596. He follows the stanza just mentioned by an appeal to the English to take advantage of Raleigh's discovery and conquer the land of gold which he had found.[1] The catalogue of rivers set out above indicates how much stimulus and variety of style Spenser could bring to the known and the unknown.

I have selected this stanza because it hardly appears promising in its content at first sight and yet proves unexpectedly rewarding when it is examined. This is true of most of the stanzas in the procession, although some obviously possess powerful imaginative appeal. These may now be considered for their own sake.

[1] See K. Koller, *E.L.H.*, I, 49, and *Variorum*, pp. 248-249.

The arrival of Thames, the bridegroom, is heralded by a passage of music which drew the attention of all the witnesses of the marriage. This was Arion playing upon his harp as he had in the past:

> That even yet the Dolphin, which him bore,
> Through the Ægaean seas from Pirates vew
> Stood still by him astonisht at his lore
> And all the raging seas for joy forgot to rore.

> So went he playing on the watery plaine.

IV. xi. 23-24

This is a moving instance of the magical power of music, assisted by Spenser's reconstruction of its impact upon the dolphin and the rough seas and by the rhythm of the stanza which continues the joy of its skill on this occasion.[1] Rhythm is one of the arts which builds up the processional character of the stanzas. It is difficult to isolate single lines since each depends upon the support of its whole context. Yet here, for Arion, there is the quiet charm of

> So went he playing on the watery plaine.

which extends the singing movement of the previous stanza.

Most of the epithets attached to the rivers preserve their watery nature, but at times they are marked by a slight element of personification. The 'stately' Severne, the 'sad' Trowis, and the 'gentle' Shure possess some nearness to living people although the context keeps them in the liquid realm where they belong. What is more impressive is the variety of epithets and explanatory phrases which Spenser finds to attach to them as rivers. The 'stony shallow Lone' (i.e. the Lune), the 'soft sliding Breane', the 'sandy Slane', and the 'spacious Shenan spreading like a sea' are all rivers he could have seen. Moreover, because their waters are productive Spenser often has a word for the kinds of fish which live in them: the Yar brought his own fish (a type of perch) to the feast; in the clean still water of the Darent 'ten thousand fishes play, and decke his pleasant

---

[1] Arion was a popular Elizabethan subject. The *Emblems* of Alciato prints early a highly competent engraving of him riding on his dolphin, although not crowned or robed.

streame'; the Trent contains 'thirty sorts of fish'; and among the Irish rivers the 'goodly Barow' is recalled

> which doth hoord
> Great heapes of Salmons in his deepe bosome.

Compassion, one of Spenser's strongest emotions, creeps into his references to rivers which have been close to battle scenes and his own personal feeling is aroused when he writes of waters he has known. For instance, when the Rowne (i.e. the Granta) enters:

> My mother Cambridge, whom as with a Crowne
> He doth adorn, and is adorn'd of it
> With many a gentle Muse and many a learned wit.

On his own property he must add to the list of Irish rivers

> And Mulla mine, whose waves I whilom taught to weep.

All these waters have been brought together to celebrate the marriage of Thames and Medway and these two occupy the most prominent position in Spenser's catalogue. The attire of Thames is of 'watchet hue' interwoven with waves 'glittering like Cristall glas' so that the impression is strangely remote. More impressive, however, is the arrival of the bride dressed in beautifully ethereal robes and moving in a dancing rhythm:

> Then came the Bride, the lovely *Medua* came,
> Clad in a vesture of unknowen geare,
> And uncouth fashion, yet her well became;
> That seem'd like silver, sprinckled here and theare
> With glittering spangs, that did like starres appeare,
> And wav'd upon, like water Chamelot,
> To hide the metall, which yet every where
> Bewrayed it selfe, to let men plainly wot,
> It was no mortall worke, that seem'd and yet was not.
>
> IV. xi. 45

The repeated 'came' in the first line creates a musical accompaniment, light and shining in its movement, and Spenser's description of her attire creates the same effect. Like Thames, she is dressed in a style which is not human but belongs to the water world of the rivers. The 'water Chamelot' places her dress outside the familiar wedding scenes (although it is, in fact,

an Eastern fabric) and looking back we realise how uncommitted the syntax has been in its '*seem'd* like silver' and 'did *like*
starres appeare'. The presence of the metal is partly concealed
as was the gold in the House of Busyrane, but here the concealment is attributed to the shot-silk quality of the 'water Chamelot'. The wealth of suggestion in this stanza is extended to those
which follow. Her hair is covered with flowers 'as a new spring',
her train, supported by two small streams, reveals her 'silver
feet', and drops of dew fall from the floral chaplet she wore
upon her head. However close this bride appears to those of
human marriages, she remains mysterious and is still truly a
river.

Spenser's art as a poet separates this particular Canto from
all the others which make up Book IV. The progress of the
story is suspended throughout although we have been reminded
of the fate of Florimell at the beginning and return to it at the
end. It is not, however, the suspension of the action which
isolates this section; it is much more the outstandingly original
quality of its verse. The ease with which Spenser handles an
apparently monotonous topic, the power of control he brings to
the sounds of names and words, the warmth of feeling he gives
to special details, and above all the appreciation of the remoteness of the rivers from any human experience combine to create
a world that lives to itself alone. Spenser has found one phrase to
describe its impersonality when he writes:

> It was no mortall worke, that seem'd and yet was not.

The bridal suite concludes with a list of the daughters of *Nereus*
in which the beauty of the sound recalls the sonorousness of the
lists introduced by Homer in the names of the nymphs who
gather round Thetis when she hears the cry of Achilles and by
Virgil imitating the phraseology of the *Iliad* in the fourth
Georgic.[1] Like both, Spenser is overwhelmed by a sense of the
boundless fertility of the ocean. It outweighs the lavishness of the
life on earth or in the sky, and the image of *Venus* reappears as it

---

[1] *Iliad*, XVIII, 38, and *Georgics* IV, 333-344. The most likely source to
Spenser is Mombritius's Latin translation of Hesiod's *Theogony*, 224-301,
and *Natalis Comes*, 8.6. V. *Variorum F.Q.*, iv, pp. 273-276. Sources can best be
supported by factual resemblances, but the poetic enchantment of the sounds
created by the Greek names must be recognised.

had in Canto x as an emblem of endless generation. (Spenser noted that it was wise of the thinkers of antiquity to maintain 'that *Venus* of the fomy seas was bred'; because their stupendous power was best measured in the numberless objects created in them.)

In Canto xi the joy of creation is conveyed in the crowded scene in the marriage celebrations, but in Canto xii another note is struck. The power of the sea can be a cause of grief as well as of joy. Marinell, having been present at the marriage, is excluded from the subsequent feast of the gods and nymphs because he is partly mortal and does not belong to their society. His curiosity leads him to explore the strangeness of Proteus's palace, and he becomes aware of the imprisoned Florimell lamenting against the roaring of the ocean. The water beats upon the rocks and Florimell, hearing it, exhorts the rocks to continue to groan in pity for her. She grieves in a characteristically Spenserian fashion:

> Ye Gods of seas, if any Gods at all
>   Have care of right, or ruth of wretches wrong,
>   By one or other way me woefull thrall,
>   Deliver hence out of this dungeon strong,
>   In which I daily dying am too long.
>
> IV. xii. 9

and at the end reveals the truth of her suffering:

> Know *Marinell* that all this is for thee.

The listener is at last touched with sympathy but cannot find any means of rescuing her. Florimell had, as he well knew, looked for him fruitlessly, while he had despised her;

> (she) him had sought through trouble and long strife;
> Yet had refusde a God that her had sought to wife.

His sensibility is called to think about the nature of love. Returning to Cymodoce's bower, he gives every sign of illness. She interprets his condition as a further development of the wound given him by Britomart, but *Tryphon* denies this to be the reason. A second opinion has to be obtained from *Apollo*. In response to her appeal '*Apollo* came' and diagnoses the source of the trouble to be love. Marinell has joined all the characters in Book III who had spent their time in search and solitude and who ultimately in Book IV had achieved their end. Florimell had been in this situation already although her time was engaged in flight from those who she suspected desired her. Now it is for Cymodoce to prevail upon Neptune to force Proteus to set her free. Neptune brings all his right over the sea to bear upon Proteus and commands him to relax his grasp of his illegally confined victim. The language in which he does this is language which looks forward to the Book on Justice. The terms are the technical terms of the law-courts which Proteus dares not disobey. Cymodoce speaks to Neptune of the 'waift' which does not 'in equitie' belong to Proteus but 'by high prerogative' to the King of the ocean and begs him therefore to 'replevie' it (i.e. to return it to its rightful owner by 'replevin', the restoration of property through legal judgment). Neptune responds by having a 'warrant' made under his 'seale autenticall' which Cymodoce bears to Proteus so that he is obliged to release Florimell, who is then brought to Marinell. Thus the remaining separation is concluded and Marinell and Florimell obtain the happiness of discovered unity. Book V, the Book of Justice, is the proper place in which their marriage will occur. As in the sequence of the earlier Books, the central theme is already hinted at in the style of the last Canto of the preceding Book.

Chapter VIII

BOOK V. JUSTICE AND POLITICS

BOOK V is in many respects the most neglected of the Books in *The Faerie Queene* and the least appreciated. In it Spenser seems to be returning to the design with which he had begun, constructing his allegory around the central figure, Artegall, who has a quest to perform and a representative companion, Talus, to guide him. Its resemblance to Books I and II does not, however, go much beyond that, and in other respects it is very different. Books III and IV had followed an independent scheme of their own, being more romantic in form and style, closer to Ariosto in technique, and introducing numerous characters to signify the various aspects of love and friendship whose adventures require development. In them, the search for emotional satisfaction had been pursued (in Book III) and fulfilled (in Book IV). Book V rightly restores the earlier form, but its structure is extensively modified to suit its content, and the content is altogether new. Artegall had already appeared in connection with Britomart in Books III and IV and consequently little space is devoted to the definition of his character. Instead, the Book plunges straight into a series of episodes illustrating the narrative in which its general theme is set out.

The theme is Justice, the virtue that should order man's life in society and govern his relations with other men. What is required between friends is outside its provenance,[1] this has already been amply treated in Book IV, but Justice includes wider and more impersonal matters, the rights and duties of men to the community at large and to individuals as members of that community. In this theme Spenser sees an opportunity, perhaps it was a temptation, to discuss subjects of immediate topical interest. Contemporary affairs enter the poem, not now

---

[1] Aristotle says that friendship is the bond that holds states together and legislators set more store by it than by justice for if people are friends there is no need of justice between them. Book Eight, Cap. 1. (Thomson, pp. 227-228.)

glimpsed in passing allusions, metaphors, and similes, nor suggested doubtfully as one of the possible points of reference for the moral allegory, but unmistakably as the principal subject for the Book. Here, for the first time, the activity of the Queen's government and the administration of public business at home and abroad, occupies the foreground; and the allegory is bent to the purposes of the pamphleteer and made a channel for the expression of political opinion.

This shift from the primarily philosophical or ethical to the primarily political—it is impossible to categorise Spenser's themes without modifications of this kind—affects the whole character of the Book. In the first place it is necessarily more episodic in structure: Artegall is to demonstrate Justice in action, as arbitrator, judge, and deliverer. Hence he is called upon to intervene in disputes between people who then disappear from narrative altogether. There are no recurring characters like Archimago or Pyrochles and Cymochles, and no interwoven stories comparable with those in Books III and IV. Each episode, apart from the hero's capture by Radigund, is self-contained and conclusive: Artegall settles the dispute, Talus carries out the sentence, and the matter is closed. Even after the Radigund scene when there is more opportunity for causal connections, these are scarcely made. Artegall may be supposed to be a wiser man when rescued by Britomart, and his support of the condemnation of Duessa attributable to his having learnt the dangers of clemency in Radigund's prison, but Spenser does not explicitly connect the two episodes; that is left for the reader to do. Moreover the events of the first eleven Cantos lack any intelligible bearing upon the 'quest', the liberation of Irena. Artegall's final exploit is simply one more demonstration of his function, neither the culmination of his experiences nor of the Book as a whole.

Secondly, there is in Book V a much greater emphasis upon narrative: each episode is recounted with a brisk competence which leaves little room for description of scenery or for reflection. Even characterisation is of small moment until we reach Britomart's reaction to Talus's report of her lover's captivity. Instead, behaviour speaks for itself and people are defined by what they do. Details in the presentation of the

action are factually informative and often curiously precise.
Artegall knocks one of the Soudan's knights 'quite two spears
length' out of his saddle; and in the final battle when Grantorto's axe becomes embedded in Artegall's shield the Giant
'tugged and strove to get it out' dragging the knight 'all about'
until Artegall takes advantage of the situation, abandons his
shield, and drives his sword home. Of a piece with this kind of
circumstantial narration is the exact localisation which is given
from time to time. Some of these details, perhaps all, are for the
benefit of the allegory, as when Britomart waiting for her lover
looks out from 'a window on to the West' and sees Talus in the
distance, or later on her way to join Artegall is taken by Dolon
to his house 'not far away but little wide by West'. Ireland is
intended, but the narrative gains verisimilitude by such precision, as it is when we are told that *Pollente's* corpse is carried
down 'the Lee', that the wedding between Florimell and Marinell is to take place in three days' time at 'the Castle of the
Strond', and that the name of Florimell's Dwarf, who gives this
information, is 'Dony'. Details of this kind occasionally occur
in the early books, and more frequently in Book VI, but never
with quite the same bare exactitude as here. They are numerous
and conspicuous and assist in forwarding the interests of the
narrative.

This change of emphasis is accompanied by an equally
noticeable change in the style. The vocabulary is often colloquial, the imagery brief and unheroic, the movement of the
verse sharp and incisive. In the first episode, for instance, Sir
Sanglier, having 'cropt off' his lady's head in preference for one
attached to a Squire, is pursued by Talus who

> to him leaping lent him such a knock
> That on the ground he layd him like a senceless block.

'Lim he could not wag' and Talus seizes him 'in his iron paw'
and carries him off to Artegall for judgment. Artegall investi-
gates the situation in language which gives the appearance of
natural speech. He asks the Squire:

> Who was it then (sayd *Artegall*) that wrought?
> And why? doe it declare unto me trew.
> A knight (sayd he) if knight he may be thought

> That did his hand in Ladies bloud embrew,
> And for no cause ...   V. i. 16

The compact, conversational syntax defines the occasion in a direct, plain fashion. Artegall suggests that the lady be divided in half, to which Sanglier agrees, but the Squire rejects such a proposal and says he prefers to pay the penalty for the crime he had not committed and to carry the head of Sanglier's victim on his saddle for a year as Artegall had required.

> Whom when so willing *Artegall* perceaved;
> Not so thou Squire (he sayd) but thine I deeme
> The living Lady ...

Justice is an active virtue speaking in the world of men, and the style is that proper to the purpose. It is Sanglier who is condemned to bear the head on his saddle and he obeys:

> As rated Spaniell takes his burden up for feare.

Pollente, in the next episode, represents the contemporary evil of exploitation and pillage in the society of England and Ireland. He 'pols and pils the poore' by demanding a passage-penny from all who cross the bridge beside his castle and thus accumulates a hoard of gold, 'mucky pelf'. This phrase is a deliberate lowering of the style for purposes of comment.[1] The bareness of the vocabulary and the bold imagery are a means of passing judgment upon the material. Justice is a heroic as well as an active virtue, and Sanglier's and *Pollente's* conduct is shewn to be unjust to the degree in which the vocabulary lowers it. It is a style which also gives impetus to the narrative. Battles are treated with a freedom and a sense of the pressure of physical effort. Verbs are frequent and forceful in themselves. There is no lingering to enlarge a specific moment. *Pollente* and Artegall fight breathlessly in the water:

> They snuf, they snort, they bounce, they rage, they rore,

and *Pollente's* feeling that he is getting the worst of it is indicated more through what is happening than through any direct statement. The dialogue is brief and to the point: 'Lo there thy

---

[1] Rosemond Tuve writing on 'Decorum and the Lowering of Style' in *Elizabethan and Metaphysical Imagery*, pp. 196-214, quotes Puttenham's observation on the employment of the word 'pelf' to imply condemnation. A similar use occurs in Ben Jonson.

hire' is Artegall's reply, with a stroke of his sword, to the ruffian who demands his passage-penny. As soon as *Pollente* reaches the bank Artegall is able to decapitate him when he rises out of the water to climb to the shore. This episode is more explicitly allegorical than that concerned with Sanglier, but the general impression remains of a firm, disillusioned statement. When *Munera*, *Pollente's* daughter, attempts to distract Artegall from his application of Justice by throwing sacks of gold over the wall, she is left to Talus to search out and punish. He moves 'like a limehound' to discover her hiding under a heap of gold:

> Still holding up her suppliant hands on hye,
> And kneeling at his feete submissively.
> But he her suppliant hands, those hands of gold,
> And eke her feete, those feete of silver trye,
> Which sought unrighteousnesse, and justice sold,
> Chopt off, and nayld on high, that all might them behold.

Munera's name agrees with her deeds, and her appearance is representative of her nature. Spenser preserves the naturalistic quality of his style in the simile attached to Talus and in the caustic verb, 'Chopt off'; repetition and amplification add force to the concept underlying her nature but they do not introduce the kind of elaboration which Spenser frequently employs in other examples of allegory. They constitute his way of building up all that *Pollente* and *Munera* stand for. The story contains an admonition to great men never to employ their power destructively and it ends in the banishment of an evil custom with the assurance that no memory of it will remain.

Missing the elaboration, the evocative rhythms, and the decorative imagery, the typically 'Spenserian' qualities, critics (apart from Upton who was interested in the political aspects of this Book) have been inclined to condemn Book V and to overlook its positive merits. But as narrative of a particular type, there is much to be said for it. What matters above everything is the story, and its conduct shows a firm grip of events to the exclusion of other demands. Spenser relies upon the dramatic possibilities of his medium and less upon the descriptive, seizing every opportunity to allow the story to tell itself. It is, of course, necessary to define the circumstances in which Artegall

is called upon to exercise his powers; but this is done economically, chiefly through the action of the characters themselves
rather than by the author's voice. Thus it is the Dwarf who tells
Artegall about *Pollente* and his deeds, preparing the reader for
what is to come and its significance, so that the episode can be
developed with full attention to it as a story. There is a sureness
in the control of the proportions, a skill in the management of
the *tempo*, and vitality in the actual narration of these first
episodes that give them a distinction within their chosen kind.

A third difference in character in Book V is seen in the
remarkable relevance of almost all the parts to the central
theme, as if the same singlemindedness as impels Spenser to
concentrate primarily on the needs of the narrative also impels
him to keep its significance clearly in view. The episodes at the
beginning are all parables of Justice: even the Tournament
becomes an occasion for the display of Artegall's virtue. Spenser
on this occasion expresses his intention openly, consciously
turning away from the individual achievements and pageantry
he had made so prominent in Satyrane's Tournament and in
the marriage of Thames and Medway in Book IV. His introduction dismisses the whole matter in one stanza:

> To tell the glorie of the feast that day,
> The goodly service, the deviccfull sights,
> The bridegromes state, the brides most rich aray,
> The pride of Ladies, and the worth of knights,
> The royal banquets, and the rare delights
> Were work fit for an Herauld, not for me.
> But for so much as to my lot here lights,
> That with this present treatise doth agree,
> True vertue to advaunce, shall here recounted bee.
>
> V. iii. 3

The determined modesty of this approach illustrates the
foundation of Spenser's scheme. Only the briefest summary of
the three days' jousting with the minimum of particularisation
and only a little collective phraseology ('Full many deedes of
armes that day were donne, And many knights unhorst', with
Marinell's 'Rashing off helmes, and ryving plates a sonder')
agrees with the present 'treatise', and Spenser moves on to the
business of righting old wrongs. The false Florimell, faced with

I*

the true, vanishes into nothing, leaving only the girdle which had been unlawfully hers to be returned to its rightful owner; Artegall unmasks Braggadocchio as an impostor, and Guyon gets back his horse. These reparations are made upon careful examination of the evidence; Artegall, maintaining that Braggadocchio's Florimell is not the real one, sets the two beside each other 'for proof'; Braggadocchio is asked to produce his sword and show the wounds he received in the battle he alleges he had won; and even Guyon's word is not enough to establish his ownership of the horse. He has to prove it by providing marks of identity. *Brigadore* cooperates by refusing to open his mouth to show the black spot shaped like a horse's shoe until Guyon called him by his name, and then he 'suffered all to see'; there is a joyful reunion when *Brigadore* 'friskt, and flong aloft, and louted low on knee'. Accusation and conviction are followed by sentence, although Guyon insists that for Braggadocchio 'It's punishment enough for all his shame to see'. Talus enforces the exposure by destroying his armour and driving him away, a disgraced knight. This is a public examination, presented in language as near to that of the lawcourts as it can be without becoming technical, introducing the terms 'proof', 'due trial', 'judgment', 'equity' and 'mitigate'. Similarly, in the episode of Sanglier, Artegall has listed the possible methods of dispensing Justice (by sacrament, or ordeal, or combat), before suggesting arbitration, and asks for a formal pledge from the disputants that they will abide by his decision.

In two other early episodes the same principles apply. The topical narrative of *Pollente* is followed by another conception of injustice, more general in its character. This is the occasion when Artegall comes upon a Giant who offers to establish equality in the composition of the world. He is surrounded by a gullible audience who accept his flamboyant outlook and believe that he can weigh everything in a pair of scales so as to restore all objects to their right proportions. On an elementary plane he argues that the sea has encroached upon the land, just as fire has swallowed up the air, and all countries have broken the bounds which had contained them in the past so that equality has been lost. This attitude, labelled 'ostentation' in a contemporary marginal note, attracts the mob who expect to

make personal gain out of the Giant's free-handed distribution
of property. Artegall identifies this egalitarianism as a miscon-
ceived notion of the origin of the universe. At the creation, he
says, God weighed all things and established them in their
proper station:

> The earth was in the middle centre pight,
> In which it doth immoveable abide,
> Hemd in with waters like a wall in sight;
> And they with aire, that not a drop can slide:
> Al which the heavens containe, and in their courses guide.
>
> V. ii. 35

If the Giant now thinks he can begin weighing them again, he is
hardly likely to establish a better version than that which had
remained unassailed for so long. Artegall is expounding the
official doctrine of the world's stability and forbids any altera-
tion of it because:

> All change is perillous, and all chaunce unsound.

The Giant's levelling examples are easily dismissed. It is fallacious to refer to the sea since it returns what it gains on the next
tide. Nor do his other views hold good: the earth is not enlarged by the death of the creatures that live upon it since they
simply return to the material out of which they were made, the
mountains do not soar abruptly above the valleys, for hill and
dale gladly accept the difference between them, and as for the
notion that the rich tyrannise over the poor only ignorance of
God's conception of the organisation of society could maintain
so foolish an idea:

> He maketh Kings to sit in soveraignty;
> He maketh subjects to their powre obay;
> He pulleth downe, he setteth up on hy;
> He gives to this, from that he takes away.
> For all we have is his: what he list doe, he may.
>
> What ever thing is done, by him is donne,
> Ne any may his mighty will withstand;
> Ne any may his soveraine powre shonne,
> Ne loose that he hath bound with stedfast band.
>
> V. ii. 41-42

This is a typically Elizabethan doctrine, closely related to the ideas of Hooker and expressed with all the emotional force which Spenser can command. If it were possible for the Giant to change the constitution of the world, he would have to understand its causes and be able to follow the conditions of the life in each thing in it. It is reverence that Artegall is trying to teach him. Nothing in the world can be measured in the way he assumes it can, and Artegall exposes his folly by suggesting that he apply his scales to the ordinary elements of existence:

> For take thy ballaunce, if thou be so wise,
>   And weigh the winde, that under heaven doth blow;
>   Or weigh the light, that in the East doth rise;
>   Or weigh the thought that from mans mind doth flow.
>   But if the weight of these thou canst not show,
>   Weigh but one word which from thy lips doth fall.
>   For how canst thou those greater secrets know,
>   That doest not know the least thing of them all?
> Ill can he rule the great, that cannot reach the small.
>
> V. ii. 13

The passion felt by Artegall echoes for the reader the answer which God gave to Job to make him understand the nature of the world in which he had been born but did not create. So, for Artegall, the Giant is applying the wrong criterion when he tries thus to expose the inequality of contemporary society. False cannot be weighed against the true nor right against wrong. The Giant tries to destroy his scales but Artegall explains to him that ideas must be assessed in the same way as physical entities:

> But in the mind the doome of right must bee;
>   And so likewise of words, the which be spoken,
>   The eare must be the ballaunce, to decree
> And judge, whether with truth or falshood they agree.
>
> V. ii. 47

Lacking any interest in right, the Giant clings to his desire to achieve a fair distribution among unequal items. Finally, it is left to Talus to remove him by pushing him off the rock into the sea.

The Giant represents a contemporary problem. He speaks

for the Anabaptists, a dangerous group in England and Germany who had attempted to put a form of communal society into practice. During the Commonwealth, the 'slaughtered saints', settled in Piedmont, seem to have been peaceable, a small group doing no one any harm. But those in Elizabethan England were more revolutionary and were anxious to spread their ideas through the country. The speeches of Artegall are constructive and moving, but the Giant gains little support from the words Spenser allows him to utter. As a Giant, he is conceived as a crude, unreliable figure, a deceiver of the multitude. The scene in which he appears takes the form of a debate, like that between the Red Crosse Knight and Despair or that between Guyon and Mammon. Yet it possesses nothing comparable in allurement with either of these. Artegall finds no attraction in him and has no difficulty in dismissing his arguments. Where there *is* difficulty is in the allegorical technique which is being used. Artegall, having momentarily pointed out to the Giant the fallacy of his principles, then takes quite seriously his use of scales and expects him to weigh concepts as he has weighed bodies. The Giant is bound to lose his case where the allegory has moved to such unacceptable terms.

Artegall occupies a stronger position because he can argue in favour of the absolute power of the Creator and the hierarchical system underlying the creation, whereas all the Giant can do is to ignore an opposite view and try to set out a society where all things will possess equal claims. Social order is divinely inspired, and the revolutionary ideas of the Giant are themselves rebellious. Artegall was maintaining a concept previously modified in the *Proem* where cosmological disarray had been manifested. The golden age of Justice had been repudiated and vice and virtue hardly distinguishable:

> Right now is wrong, and wrong that was is right,
> And all things else in time are chaunged quight.
>
> Proem 4

In these circumstances the Giant had been encouraged to enlarge his seditious opinions.

Spenser clearly had no wish to support the irreverent Giant, but Artegall's piety scarcely stands in view of what had been described in the *Proem*. The aspect of injustice he is identifying and attacking would have been sounder if the terms in which the positive side of the case had been more convincing. The form of debate which Spenser is using promises well since it treats general ideas and ranges more widely than any of the other topics which surround it. It is a form in which Spenser excelled elsewhere, but it scarcely achieves excellence here. Its failure is partly technical since the two aspects of allegory, the literal-physical and the spiritual-conceptual do not conform satisfactorily with each other; there is, in fact, a complete absence of consonance between them. But it is also a failure of substance in that the beliefs which Artegall sets out so firmly had already been qualified in the *Proem*. Yet, in spite of these objections, the ideal Artegall expounds gains considerable strength from its warmth of expression.

The remaining episode offers a narrower and more easily solved problem of Justice than that raised by the Giant. Based upon an Irish legend, it is also a question of property. Two brothers, Bracidas and Amidas, are found fighting over two islands inherited from their father, and two dowries brought by their future brides. Bracidas's island has been largely devoured by the sea and little remains of it. His bride-to-be, Philtera, despatched with a coffer of treasure for her intended husband, breaks off the engagement when she sees how small his property has become and attaches herself to Amidas, the younger, whose island has become expanded as Bracidas's has diminished. Her name suggests that it is the possession of land that she is most interested in. Amidas accepts her, deserting the ill-endowed Lucy, who determines to drown herself. Philtera, however, is shipwrecked and her treasure is washed into the sea where Lucy takes it as a raft to preserve her life and floats on it to Bracidas's tiny island. Artegall, asked to decide between the claims of the two brothers, requires each to lay down his sword and then courteously asks the grounds upon which each makes out his right to the objects of dissension, the enlarged island and Philtera's coffer of treasure. Amidas defines his claim to the island:

> What other right (quoth he) should you esteeme,
> But that the sea it to my share did lay?

> Your right is good (sayd he) and so I deeme,
> That what the sea unto you sent, your own should seeme.
> V. iv. 17

Bracidas establishes his claim to the treasure in identical terms:

> What other right (quoth he) should you esteeme,
> But that the sea hath it unto me throwne?
> Your right is good (sayd he) and so I deeme,
> That what the sea unto you sent, your own should seeme.

Each brother has committed himself inescapably, and Artegall draws the difference in the matter of principle:

> For equall right in equall things doth stand,
> For what the mighty Sea hath once possest,
> And plucked quite from all possessors hand,
> Whether by rage of waves, that never rest,
> Or else by wracke, that wretches hath distrest,
> He may dispose by his imperiall might,
> As thing at randon left, to whom he list.
> So *Amidas*, the land was yours first hight,
> And so the threasure yours is *Bracidas*, by right.

This seems a just conclusion, although Amidas and Philtera feel they have got the worst of the judgment. But it had to be admitted that each one had his right.

This interest in the methods of justice at work gives intellectual quality to the first part of Book V which outweighs any emotional appeal the stories might make if differently presented. There is no grief for the death of Sanglier's lady such as Guyon felt for Amavia (II. i), no pity for the treasureless Philtera, no sympathy for *Munera*, *Pollente's* golden-handed daughter. Instead, the issues are posed impersonally; demonstration, not exploration, is Spenser's object. Only *one* theory of virtue is involved in each case. Admittedly Artegall is granted a genuine quality of emotion when he describes the order of the universe as God-given, and the versification conveys the existence of his emotional response to it. But it is not until the later sections of the Book that full scope is given to individual feeling, either because the problem is more complicated, as in the Mercilla episode, or more serious as with Malengin, or because Britomart comes on the scene with her deep love for Artegall. Yet the tone of the Book as a whole is set by the rigorous concentration upon the practice of Justice rather than its nature, and by the presence of Talus as its hard-hearted agent. Thus the Tournament is occupied with theoretical issues, and not even the sea which was so powerful an imaginative factor in Books II and III can entice Spenser away from his commitment to legality. Artegall crosses it, but the journey is not described, and in the narratives of the Giant and of Bracidas and Amidas it remains an external point of reference, a mighty, devouring force as impersonal as the rule of Justice itself.

ii

At the end of Canto ɪv, Artegall reaches the fatal moment in which he is tempted, and succumbs. He finds the knight, Terpine, with his hands bound and his face covered on the way to execution at the hands of an army of women. Recognising the captive, he enquires how he had come into so shameful a condition—a query which proves ironic in view of his own future state. He hears of the monstrous regiment of women, the power of Radigund who had overcome many brave knights 'by force or guile', and had committed them to the domination of women, abandoning their masculine duties to the feminine society of which she was ruler. 'Force or guile' is the keynote and it is repeated in the generalised vision which Britomart experienced in the Temple of Isis, where Isis stands with one foot upon a crocodile and the other upon the ground, thus representing her nature which can 'suppresse both forged guile and open force'. Artegall's knowledge of his function is still too much limited to realise the danger he is in and he goes confidently with Terpine to Radegone, the city which owes its name to its queen. Here they are met by an onslaught of sharp arrows (a term which Milton was to remember in delineating the Parthians' battle methods in *Paradise Regained*), and a savage attack from Radigund who throws Terpine to the ground and brings equal violence against Artegall. Only the coming on of night breaks off the battle, but Radigund is prepared next morning to issue a challenge accompanied with terms by which Artegall is required to accept her régime if he is defeated. Artegall foolishly accepts what he regards as an opportunity to avenge Terpine and to establish his own military superiority, a response to which Britomart will not descend when the chance is later offered to her.

Artegall might have conquered had he not removed Radigund's helmet and been overpowered by the beauty of the face he uncovered. Radigund's victory was assured. Artegall became her captive. His fate is likened to that of Hercules under *Omphale* (or, as Spenser's customary casualness about classical narratives, or his fidelity to Natalis Comes, prefers to label *Iole*) and his time is now spent with distaff and loom. He had to attire himself as a woman, in what he had referred to with Terpine as 'squalid weed' and fulfil the promise he had made before the battle. It was attraction which destroyed his judgment, attraction which drove him to submit to the evil order of society to which many able knights known to him already had become victims. Its evil was exposed both in its false conception of the relation of woman to man, and in the fact that the unfortunate Terpine, once rescued, was carried off and hanged.

In this episode it is evident that Artegall has abandoned the virtue of which he is patron, and has been conquered not by Radigund's strength but by her beauty. Her feminine colony reversed the order of nature which he had so firmly defended in his argument with the Giant. Now he yields to her for no reason related to Justice but simply because he had succumbed to the promptings of her physical attraction. The incident creates difficulties because it scarcely appears to belong to Book V as regards narrative or allegory. It is, in fact, nearer to the style of Ariosto and to Book IV. Only when Britomart, fetched by Talus, comes to his rescue, can Artegall return to his masculine dignity. His fall might be called a misapplication of the principle of mercy and a failure on his part to see when the rules of strict Justice might be waived in favour of clemency and when not, but if this is what is in Spenser's mind, it is not brought out either directly nor by implication. For when Artegall parted from Britomart after she had killed Radigund and rescued him, he was praised for his manly respect to duty, in contrast with those who like Samson, Hercules and Antony had allowed themselves to forget theirs and to remain 'wrapt in fetters of a golden tresse'. His failure might never have occurred for all the notice that was taken of it when he parted from Britomart or when later he apologised to Sir Sergis for his delay in coming to the rescue of Irena. His view then appeared to be that he had been driven by fate into a thraldom like that in which Irena now stands and he was not himself in the least to blame. This excuse was strongly condemned by him when Terpine offered it as an explanation for his captivity by Radigund's army and it is not easily forgotten considering that Terpine ultimately suffered the death from which Artegall had previously saved him. To Britomart, to Burbon and to Irena, he behaves as if his conduct had been wholly blameless, whereas in the Radigund scene it is explicitly stated that his defeat was entirely due to his own misguided choice. This is one of the occasions when Spenser interrupts the narrative with direct comment:

> So was he overcome, not overcome,
>   But to her yeelded of his owne accord;
>   Yet was he justly damned by the doome
>   Of his owne mouth, that spake so warelesse word,
>   To be her thrall, and service her afford.
>   For though that he first victorie obtayned,
>   Yet after by abandoning his sword,
>   He wilfull lost, that he before attayned.
>
> V. v. 17

This comment, because it holds up the development of the story and is based upon the conviction that no knight should ever abandon his sword, gains exceptional force. A similar interruption can be found in *Paradise Lost* when Milton comments upon Adam's decision to share Eve's fate which also breaks into the swing of the narrative:

> he scrupl'd not to eat
> Against his better knowledge, not deceav'd
> But fondly overcome with Femal charm.

Adam's action is here what the whole design of the epic had been leading to, whereas Artegall's choice is less central to the Book. Each occasion is, however, dramatic and if Artegall's action had been made more intelligible in relation to his character and function it would have carried greater plausibility.

The advantage of putting it beside a similar event in a greater work provokes a general problem of consistency. Admittedly, having made the wrong decision Artegall behaved as an honourable knight should and accepted his humiliating situation with grace and dignity, but this is a mere palliation and can scarcely release him from the moral implications of his conduct as the patron of Justice. The Red Crosse Knight, having made similar mistakes in relation to Duessa had to form his life again in the House of Holiness and to pay heavily, both in Orgoglio's dungeon and in his contact with Despair, for all the sins he had committed. Artegall's submission to Radigund cannot be explained away so easily. It does not appear satisfactorily integrated with the rest of the Book's design. The fact that Talus had to abandon his lord and to some extent his rôle by becoming, for the only time in the Book, a messenger charged with the distasteful task of carrying ill news to Britomart and so losing temporarily his inflexible iron nature and his silence, is further evidence that the episode does not synchronise with the rest.

There are, of course, other ways of meeting this difficulty. The Radigund episode may belong, as Josephine Waters Bennett thinks, to another layer of the composition and has been pushed into the place it now occupies to supply more material to this plot; or Spenser may have made an unfortunate choice of allegorical material. Certainly, considered independently of the character of the hero, the introduction of this scene might be justified: it treats one form of injustice, the wrongful sway of women, particularly of women in the places assigned by general usage to man. It was quite legitimate therefore that Spenser should select this instance as an example of unjust dealing: the trouble is that he appears to have attached it to the wrong person. No doubt, in order to show the perverseness of such subjection, a knight as prominent as Artegall was needed; but Artegall's other commitments in the rest of the Book precluded, or should have precluded, this employment of him. Whatever the reason, whether Spenser is using old Ariostan material—a suggestion supported by the linking techniques at the close of the relevant Cantos—or whether character and narrative are being sacrificed to the demands of theme (allegory gaining priority over the subjects chosen for the Book's content), the Radigund affair appears out of key with the rest. There is much which gives it power, but it seems impossible to support this particular flaw in the interpretation of the hero. One can accept easily the remaining parts of the narrative in Book V, but this unexplained event in Artegall's life makes a regrettable impact. It is one of the rare moments when one tends to agree with Yeats that allegory did not come naturally to Spenser.

The news reaches Britomart at a time when she is ready to receive it with characteristic impetuousness. She had been waiting patiently for Artegall, sometimes suspicious of his constancy, sometimes fretful for his safety, always longing for his return with his quest in Ireland successfully accomplished. Her attempt to sustain his absence had been recounted with Spenser's tenacious sense of her individuality. She had tried to count the time in terms of months because they seemed to go faster, yet every hour seemed like a month, and every month a year. Spenser always demonstrates his gift of personal understanding whenever states of mind are involved, and here he portrays Britomart's consciousness of isolation with his customary perception. Trembling in mental hesitation she goes up to look through the window towards the direction from which Artegall must appear, and sees at last Talus riding towards the castle. Typically she descends to meet him and pours out a flood of questions which gives him no time to deliver his message plainly:

> And where is he thy Lord, and how far hence?
> Declare at once; and hath he lost or wun?

This is a direction which the naturally mute Talus is incapable of following. All he can achieve is a mis-explanation. Spenser brings liveliness and humour to the occasion and describes the effect of the deception upon Britomart's mind in the type of imagery he is accustomed to apply to her. She is like a child disturbed by a nightmare:

> Ne can be stild for all his nurses might,
> But kicks, and squals, and shriekes for fell despight:
> Now scratching her, and her loose locks misusing;
> Now seeking darkenesse, and now seeking light;

Then craving sucke, and then the sucke refusing.
Such was this Ladies fit, in her loves fond accusing.

V. vi. 14

This image is appropriate to Britomart and builds up the intensity of her feeling for Artegall. In milder mood she returns to Talus and elucidates the truth from him. Her suspicion was allayed and she accepted his interpretation of Artegall's present condition, that he was

> Not by strong hand compelled thereunto,
> But his owne doome, that none can now undoo.

Yet that is something which she *can* undo and guided by Talus she rides to the rescue, too angry with Radigund to look about her or express her emotions.

The ensuing Cantos are Britomart's. Going on, accepting hospitality from a seemingly pleasant elderly knight and finding herself entrapped by his villainous companions, she is able with Talus to drive her attackers away. This stage of the narrative is entirely consistent with Britomart's outlook. She will not remove her armour, sees her bed let down by a trap, remains ready to defend herself, assisted by Talus who had been watching like a spaniel outside her door, and drives away the two knights who had come to destroy her. The explanation of the event is a matter of mistaken identity. *Dolon*, the old Host, a wicked, fraudulent figure, the father of Guizor whom Artegall had killed during his adventure at *Pollente's* bridge, seeing Talus with Britomart, concludes that she must have been the knight who had killed his son.[1] The surviving brothers wait for her at the head of the bridge and Britomart, mystified by their obscure accusations, charges straight down the narrow road and kills one on the bridge itself and throws the other into the river. Spenser gives vigour to this event by the imagery which individualises Britomart:

> The glauncing sparkles through her bever glared,
> And from her eies did flash out fiery light,
> Like coles, that through a silver Censer sparkle bright.

V. vi. 38

[1] Since there is so strong a reference to politics in Book V it is not unlikely that the reference to 'Guizor' may be to the Guise family. Alternatively, it has been suggested that *Dolon* represents Philip of Spain.

Bright, moving lights are associated constantly with Britomart whereas for Una the light is slower and broader in its extent. Britomart's actions are symbolised by lightning which can uproot trees, and her appearance by flames and fire.

iii

In each Book of *The Faerie Queene* there is always, as C. S. Lewis has pointed out, a scene which represents the positive aspect of the virtue it embodies. The House of Holiness, the Castle of Temperance, the Garden of Adonis, and the Temple of *Venus* stand for the ideal quality upon which the allegory turns. These are not necessarily the most memorable scenes in the Books. Poetically they are eclipsed by the House of Pride and the Cave of Despair, by the Cave of Mammon and the Bower of Bliss, by Malbecco's home and the House of Busyrane, and even by the blacksmith's hut of Care and Timias's solitary cabin. The fact remains that the scenes which represent the opposite of the good are more powerful and carry greater emotional pressure. Spenser quite properly preferred to tone down the images of virtue and allot the vigour and the force of imagery to the bad figures, just as one finds Milton keeping the Lady in *Comus* and Christ in *Paradise Regained* upon a quieter, sparer, level than the formulations applied to Comus and to Satan. The reasons for this variety in both poets are not hard to seek: they depend upon the poetic style adopted for each rôle.

In Book V the theme of Justice was embodied in several scenes in which Artegall applied the virtue of which he is patron against those who either behaved unjustly, such as Sanglier and the Giant, or those whose conduct required him to make difficult decisions, such as the arguments at the Tournament or in the Bracidas-Amidas quarrel. His failure to carry out his principles in the scene with Radigund was different. It had been successful in another way, in that it had forced Britomart to offer the good which he might have provided to Radigund's captives. Before she could do this, however, she had first to destroy the guardians of *Pollente's* perilous bridge and then to meet the virtue of Justice in the special form of Equity which more properly belonged to herself. This section provides the positive core to Book V, comparable with the description of

ideal qualities which made the centre of the earlier Books. The
reason why it had been Britomart and not Artegall who
received this experience depended upon the development of the
plot. Artegall, after all, had cut himself off from the significance
of the virtue he had so far been representing by his subjection to
Radigund. More charitably, it may be added, that Artegall and
Britomart were united in their political and moral futures and
this was the occasion when Britomart could see her destiny in
her dream in the Temple of Isis. It was appropriate that Talus
should be excluded from entry, for he is committed only to the
exercise of Justice and its narrower and more cruel aspect.

Britomart's dream took place in a framework of Egyptian
mythology, derived from Plutarch. Spenser here made his rare
employment in Book V of uncommon imagery so as to shift the
narrative into an unknown strange world. The first stanza acts
as a bridge between all that had preceded it and emphasises the
desire felt by human beings and by Gods for true Justice. The
second moves to a euhemeristic concept of Osyris, who in his
lifetime was 'the justest man alive' and after his death became
the God of the virtue he had so nobly embodied. Isis, his wife,
also became a symbolical figure, the goddess who represented
'that part of Justice which is Equity'; and since both are transported to the heavens they were related to heavenly bodies—
Osyris had the Sun for his emblem, and Isis the Moon.

Britomart's vision was characteristically Spenserian in its
combination of literalness, which had been clearly carried
throughout Book V, with the vague distancing which was less
usual there. The Egyptian crocodile was doubtless acceptable
emblematically. It had its place in Plutarch's *De Iside*; and it
appeared in Peacham's *Basilikon Doron* which has a marginal
note on Plutarch.[1] The priests were, like Isis herself, clad in
white linen robes hemmed with silver; they wore moon-shaped
mitres and lived an ascetic, ritualisite life in worship of their
goddess. Britomart, brought by them into the presence of Isis,
slept at her feet and dreamed of herself clad in priest's robes
ready to take part in the sacrifice to her. Her dreams became a
vision in which she found herself clothed in royal scarlet with a

[1] The emblem is based on a quotation from James I; *Basilikon Doron*,
Cap. II, p. 35.

golden crown, and the Temple was filled with flames blown from the holy fire at the altar. In this curious episode the crocodile, aroused by the storm, ate 'both flames and tempest', in Spenser's strange non-visual phrase, and would have included Britomart in his feast had Isis not deterred him with her white wand. Britomart then became pregnant by him and bore a lion strong enough to conquer all the other beasts of creation. The greatest of the priests then interpreted this dream to her: she could not, he explained, conceal herself from the omniscient Gods. They knew her lineage and the fate of her lover within the power of Radigund. The crocodile is a double symbol: he represents Osyris and sleeps always at the feet of Isis:

> To shew that clemence oft in things amis,
> Restraines those sterne behests, and cruell doomes of his.
>
> V. vii. 22

He also represents Artegall, whose Justice, like that of Osyris, requires order and proportion. The flames of the tempest were the dangers within her own country, and these Artegall would destroy, taking Britomart for his bride and absorbing all her inheritance. Their union would produce a son whose power would equal that of a lion.

This scene has invoked much enthusiastic comment. Its mystery, its consistently literal elements, and its rhythmical power gave it the weight expected for the positive factor at the heart of the Book. Yet its remoteness and obscurity separates it from the narrative in which it appeared. One feels that Spenser had entered a new and unfamiliar world where even the support of Plutarch failed to prevent him from making his portrayal of Justice convincing. The crocodile needs explanation and nothing appears to make it imaginatively satisfactory. Angus Fletcher in *Allegory* placed it in his chapter upon 'The Daemonic Agent' where it is both good and evil—'the crocodile is both fawning and threatening, both amorous and hostile'.[1] Elsewhere he classified the scene in which it occurs as an example of Spenser's intentional shift from allegory to myth. The allegory in his view here, as in the Garden of Adonis, became 'mythical and dreamlike'. He, in my view rightly, argues that

[1] p. 47, note 43.

the reader is required to accept an 'overwhelming paradox, since these moments create an ultimately inexplicable knot of imagery and action. Ultimately the reader has to give a mythical account of the Gardens and the Temple, yet their resistance to rationalisation does not imply a lack of signifying power.' He then establishes a distinction between myth and allegory: 'It is the peculiar character of true myth, we may say, to enforce acceptance of a totally ambivalent imagery, whereas true allegory would achieve a rigid displacement of one aspect of the ambivalence, by arguing that either death *or* life predominated in the Gardens, either justice and clemency *or* injustice and draconian rigor predominated in the Temple of Isis. But such displacement does not occur at these moments in Spenser's poem. Rather he maintains an equality between the polar opposites of the ambivalent attitudes and almost insists that they must be joined, the apocalypse being thus gained in a moment of total consciousness.'[1] This is an interesting suggestion which tends to justify a reader's suspicious response to the difficulty of the Temple of Isis scene. For those to whom 'Ambivalence' is not the final virtue of literary achievement, whether in Spenser's work or elsewhere, the Temple of Isis scene remains limited by the dubious rôle of the crocodile and is surely outweighed by other scenes which are more intelligible. One might wish to emphasise more strongly the subsequent scene with Malengin as 'myth', or that with Mercilla as 'allegory', for both possess significant qualities of imagery and, in their own way, are outstandingly mysterious. But, admittedly, nothing can compare with the magical situation of the Temple of Isis and for those to whom 'ambivalence' is a most important characteristic of poetry this situation will give the greatest distinction to Book V.

Britomart and Talus continue their journey for the succour of Artegall imprisoned by Radigund. A rapid battle with her quickly disposes of her power, for Britomart will have nothing to do with her suggested truce and conducts a solitary duel in which her enemy is soon defeated. Britomart, victorious, follows Talus to *Radegone* where he has already slaughtered many of the women who had gathered to witness what they are

[1] *ibid.*, p. 321.

certain will be their Queen's success. She forces Talus to cease his attacks and moves to the prison where she found the captive knights in their misery and her own Artegall among them. Here she turns her glance aside

> as nothing glad
> To have beheld a spectacle so bad.

Generosity, or more characteristically the pride of her royal descent, leads her to deprecate the shaming condition in which he now appears. It is left to her to restore him and the other knights to their proper station, to make them rulers in Radigund's town, and to swear loyalty to Artegall. Justice has returned under her sway and its reappearance recalls him to his quest and the virtue he represents. Britomart, conscious of his honour, is sensitive enough to reduce her personal grief when he decides to ride away in pursuit of the conquest he had agreed to undertake. The Book was no longer Britomart's Book but had again become preoccupied with Artegall, its hero, and Britomart can only leave *Radegone* and find another place where she would be less conscious of missing him. Meanwhile it is for Artegall to put Justice into practice and rescue Irena to whose safety he is committed. His journey in search of her brings him into contact with other problems of injustice and it is to these that the Book turns.

When Artegall sets off on his quest after he had been released from his captivity under Radigund, the plot of Book V becomes more openly linked with topical events. The relation between England and Spain and the Netherlands was the determining factor in the material which Spenser had now to explore. It was not for nothing that he was working and writing in Ireland, for there he saw the activities of the Spanish power operating in the country which could best be used as a base for attacking England. There was the constant element of rebellion among the Desmonds and the O'Neills and there were the ports into which the Spaniards could bring their armies. It has been argued that in Book V 'the most important events in the history of Elizabeth's development of a powerful government are treated, not badly and incoherently as in the chronicles, but in an allegory that unifies and interprets'.[1] It is in the second

[1] Greenlaw, 'Spenser and British Imperialism', *Variorum* Book V, p. 306.

half of Book V that the closest study of the serious problem of foreign affairs facing Elizabeth's Government is followed out. Here are developed the episodes of Canto vIII—the narrative of the Souldan and his wicked wife Adicia; in Canto Ix—the struggle with Malengin and the visit of Mercilla with the arraignment of Duessa and the appeal for help from two representatives of the Low Countries; in Canto x—the rescue of Belge; in Canto xi—the story of Bourbon; and finally in Canto xII—Artegall's completion of his quest by the redemption of Irena. As Greenlaw has pointed out, the allegory is essential as a means of unifying and interpreting the action. It is not only the substance but its design and technique which gives Book V its attraction and artistic interest. It also gives it its problems, for this is esssentially a topical volume creating inquisitiveness in the mind of a critic gloomily conscious of a lack of sufficient historical knowledge.

Each event requires explanation. The first is unusually gruesome. It describes the danger in which the Queen, Mercilla, is placed by a neighbouring ruler, a Souldan, who attempts to destroy the justice with which she governs her country. The envoy she has despatched, Samient, is seen fleeing from attacks by the Souldan's pagan knights encouraged by his wife, Adicia. Her rôle as messenger has been ignored—'Me like a dog she out doors did thrust'. Artegall comes to her rescue with another knight, who proves to be Arthur.

The fight is savage since the chariot-wheels are armed with hooks. (Arthur cannot move near enough since the Souldan is perched up so high that he cannot attack him.) Finally he takes the only means available to him and withdraws the veil from his shield. The horses thus become uncontrollable, and the Souldan cannot direct them:

> He to them calles and speakes, yet nought avayles;
> They heare him not, they have forgot his lore,
> But go, which way they list, their guide they have forlore.
>
> V. viii. 39

Eventually they throw him to the ground so that he is torn to pieces by his own hooked wheels, leaving nothing but his broken armour to be gathered up by Arthur and hung outside his door as a monument to the power of tyranny. Spenser has, however, introduced into this episode imagery which is suitable to the ferocity of its tone. He grounds it upon classical events and upon events of hunting. The expanded similes add to the notion of savagery; they include the 'Thracian Tyrant' who gave his guests to his horses to eat, the disaster of Phaeton when driving the horses of the sun, an analogy for the refusal of the Souldan's headstrong steeds to obey him; the cruel death of Hippolytus likened to the end of the Souldan, although here the treatment is gentler, for Spenser recalls

> That for his sake *Diana* did lament,
> And all the wooddy Nymphes did wayle and mourne.
>
> V. viii. 43

whereas there is no grief at the destruction of the Souldan. Apart from classical analogies, liveliness appears in the use of colloquial vocabulary. The horses 'have all overthrowne to ground quite topside turvey'—a phrase which dispels any sense of remoteness.

Not at all remote, however, is the rôle of the Souldan. He probably represents Philip of Spain who made Ireland his political victim. But the precise equivalent of the chariot with its wild horses is open to further enquiry. It was Arthur who fought the Souldan, which is customarily Spenser's method of indicating the importance of a conflict; moreover it is one of the rare occasions when he is forced to unveil his shield in order to reduce his enemy's power. The reason for the adoption of this method is revealed in the contrast between the purposes of the two warriors. The Souldan aims only at 'slaughter and avengement', whereas Arthur sought to establish the truth he represented. The political implications are beyond the identification of the figures who make up the savage group. It was suggested by Upton that the Armada ships were the focus of the battle. They were admittedly much taller than the English vessels, they were armed with hooks and spikes and, in the event, they failed to carry out their duties successfully. Alternatively the ships at Antwerp, kept ready by the Prince of Palma, which were also equipped with hooks, might have resembled the Souldan's chariot.[1] That there is at least a topical reference wherever it

---

[1] See references to Upton quoted in *Variorum*, Book V, pp. 226-228.

can be traced is clearly acceptable; without it, the allegory reads as only a peculiarly violent story.

More imaginative is the event which appeared in Canto ix. It begins with Samient's description of a villain who lived in a rock nearby and pillaged all he could snatch up in the country round. He resembled a juggler, capable of every kind of deception, skilful with his hands and ready to capture anyone who believed in him. He was known as Malengin, or according to the introductory rhyme Guyle, and his presence at this stage of the narrative provides an anticipation of the trial scene at the end of the Canto. He partakes in the type of wickedness expressed in other figures in *The Faerie Queene*. Like Archimago and Proteus, he relies upon disguise for his strength, regularly changing his form during his struggle with the two virtuous characters. He is an example of Spenser's way of regarding all detail as potentially symbolic, a technique which gives intensity to a figure conceived realistically:

> Full dreadfull wight he was as ever went
> Upon the earth, with hollow eyes deepe pent,
> And long curld locks, that downe his shoulders shagged;
> And on his backe an uncouth vestiment
> Made of straunge stuffe, but all to worne and ragged,
> And underneath, his breech was all to torne and jagged.
>
> And in his hand an huge long staffe he held,
> Whose top was arm'd with many an yron hook,
> Fit to catch hold of all that he could weld,
> Or in the compasse of his clouches tooke;
> And ever round about he cast his looke.
> As at his backe a great wyde net he bore,
> With which he seldome fished at the brooke,
> But usd to fish for fooles on the dry shore,
> Of which he in faire weather wont to take great store.
>
> V. ix. 10-11

With his ragged attire, his staffe and his net he could be one of those recurrent solitary figures of literature, like Cain or Wordsworth's Leech Gatherer, who wander about the world, an eternal manifestation of self-sufficient humanity. His cast-down eyes, his hooks on the top of his staff, and the great wide net used for fishing upon land signify something more. They are symbolical of guile, not merely pictorial, and as the narrative develops he proves to be one of those Protean figures of evil who can transform themselves into other shapes and move further and further into the realm of allegory. Spenser in introducing him into the Book had said that his cave in the rock plunges below the surface:

> A dreadful depth, how deepe no man can tell;
> But some doe say, it goeth downe to hell.

The transition from the naturalistic portrait to symbolism is managed first by an account of his expression when he looks at the knights 'with Sardonian smyle'[1] and then by a simile of the fowler's guileful ways, until his changes of shape are readily accepted. The forms which he adopts are typical of villainy; he becomes a wild goat prancing over the rocks until Talus has to undertake the pursuit, since physical chase is impossible for the armed knights. He then becomes a fox, a bush, a bird, and in reaction to Talus's throwing rocks at him, a stone; picked up he turns into a hedgehog pricking the hand that holds him, and finally he tries a snake when he is beaten to death by Talus's flail. Most of these objects of metamorphosis are creatures which Spenser associates with evil. The goat appears in Book I as the beast for Lechery to ride upon in the procession of the Seven Deadly Sins and is also the form which Malbecco resembles when he joins the satyrs with whom Hellenore has run away in Book III. The fox was one of the figures Archimago thought of adopting when he wished to deceive Una, and in *Mother Hubberds Tale* and in the May episode of *The Shepheardes Calender* he is an exemplar of craft, and wiliness, and, as the Kid's mother warningly informs him 'a maister of collusion'. The other items appear comparatively harmless except for their link with Guile, but all may possess emblematic connections. The panther, for instance, hides himself within a bush to disguise his dangerous appearance from his prey (*Amoretta*, LIII) and the stone is labelled by Spenser as 'a senseless stone' and since the Golden Age we are told men have been transformed into hardest stones. Of the snake, little need be said: like his contemporaries Spenser regarded it as the source of the world's

---

[1] Upton explains this as a form of guile, laughter from the lips only, which was the legendary effect of eating a herb in Sardinia.

wickedness and an embodiment of Satan; it was 'hateful' and filled with venom. Talus rightly destroyed it for 'so did deceipt the deceiver fayle'.

The appearance of Guyle is a prelude to the rôles of artifice in the succeeding narrative. He has been identified as an example of the wild attacks of the Irish Kerns against Lord Grey and the kind of guerrilla warfare they carried on. It is easy to press the analogies between the events in Ireland which Spenser witnessed and the episodes in Book V which is openly connected with justice and politics. The sole objection to this interpretation is that it over-simplifies. Guyle is a form of personification which runs all through *The Faerie Queene*; to confine him to one aspect consistent with one Book is to narrow the impact he makes on the reader. Irish Kerns are certainly implied but their presence does not account for the power of this particular scene. Spenser's gift of uniting fact and idea is at the root of it. It is remembered not for its political associations but for its visual artistry.

All the subsequent episodes also have close bearing upon politics. The Mercilla story stands out very strongly and its topical relevance is supported not merely by the internal evidence of the allegory but by an external pointer in the complaint from James I (and VI) that Spenser should be tried and punished for his hostile portrayal of Mary, Queen of Scots. It was also to Mercilla that Spenser gave his deepest attention. He was determined to draw his Queen in the most exalted style. The palace which Artegall and Arthur reach had the grandeur of its time: it was necessarily 'stately', decorated with high turrets, and terraces along its walls; and because it was a 'palace', surpassing the Burghley and Hardwicke houses of the age, it had a fairy-tale magic about it so that all the towers were 'bright glistering with gold'. Mercilla as well possessed this magic: she was seated on a golden throne embossed with lions and the heraldic *fleur de lys* a feature which remained in the English coat of arms from Edward III to George III. The splendour of her appearance was magnified by the mysterious quality of the cloth of state spread over her. It was none of the material the Elizabethans would instinctively think of, 'rich tissew' or 'cloth of gold',

Nor of ought else, that may be richest red,
But like a cloud, as likest may be told,
That her brode spreading wings did wyde unfold;
Whose skirts were bordred with bright sunny beams,
Glistring like gold, amongst the plights enrold,
And here and there shooting forth silver streames,
Mongst which crept litle Angels through the glittering gleames.

These Angels were not fictitious, for they upheld the cloth of
state and they belonged to the same world as the Angels who
sang hymns to God. The Queen, whom they surrounded, was
also Angel-like, 'the heyre of ancient Kings', holding a sceptre
as a promise of the peace and prosperity with which heaven had
blessed her land and keeping at her feet a sword which could be
used when it was needed.

The description of Elizabeth was keyed high; yet in a characteristically Spenserian way realistic details are incorporated
into its setting. The door was kept wide open for all subjects
freely to enter; it was guarded by a porter to keep out enemies
and those who might interfere with the daily occupations of the
court. The scene remains recognisable in its literalness, but it is
not left so. The porter is named *Awe*, Guyle is one of the figures
who must be kept outside, and a poet is presented as a warning
to others who might have found their way within. He was once
called *Bon Font* but now stands with his tongue nailed against
the wall, with *Mal* correcting the name that formerly was his.[1]
The magnetism of the allegorical style draws every realistic
particular into its ken. Consequently normal situations prepared the reader for the controversial issues which Mercilla had
to encounter. Surrounded by representatives of Justice and good
government, she had to discriminate between the merits of the
cases set before her, and here, in the presence of the two strange
knights, she was faced with the beauty and dishonour of the
great, brilliant, and often widely suspected prisoner whom she

[1] Attempts have been made to identify this poet, and if identification is
necessary the most plausible is that of Richard Verstegan who was punished
for attacking Elizabeth in 1587. See the discussion by Kerby Neill, 'The
Faerie Queene and the Mary Stuart Controversy', summarised in Appendix
II of the *Variorum Book V*, pp. 319-324. Mr Neill, however, prefers to believe
that the reference is to all attacks upon the Queen, not to those of a single
person.

had to judge. This figure was Duessa, now brought to trial for her treason and plots against Mercilla.

On this occasion Spenser draws together some of the strands of Duessa's actions in Books III and IV, attributes to her a conspiracy with Blandamour and Paridell and an association with *Ate*, but the assessment had little connection with Duessa's conduct in the previous Books, and here stands as a completely separate study of the trial of Mary, Queen of Scots. The accuser, *Zele*, outlined all the arguments which had been extended against her. She was now an 'untitled Queene' (she had abdicated from her throne in Scotland in 1567), she had, it was alleged, schemed to deprive Elizabeth of her royal position, had been involved in several murderous plots in which the principal figures had been identified and executed, she had ignored the law of nature and neglected the religion of the England which had sheltered her (i.e. in the Throckmorton Plot designed to enable the invasion of the country with the assistance of the Spanish Ambassador, Mendoza). Last of all, the people had risen to demand her death after the Babington Plot (1586) and the House of Commons issued a statement insisting that there could be no stability while Mary lived as heir to the throne. The attack was made by various personifications which can, or cannot, be related to particular figures of the time—*Zele*, the *Kingdom's Care*, *Authority*, the law of *Nations*, *Religion*, and lastly *Justice*. If this weighty set of arguments in favour of the death of Mary appeared to establish the decision, as indeed it did in historical fact, there were other arguments to set against the execution. They consisted partly in what occurred in Elizabeth's mind—her pity, her regard for Mary's womanhood, the consciousness of danger from France and Scotland, her sense of the nobility of the queen she was to destroy, and finally, personally, a feeling of grief. More objections had been raised by *Zele*, until Arthur and Artegall favoured the belief that condemnation should follow even though Mercilla still hesitated. This situation appears to give a reasonable account of what in fact happened, with Elizabeth's refusal to agree to the death of her enemy, then her signature to the death warrant after pressure from the Commons, then her recalling of it, and fears when it was carried out too quickly for

K

her to repeat her recall. It was, as all historians think, a terrible decision to have to make—politically inevitable, humanly cruel. Spenser emphasised at the end of the Canto Mercilla's unwillingness to allow public vengeance to light upon her victim and her natural instinct to weep for the sadness of the fate which would have to come, delayed the conclusion until Canto x. There he gave himself time to expand the theme of the place of mercy in the practice of Justice. Justice, he explained, should find a place for Mercy:

> For if that Vertue be of so great might
>> Which from just verdict will for nothing start,
>> But to preserve inviolated right
>> Oft spilles the principall to save the part;[1]
>> So much more, then, is that of powre and art
>> That seekes to save the subject of her skill,
>> Yet never doth from doome of right depart,
>> As it is greater prayse to save, then spill,
> And better to reforme, then to cut off the ill.

V. x. 2

This analytical passage only anticipated the ultimate sentence. Mercilla's reputation for clemency had stretched far through the known world, yet even so she had to pronounce the right decision. She remains constrained in her conception of it:

>> And yet even then ruing her wilfull fall
>> With more then needfull naturall remorse,
> And yeelding the last honour to her wretched corse.

V. x. 4

This is historical fact, although Elizabeth was not at Fotheringay, for orders were given for the suitable conduct of the execution and the burial, and the presence of her servants was permitted. Spenser's treatment of this event is marked by its sympathy and dignity, and one feels that James I was going out of his way to criticise it. For him, the use of the repugnant portrayal of Duessa in Book I, Canto viii, stanzas 46-48, was an additional factor. No doubt the reference to her employment of Blandamour and Paridell as agents for the acquisition of Mercilla's crown and her use of them as paramours were

---

[1] That is, Justice cuts off the greater, violated centre in order to preserve the whole.

offensive, yet the impression of the whole had been as much in
Mary's favour as the facts allowed. Spenser's experience of
political affairs in the wildly uncontrollable state of Ireland left
him with a genuine sense of the rights and wrongs of each event
as it occurred, and it is here, in connection with Mary, Queen
of Scots, that this sense of truth remains still in power.

The three final Cantos follow much the same pattern. They
are concerned with foreign affairs, with the Netherlands and
with Ireland rather than with episodes in England, but they
are characterised by a determination to state events rightly and
to find a real sense of compassion within the scene being treated.
The problem of the Netherlands is illustrated at length, and,
finally, in Ireland there appears at last Artegall's long post-
poned quest. On both these topics the allegorical method is
somewhat unhappy, for it is based upon the activities of
Giants, Geryoneo and Grantorto, a device with which Spenser
never much enjoyed. Crudities were essential in his scheme, of
course, and these figures emerge as crude as their natures make
them. In the first study, that of the Netherlands, the account of
Geryoneo is conspicuously repulsive. *Belge* is brought a rescuer
in Arthur by her two sons who have been to Mercilla for help.
Allegorically, these represent the provinces of Holland and
Zealand which took the lead in negotiating political assistance
against Spain.[1] The Spanish occupation had driven the Dutch
into the country away both from their flourishing cities and
from their prosperous agricultural lands. Tyranny was powerful against the Protestants, and it is in the voice of *Belge* that the
suffering of the makers of the civilisation in the towns and farms
finds utterance. Arthur has suggested a private conference to
decide on the best means of restoring peace to her nation. Her
reply is the reply of all victims of military aggression, as familiar
today as it was three centuries ago:

> Ay me (sayd she) and whether shall I goe?
> Are not all places full of forraine powres?
> My pallaces possessed of my foe,
> My cities sackt, and their sky-threating towres

[1] A contemporary annotated copy of *The Faerie Queene* notes that the
appeal to Elizabeth was made when 'They had audience 9 Julii 1585'.

> Raced and made smooth fields now full of flowres?
> Onely these marishes and myrie bogs,
> In which the fearefull ewftes do build their bowres,
> Yeeld me an hostry mongst the croking frogs,
> And harbour here in safety from those ravenous dogs.
>
> V. x. 23

This is the plainest statement ever written of the adversities of occupation, every part full of the enemy, danger concealed for each person in the land. Spenser has sounded the flat note of desolation in this stanza with its falling cadences and spare language. *Belge's* blunt questions can obtain no answer. The pathos of the sight of the 'smooth fields now full of flowres' has transformed the experience of the moment into knowledge of universal grief. Her lament springs from feelings for which other poets have found a voice: it comes from 'depths of some divine despair' and it is what readers of Thucydides recognise as κτῆμα ἐς ἀεί. The phrase revives the gasp of surprise with which we first encountered it. Spenser has made out of the texture of his own extraordinary creation something that will remain a 'possession for ever'. And because *The Faerie Queene* is an extraordinary creation he goes on, as he so often does without hesitation, to add yet more to the distressing activities of his objectionable giants.

Their operations eventuate in the damaged city of Antwerp. Here there had been violence in the massacre of the inhabitants, the destruction of buildings, the ruin of trade through the harbour, and the replacement of mercantile activity by the establishment of a castle and citadel which interfered with the dealings of the merchants and required fulfilment of stiff regulations. This had been the work of Alva, acting as Regent, who imposed what Spenser calls 'the yoke of inquisition' (X. 27), burning to death those who would not submit. Spenser does not specify the conduct of the Inquisition, but leaves it, as it was intended to be, secret and sinister.

When Arthur has disposed of Alva's seneschal, he finds three knights spying upon him at the entrance to the castle. Here reliance upon the employment of circumstantial detail defines the intricacies of the fighting. Arthur chases the three, killing the first just outside, the second at the Postern gate, and the third, who manages to get into the hall 'at the skreene'. The second causes the most trouble because his body

> Right in the middest of the threshold lay,
> That it the Postern did from closing stay:

The castle proved deserted and Arthur was able to welcome *Belge* into her home. This was not the end of the episode, for Geryoneo descended upon Antwerp and challenged Arthur to a single combat. Geryoneo had been described at the beginning of Canto x: a caricature of a Giant, he had three bodies combined in one waist, with arms and legs for three. His weapon was an enormous iron axe which he used with each arm turn and turn about. Arthur observed his methods and at last succeeded in slaughtering him during a blood-stained struggle. Death carried the black corpse down to hell covered 'with a cloud of night'. The final stage involved Arthur's fighting against a monster, which was like a sphinx and devoured those rejecting Geryoneo's Idol. As with the battle against Orgoglio in Book I, and against the Souldan in Canto viii of this Book, Arthur is forced to use his shield to destroy this creature. The Idol was evidently the symbol of the Spanish doctrine and the annotator of the Folio text has underlined the words 'the deformed Masse' to indicate its significance. Arthur's success is celebrated in Spenser's customary fashion in the dancing, singing, and the scattering of garlands by the released people. We have met this scene often before, particularly at the end of Book I, and nothing new is added to it here, but it creates a due ending to a familiar situation.

More is left to be done in Book V. Ireland remained the inescapable problem, the Elizabethan nightmare, and it was upon Artegall responsibility falls. He reached the sea which he must cross to carry out his quest and on the shore meets Sir Sergis,[1] 'the aged wight' who clearly has had long experience with Irish rebellion. He learned of the situation which he now must encounter. The unfortunate Irena, to whom his promise

[1] Sir Sergis has been identified with Sir Henry Sidney, Lord Grey's predecessor, or with Walsingham, active in the colonisation of Ireland.

had long ago been given, had been imprisoned by Grantorto and was in danger of death. Ten days are all the length of life which she could hope for and these appeared too short for any chance of rescue. Artegall recognised that his delay had placed her in this position, tried to excuse his failure to arrive at the expected time, and undertook to tackle the issue with all the energy granted to him. Even so, on his way, he was distracted by another demand for assistance which he could not neglect, a demand which had an ironic connection with his own fault, and the narrative was suspended yet longer while this matter was dealt with.

What impeded Artegall's activity was the discovery of a riotous mob attacking a knight (Burbon) whose lady stood watching the affray, helpless and unprotected. The knight had parted with his shield, and had Sir Sergis and Artegall not arrived to restore him to safety, he would have been lost. Burbon's explanation adds something further to the understanding of Elizabethan politics with which Book V is concerned. It is the episode of Henri IV's acceptance of the Roman Catholic faith in order to gain French sovereignty. 'Paris is worth a mass' had been his cynical observation, a gesture strongly deplored in England. This is an instance of Spenser's tendency to transform a controversial issue into a universal one. He linked the occasion with Book I because the Red Crosse Knight, the representative of Holiness and of the Protestant faith, had given Burbon his shield and made him a knight; he also linked it with the theme of constancy and with the concept of the unity of truth as expressed in Book I and in debates elsewhere. The generalisation about ambition in the opening stanza of Canto XII supports this. It may be noticed that this particular scene was originally written as a separate passage intended to be combined with the Grantorto narrative, as the Canto-head shows, and as the first two stanzas make evident. But the account of Henri IV's conversion is set out in Canto XI. The lady for whom Burbon was fighting was Flourdelis (i.e. France) who had abandoned him for the sake of Grantorto (presumably the Pope or possibly Philip II), a wealthy, guileful tyrant, the same figure who had captured Irena. Artegall rebukes Burbon for having cast aside his shield. He has his answer:

> Not so; (quoth he) for yet when time doth serve,
>   My former shield I may resume againe:
> To temporize is not from truth to swerve,
>   Ne for advantage terme to entertaine,
>   When as necessitie doth it constraine.

V. xi. 56

Artegall, plainly the knight of Justice again, makes a memorable profound response to this argument:

> Fie on such forgerie (said *Artegall*)
> Under one hood to shadow faces twaine;
> Knights ought be true, and truth is one in all:
> Of all things to dissemble fouly may befall.

This is the proper recognition of integrity which places Artegall in the rôle he is required to champion. His definition of truth recalls his carlier dismissal of the Giant's false criterion of equality:

> For truth is one, and right is ever one.

V. 2. 48

These phrases belong in effect to one of Spenser's deeply-felt ideas of intellectual and moral worth which is part of the texture of the faith of *The Faerie Queene*. It expresses the fundamental certainty of human values and was stated later by Clough in a simpler style:

> It fortifies my soul to know
> That, though I perish, Truth is so.

In *The Faerie Queene* straightforward statements are powerful whenever they occur and, undoubtedly, gain in strength against the more complicated, often involved, metaphors which embody the arguments of Book V. Historiographically, Spenser is ultimately concerned with matters of serious importance, but his commitment to a chosen allegorical form can result in a reduction of acuity. Durbon's elusive assumption that his religious beliefs come or go with time are open to direct condemnation, and this condemnation is implied both in the language he uses in relation to his shield and in Artegall's instant objection. This is a stage in the allegory when the choice of formulation, the shield associated with the Red Crosse Knight, brings strength to the situation. Where the design weakens is at the entry of Grantorto. Flourdelis is still unwilling to accept Burbon's plea, and Artegall insists on interpreting her refusal as a desire for wealth and worldly success. His generalised comment is as moving as other comments he has made:

> Dearer is love then life, and fame then gold;
> But dearer then them both, your faith once plighted hold.
>
> V. xi. 63

We should be more willing to accept his argument had a haunting recollection of his earlier neglected promise to Irena not undermined its force. Henri IV had brought France with him to the side of the Roman Catholics, and the foreign policy of Elizabeth was consequently damaged. The Netherlands remained Protestant as far as was possible, yet the South clung to its Catholic faith, and Spenser was well aware of the foreign policy which brought both the newly converted Henri IV and the realm of Belgium together in unity with Spain on the one side and the fiercely independent Netherlands battling on the other. Grantorto ('Great wrong', as Upton translates) stands for what Spenser saw.

The whole character of Artegall's nature, like the whole character of the Elizabethan interpretation of the Irish problem, is summed up in the duplicity of his outlook. The situation recalls many doubts and uncertainties in the relation between England and what Spenser calls 'the salvage Isle'. The future will produce many people of political experience and human imagination who will give their minds and ability to the struggle—men like Swift, Burke, or Yeats. The wisest contemporary conclusion made today after the creation of Eire is surely that the history of Ireland is a history for 'England always to remember and for Ireland to forget'. Spenser perhaps thought that too; *A View of the Present State of Ireland* gives a picture of extreme complexity, yet is sufficiently balanced as far as the circumstances of the time could allow. His view has been condemned as cruel and exceptionally ferocious, but yet it is a view which attempts to take into account not only the desires of the English settlers, but also the interests of the Desmonds and other powers in the country.

What Spenser first saw in Ireland is probably indicated in Camden's account of Lord Grey's arrival in Dublin and his immediate march against the rebels. Whether his secretary was with him is not certain, but Alexander C. Judson[1] suggests that this may have been so and Upton long ago noticed the similarity of the landscape. Grey ordered all the captains who had come to welcome him to gather their troops and accompany his against the rebels in Glandilough, some twenty-five miles south of the Wicklow Hills. The contemporary commentator in the first edition of *The Faerie Queene* includes a reference to Camden 'An. 1580 Camden's Eliz eodem an.' He also identifies Grantorto as 'Giraldus Comes Desmond' and adds another piece of information beside the same stanza '1579 near [? Smer]wick ye Castle [ ] subdued.' This probably refers to the destruction of Font del Oro where the Spaniards who were holding it were massacred. The date is wrong, but as he has twice deleted 1578 from the beginning of the episode this is hardly surprising, He perhaps went to Camden, discovered that Grey had landed in 1580, and failed to correct his first guess. He offers a new candidate for Sir Sergis as

'C Cosbie le[ader]
of ye kernes [ ]
yeres old.'

Cosby was killed in the ambush, and was still, despite his seventy years, an active soldier, and this may be an occasion where a reputable figure in Spenser's experience found his way into the poem. Equally it may be an occasion where the annotator is relying upon the information Camden could give him and not upon any first-hand knowledge of his own, in which case we can at least conclude that the identity of the 'aged wight' was not obvious to a reasonably well-informed reader of his day.

Artegall's quest concludes in a personal duel with Grantorto. His enemy is attired in iron armour, wears a rusty brown steel

---

[1] Alexander C. Judson, *The Life of Edmund Spenser*, 1945, p. 88. The correct name of the place is Glenmalure. See J. M. Froude: *History of England from the Fall of Wolsey to the Defeat of the Spanish Armada.* 12 vols. Vol. XI, 1870, p. 229.

cap, and bears a huge Polaxe. Grantorto's axe becomes embedded in Artegall's shield:

> Long while he tug'd and strove, to get it out,
> And all his powre applyed thereunto,
> That he therewith the knight drew all about:
>
> V. xii. 22

This difficulty tends to occur in single combats: the Dragon with the Red Crosse Knight had a similar problem when his claw became fixed to the Red Crosse's shield, and the monster in its battle with Arthur was defeated only by Arthur cutting off its gripping lion's claws. Nothing removes the dignity of Grantorto quite as effectively as this awkward struggle with an obstinate axe. Readers of the last part of Book V are forced to admit that the introduction of Giants and physically distorted beasts does little good to the narrative. To compare the Henri IV episode with the portrayal of Dutch and Irish events is to realise how much of a trap certain forms of allegory could prove for Spenser.

The end of the Book contains yet another failure. Artegall sets off for Gloriana's court, but cannot enjoy his success because he becomes the victim of two personified figures of evil, *Envie* and *Detraction* despatched by the Blatant Beast. These creatures are familiar from previous Books: *Envie* had appeared in Book I and *Detraction* is reminiscent of *Sclaunder* in Book IV. As for the Blatant Beast he is a future pleasure reserved for Book VI. All three are topical additions, being governed by circumstances from outside rather than by anything essential inside the poem. They are close to the experiences of Lord Grey in his attempt to carry out his unrewarding appointment. Spenser had already provided readers with a well-defined pair of personifications in *Envie* and *Sclaunder* and enough has been established about them. The Blatant Beast is another matter, for its appearance looks forward rather than backward, and it signifies one of Spenser's methods of unifying his poem. The Red Crosse Knight stepped into the beginning of Book II, Guyon into Book III; III and IV have several characters in common, Artegall has already appeared in Book IV with Britomart as his future bride, consequently some sort of linkage is needed for Book VI. The link here is unnecessarily rudimentary for it is largely a matter of contemporary reference. As the climax to the Book and the fulfilment of the quest, the Grantorto scene had been in itself inadequate, an anticlimax after Arthur's exploit from which it was insufficiently differentiated. The Blatant Beast episode merely brings a final element of clumsiness into the treatment of the last Canto. Granted its intrusion, one could never agree that 'the end crowns all', for that was never the expected culmination of so immediately radical a Book.

Chapter IX

BOOK VI. HUMANITY AND COURTESY

THE style of Book VI is a delightful change from the pragmatic representation of the action of Book V. Spenser, one
feels, has returned to the scheme in which he was naturally at
home. In Book V there had been much which deeply involved
him through his relationship with Ireland. This, we must
accept, was the result of his close association with Lord Grey
and all the problems with which the ruler had to struggle—
matters which prove to be sociological and political, matters
which bear the brunt of issues at stake for the English governors,
issues which were inescapable and were ultimately forces upon
his life. Their culmination lies in Spenser's final consciousness
of what was most serious in the Irish world in which he himself
was embroiled. The rise of the Desmonds, and Tyrone's rebellion drove him from his castle at Kilcolman back to England
and perhaps, but we do not know, destroyed the next stage of
his epic.

But his poem was developing in a way which was nearer to his
heart: it became focussed upon the pastoral world and upon
simple virtues. Consequently in Book VI the characters and the
design are derived from a rural society, from shepherds and
shepherdesses, or from primitive creatures, either perfectly good
and unformed like the Salvage Man or perfectly evil and
cannibalistic like the barbarians who captured Serena and the
pirates who descend upon the shepherds and carry them away.
Among the varied figures is the retired knight living a life of
a hermit, virtuous and thoughtful, the opposite of the disguised
Archimago, the childless couple who receive with gratitude the
baby rescued by Calepine from a bear, the parents of the lost
Pastorella, or, more than these, the old gardener Melibœe who
has rejected the life of the court to retreat to the unspoilt rural
land.

Granted this kind of life, the scene is principally normal and
the language plain. It is drawn from country pursuits and

remains in tune with the whole note of the Book. Much of it is pictorial, relying upon visual aspects which remain memorable. The settings and backgrounds, woodlands and forests, are what the reader recalls. There is a feeling of leisureliness because the descriptions are concerned with the elaboration of slow movements. Even the cannibals prepare their ritual gradually before they can take the captured Serena to their altar. Many elements produce a static effect. What stands out is the scene of Calepine examining the baby he has carried away from the clutches of the bear, and the Salvage Man coming with his arms crammed with wild fruit in time to find Arthur asleep. It is a peculiarly tranquil moment where Arthur, freed of his armour

> in silver slomber lay,
> Like to the Evening starre adorn'd with deawy ray.

It cannot remain long like this, for Arthur wakes and the Salvage on seeing the threatening gesture of Turpine begins waving his only weapon, an oaken shaft, and Arthur snatching up his sword casts Turpine to the ground. Even here, the villain has no word to say but prays for mercy, holding up his hands in silence. Arthur deprives him of his knightly appurtenances and hangs him up by his heels in condemnation of his treachery.

As is customary, Spenser opens Book VI with a *Proem*. In it he defines the nature of courtesy. This is the occasion to look back upon the content of the world of *The Faerie Queene*. Its ways

> Are so exceeding spacious and wyde,
> And sprinckled with such sweet variety,
> Of all that pleasant is to eare and eye.

Yet his failure to reach its conclusion had been a burden to his mind. For this he had already apologised half-comically to Lodowick Bryskett in a sonnet in *Amoretti*:

> But lodwick, this of grace to me aread;
>   doo ye not thinck th'accomplishment of it,
>   sufficient worke for one mans simple head,
>   all were it as the rest but rudely writ.
>
> Sonnet, XXXIII

The poem is certainly not 'but rudely writ'. Its panoramic nature had drawn from its author all the insights he possessed for its making, and it is out of a sense of the vastness of the demands it had made that Spenser appeals to the spirits of poetry in Parnassus for their assistance:

> Guyde ye my footing, and conduct me well
> In these strange waies, where never foote did use
> Ne none can find, but who was taught them by the Muse.
>
> Proem, vi. 2

He is pleading for himself and also for his readers for they too must be taught by the Muse. Other *Proems* indicate the moral and intellectual qualities of the Books to which they are attached but this is the only one which contains a passage of literary criticism. The topic of Book VI, the Virtue at its centre, is naturally referred to also, in terms of a Platonic source, but the greatest emphasis rests upon the art of poetry. It is this aspect which emerges most powerfully in the content of this particular Book.

The *Proem* provides us with a clear idea of what the virtue of Courtesy consists in. It is allied with humility and it is found wherever men are civilised. There was more of it in the past, according to Spenser's retrospective attitude, for the golden age possessed it most fully. Yet true courtesy does not show itself in worldly appearances, but lies within humanity itself. Or, to cite one of Spenser's most quotable sentences:

> But virtues seat is deepe within the mynd,
> And not in outward shows, but inward thoughts defynd.
>
> VI. Proem, 5.

That is, it lies in the mentality, not in the manners of men.

This introduction prepares the reader to discover the nature of courtesy and the form it will take in the Book. By the time he has reached Book VI, having travelled so far through the spacious and wide paths of five Books, he is ready for whatever design is proposed. Here is the main structure, of the Knight—Quest—Main-virtue type, but modified of course: the Knight is Calidore, the Quest is the search for the Blatant Beast. The modification ensues when Calidore departs for a considerable period and his place is taken by Calepine. Calidore is seen and rapidly characterised after the *Proem*. He possesses the central virtue 'by kind', a gift of nature which provides him with personal charm. There is, in him, an individual attraction which like that of Absalom 'did steal men's hearts away'. He is endowed with a special sort of courtesy, given not attained, whereas in Calepine the merit has to be acquired. We are informed fully about the charm of Calidore:

> Whose every deed and word, that he did say,
> Was like enchantment.

VI. ii. 3

Others lacking this particular quality need to impose it upon themselves with struggle and pain. Calepine is a member of that category; he is an ordinary person, who takes a substantial share of the virtue upon which the plot turns. Calidore was not; his character is said to have been derived from that of Sir Philip Sidney. All the associations with which the Elizabethans had endowed their beloved lost hero bear upon this interpretation of Calidore. The gifts which Sidney possessed, his zeal for the Arcadian and the pastoral scene, are those in which the Knight of courtesy also shared. He is as much at home with the shepherds as with the imaginative world of Colin Clout. Both embody the flower of virtue in the Faerie or the Elizabethan court and both unite personal charm with the unboasted heroism of chivalry.

The narrative begins after the *Proem* in an encounter between Artegall and Calidore. It is a courtly meeting when Calidore explains that he is beginning just when Artegall has ended his quest; that he is unable to ask for support and that he does not even know where the Blatant Beast, which he is committed to destroy, is to be found. Artegall helpfully offers his own memory of the Beast which he had seen with *Envy* and *Detraction* after his rescue of Irena. He then gives Calidore a clue as to where the creature may be sought, and after discussing its horror they part, with a valediction to Calidore from Artegall.[1] The Beast is Spenser's invention and its nature is expounded in the course of the action. Its origin is from hell. It has a spiteful malicious

---

[1] This is the conventional mode of parting between the oncoming and outgoing knights:

> 'Now God you speed . . .
> And keepe your body from the daunger drad'

is Artegall's blessing;

> 'God guide thee, Guyon, well to end they worke',

is that of Red Crosse.

tongue and its bite is deeply wounding. According to the *New English Dictionary* its name is an archaic form of 'bleating', equivalent to 'blaterare', 'to make a noise'. The form 'blatant' was used in the seventeenth century as the adjective 'noisy' and 'clamorous'. When Artegall describes it he indicates its association with spite and slander. Later it is more specifically characterised with its 'great wide mouth', its ugliness, and its capacity to make physically incurable wounds. Even the Salvage Man can do nothing for its two victims, Serena and Timias, and it is left to the Hermit to produce a profounder diagnosis. They are suffering from an injury to the moral fabric which, he tells them, they alone can treat for themselves by temperance and restraint. The inwardness of the wound is peculiar to the subtlety of the Beast's mode of attack.

Its concern had been at first with two individuals but by the end of the Book it is shown to operate upon all 'estates'. The dissolution of the monasteries and iconoclasm in the Church are also within its range. Its menace is directed to many fields; hence its early meeting with Artegall, whose success spares him from its grasp. Spenser's sense of proportion specifies the objects of the Beast's attacks. It is not violently evil but, like courtesy, is associated with ordinary phases of daily life. That it can be cruel and destructive is apparent, and a hero of Calidore's ability is needed to diminish its power in the world. Yet it is not killed, merely tied up and temporarily diverted from its dissemination of harm. What it stands for can recur, and it will escape and occupy itself in its habitual manner. Calidore's victory over it was as sure as possible and he led it by a chain over the land which it had so irresistibly threatened.

Inexplicably, it becomes free again, and Spenser draws a new vision of what it could do when at large once more. Its terror comes nearer home now for it is upon the men of imagination that it pounces:

> Ne spareth he most learned wits to rate,
> Ne spareth he the gentle Poets rime,
> But rends without regard of person or of time.
>
> VI. xii. 40

Its escape brings a melancholy conclusion to the Book which had recorded so memorable a tribute to the art of poetry. The scene on Mount Acidale where Colin could create the dancing rhythms for the Graces and for his own Love, the handsomeness and charm of the boy, Tristram, and, strangest of all, the Salvage Man whose compassionate lore of the woods is so remarkable, had been evolved from the magic of the poetic mind. Spenser has chosen to end on a sad note. Pope perhaps recalled the personal voice of the poet whom he admired when he brought the *Elegy to the Memory of an Unfortunate Lady* to end on a reminder of the creator and his subject:

> Poets themselves must fall, like those they sung;
> Deaf the prais'd ear, and mute the tuneful tongue.

The writer has a relatively small place in his work, and yet, like Pope, Milton, Johnson and Gray, Spenser found the occasion when it was right that he should enter.

As before, the design of Book VI combines an organised structure, a brave central character, and a quest, to express its essential theme in terms of exposition and contrast. Yet, unlike its predecessors, this Book consists of studies of people who are much more realistic, not only in individual detail but also in their presentation. They are *not* personified abstractions, apart from Mirabella and her companions, *Disdain* and *Scorn*, but real human beings. The scheme in which they occur is partly that of a series of chivalric episodes illustrating aspects of courtesy or its opposite, partly that of single ways of life like that of the Salvage Man or the Hermit, partly that of societies, primitive or ideal. Among the last is the long pastoral section where a satisfactory and nearly perfect world is set out. It is a world where the Blatant Beast is unknown and where Calidore is content to remain for a long period.

The first episode is a prelude to others of the same kind. It is set in a Castle, one of the recurring features for many events in this Book. Its plot derives from a story in the *Mort d'Arthur* in which King Ryence demanded Arthur's beard to complete the weaving of his cloak. Here *Crudor*, the discourteous knight, rejects Briana's love and forces her to line a mantle for him with the locks of the women and the beards of the men who pass his Castle. Calidore discovers this despicable custom when he finds a Squire tied to a tree. He releases him, hears the reason for his captivity, kills *Crudor's* Seneschall who is putting this custom into practice, and interviews Briana, whose pride and abusiveness contrast with Calidore's perfection of manner. She has sent for *Crudor* who comes to attack this unmanageable knight. When *Crudor*, unhorsed, is forced to beg for his life, Calidore grants it and gives him a lesson in courtesy:

> Who will not mercie unto others shew,
> How can he mercie ever hope to have?

He has already improved Briana's outlook in pointing the moral insufficiency for her conduct for

> No greater shame to man then inhumanitie.

From *Crudor* he demands that the wicked custom should cease and that he should take Briana for his wife. This is an entirely constructive story since it ends in happiness, both for Briana and *Crudor* and for the Squire and his lady to whom Calidore hands over Briana's gift of the Castle. The tale turns on Discourtesy Reformed.

A theme which is persistent in Book VI is the theme of education. Many situations arise from its absence, or from its presence, among the characters. The event which follows the Briana story is centred upon it; and several other incidents raise similar issues. For instance the Salvage Man possesses only a personal version of it, Meliboee among the shepherds rebuts what he has seen of the lack of education in the court; and, of course, the cannibals who try to sacrifice Serena to their primitive creed and the brigands who break up the pastoral group and kill Meliboee are proofs of the danger of its absence in society. And one may reasonably add the figures of positive discourtesy such as Briana, who is well enough educated to argue against Calidore, and Turpine who neglects all the knightly codes in which he has been trained, both characters immune to the advantages of the cultivated intelligence they possess.

Especially interesting on this particular subject is the young man whom Calidore meets after his adventure in Briana's Castle. In him Spenser finds an opportunity of portraying a virtuous character who illustrates a natural instinct towards chivalric behaviour. He proves to be Tristram, son of Melogras, King of Cornwall, who has been sent from Lyonesse to the Faerie land. Here he has learnt all that belongs to a rustic life. Calidore sees him dressed in a woodman's jacket of Lincoln green, with spangled hood, a hunter's horn hanging by his side, darts in one hand and a boar-spear in the other.

> Buskins he wore of costliest cordwayne,
> Pinckt upon gold, and paled part per part,
> As then the guize was for each gentle swayne.

VI. ii. 6

This exquisite impression astonished Calidore mostly because he had seen him fighting and killing the knight who lies dead at his feet. Tristram had been breaking the knightly code in which only a knight ought to fight another. Then Tristram explains matters and disperses Calidore's mystification. The knight had abandoned his own lady for another whom he liked better. He learns much about Tristram's own life in the forest, his knowledge of its beasts, and his experience of hawking:

> Ne is there hauke, which mantleth her on pearch,
> Whether high towring, or accoasting low,
> But I the measure of her flight doe search,
> And all her pray, and all her diet know.

VI. ii. 32

He had long desired to live in a knightly world and join the society for which he knows he had been born. Calidore, therefore, makes him a Squire and gives him the armour of the dead knight, but as he cannot take any companion during his search for the Blatant Beast he can only ask the newly-appointed Squire to accompany the neglected lady.

What gives this episode its merit is the quality of its descriptive passages. Not only is there the decorative appearance of Tristram but there is also the beautiul imagery attached to his joy at being dubbed Squire:

> Like as a flowre, whose silken leaves small,
> Long shut up in the bud from heavens vew,
> At length breaks forth, and brode displayes his smyling hew.

VI. ii. 35

There is, too, his fascination at the sight of the armour which he has gained:

> Long fed his greedie eyes with the faire sight
> Of the bright metall, shyning like Sunne rayes;
> Handling and turning them a thousand wayes.

For Calidore it was a delightful contact and, having left the desolate lady in Tristram's care, he turns his attention to the other lady and her wounded knight. Here he shows genuine imagination when he realises that she is hesitant to ask for his assistance in bearing the victim off to safety. Together they transport him back to the castle where his elderly father is anxiously awaiting the return of his son. He laments his arrival with wounds seemingly so serious in a way reminiscent of that of Egeus in the *Knight's Tale*, a tactful reminder since the Canto had begun with an overt reference to Chaucer.[1] Spenser does not quote exactly but the emotion has much in common with that of Chaucer. Egeus says:

> This world nys but a thurghfare ful of wo,
> And we been pilgrymes passynge to and fro.
> Deeth is the ende of every worldly soore.
>
> (*K.T.*, 2846-2848)

And Spenser gives to Aldus, the father of Aladine (their names are at last offered) a feeling of the same kind:

> Such is the weakenesse of all mortall hope;
>   So tickle is the state of earthly things,
>   That, ere they come unto their aymed scope,
>   They fall too short of our fraile reckonings,
>   And bring us bale and bitter sorrowings.
>
> VI. iii. 5

Egeus makes a more universal comment, but Spenser is concerned as much with the personal attitude of a father to the threatened death of his own child as was Chaucer. Aldus has welcomed Calidore and his son's lady and takes them into his hospitable castle while his son is cherished by her. Calidore is prepared to leave next morning and undertakes to return the

---

[1] Chaucer's *Wife of Bath's Tale*, lines 1109-1124, and *Balade de Bon Conseyl*, 'Flee fro the prees, and dwelle with sothfastnesse'. Chaucer's view is essentially more democratic than that of Spenser, whose 'gentleness' is always connected with birth.

lady to her parents' castle and to invent a suitable explanation for her absence. She is then received without more being said.

Calidore is now free to continue his pursuit of the Blatant Beast. He rides on in search of it and comes upon a couple, Calepine and Serena, who are enjoying their solitude in an unoccupied part of the forest. Calidore apologises for his unexpected appearance, and has no desire to make any personal use of his presence. It was 'his fortune not his fault' that has brought him there and he does all he could to make friends with the pair by discussing knightly experiences with Calepine while Serena wanders into the forest. She is then attacked by the Blatant Beast, whom Calidore hastens to pursue, leaving Serena to be cared for by Calepine. This is the last we see of Calidore for a long interval; he next appears in Canto IX, while the virtue of courtesy he has represented is carried on by Calepine.

ii

From Cantos III to VIII Spenser continues the episodic method of the Book's form, as he is entitled to do on the understanding that in it the main theme would be recognised with a different central character. He describes, and the reader is expected to follow, a series of happenings focussed upon Calepine, some as complicated as that concerning Tristram, others easier and full of surprises. To the critic there is the requirement to follow a straightforward narration and to combine it with the comment the interest of the story deserves. One finds oneself constantly turning back to re-read in order to discover what exactly has happened and why that so far unexplained new character has behaved in such a way. Sometimes the return to the text seems hardly worth the effort; but at least one can conclude that it has enabled one to find out more about the material and about Spenser's treatment of it. If one's report appears to have become somewhat flat-footed in consequence, one can always see whether a second thoughtful exploration might produce a more perceptive result. Book VI is as problematical in form and execution as are the other Books in *The Faerie Queene*, and it may be that the failure of the critic has come from the problems he has had to encounter. Or from a failure on the part of Spenser himself. No author is flawless, and the faults which abound in this particular Book sometimes leave an effect of dullness, repetition, and general lack of inspiration. Yet no commentator can stop there. The vague, unstated feeling of the presence of the author behind the text is corrective, and must illuminate the conduct of the exploration. After all, one thinks, the section was not as bad as it first appeared, it has a link with what was admired so strongly in an earlier Book. To read Spenser successfully is always to discover and to qualify. To begin the next stage of Book VI is to begin once more the hard work of interpretation: laborious apologies for clumsiness and the hopeful proffer of critical suggestions inevitably ensue.

It is with Turpine that the next event starts and with it an example of discourtesy at its worst. His name announces this estimate and so does his conduct. He lives in the 'Castle of the ford', he will not assist Calepine to bring the injured Serena into a comfortable lodging, he mocks at his attempts to carry her across the ford. When the castle is reached, its gate is slammed in Calepine's face by the 'rude Porter that no manners had' and he is forced to sleep outside, protecting Serena from the cold as best he can. Nor is this the end of Turpine's loutish behaviour. He attacks his visitor next day, chasing him round his horse, and terrifying the enfeebled Serena. His deplorable nature is displayed in a later Canto in his dealings with Arthur. He is ultimately disgraced and punished.

Meanwhile a strange powerful figure has come to the aid of Calepine. One of Spenser's unforgettable inventions, the 'Salvage Man' is a creature who brings the romantic associations of another level of being. What we learn about him enlarges the impression of his other-worldly nature. He wears no clothes, carries no weapons other than an oaken staff, he has no language apart from signs, and is physically invulnerable. Yet he, too, is an example of the practice of courtesy. His virtue has no connection with that of 'courtiers' of whom he has never heard. It consists in genuine compassion and gentleness. He is skilled in the lore of the woods and he applies his knowledge to stop the bleeding of Calepine's wound and to produce restorative sustenance for him. The solitary occupant of a dwelling 'farre in the forest by a hollow glade', safe from wild beasts, he depends upon what grows near him for his life, fruits of the

earth for food, moss and shrubs for furniture. To describe him
as 'a noble savage' is to draw a false analogy for he does not
belong to the period from which that label arose. Spenser's
attitude to him is laudatory but only within limits. He is simply
a man who does the best that absence of civilisation can do,
and that is better than some of those who are allegedly 'civilised' had done. Turpine, with his knighthood, and the cannibals, with their far from noble savagery, have to be measured
against him. Yet, for all his mildness and instinctive humanity,
he is shown to be lacking in one quality which might have been
expected of him. He is 'a bad steward', presumably because in
Spenser's view he does not take any heed of the surroundings
from which he draws his livelihood. Still, his portrayal is such
as to transform him into a rare creature. Appreciation of his
character depends partly upon the fact that he was of gentle
birth; the explanation we have yet to hear:

> For certes he was borne of noble blood,
> How ever by hard hap he hether came;
> As ye may know, when time shall be to tell the same.
>
> VI. v. 2

Time never did tell that part of his story so we have to trust in
Spenser's belief that the Salvage Man's thoughtfulness was an
aspect of his birth as well as of his life in the sylvan world.

As the plot develops, further elements of the contribution to
the idea of courtesy are provided by this fascinating man. He
understands Serena's misery at the disappearance of Calepine
and is ready to encourage her in her desire to find him by riding
on the stalwart horse he has left behind. He puts on Calepine's
armour in order to accompany her suitably. Swordless (since
Calepine had concealed that weapon when he left the Salvage's
dwelling) he walks beside Serena's steed until they meet Prince
Arthur and Timias. Here Serena is forced to explain the misleading action of her escort, who is rectifying the fitting of her
saddle, without the armour which he had found an encumbrance.
The scattered weapons and the rough appearance of the
creature accompanying her reasonably create a suspicion in the
mind of the two figures from the world of chivalry. Serena
becomes the voice for her silent companion. She can only tell

them how in the setting of wild animals and the threatening environment of the forest,

> It is most straunge and wonderfull to fynd
> So mild humanity, and perfect gentle mynd.

Her explanation diminishes Timias's inclination to attack, and they proceed placably together in search of some hospitable place where each may recover from the injuries inflicted by the Blatant Beast.

Here the inevitable need for expository narrative rears its head again. Why is Timias in this scene? Spenser, well aware of that need, provides it in an interpolation. A feat of memory, he knows, is not to be expected of an ordinary reader however much he had been concerned with the events in Books III and IV, and so a reminder must be supplied. A little help will enable him to recall that Timias had killed three foresters who had been pursuing Florimell, that Belphoebe had cured his wounds but her treatment had proved not so much a cure as the beginning of another disease, injury to the heart, not to the body, probably also remained vividly in his memory. The position of Timias as an important character in the whole poem stays vaguely in his thought and a little further effort will restore the ultimate recollection, this time to Book IV (Cantos VII, 36-47, and VIII, 1-17) when Belphoebe stumbles upon Timias's embrace of Amoret and leaves him with her incredulous, tragic phrase:

> Was this the faith?

It was a long tale. The image of the dove carrying a jewel which enabled Timias to regain his lost reputation will perhaps bring back the rest of the sequence. Here in Book VI the story is revived, or probably rewritten, for another purpose. This time three men attack Timias, not foresters but malignant enemies, *Despetto* (Malice) *Decetto* (Deceit) and *Defetto* (Detraction). They had decided to use the Blatant Beast to victimise him, knowing that Timias would not hesitate to pursue any wild animal in the forest. He, in fact, chases it until it bites him, he then falls into the ambush they had set for him, and is rescued only on the arrival of Arthur whom they have heard riding through the forest. This event is usually interpreted in a historical context, by the identification of Timias with Sir Walter Raleigh whose marriage to Elizabeth Throckmorton had thrown him into disfavour with the Queen. Her friendship was recovered as was Belphoebe's with Timias, but he remained at the mercy of the slander exerted by the three attackers.

The journey of the four characters brought them next to the dwelling of a Hermit, an ex-knight. His past had instilled in him broad experience and much knowledge of men and their ways. To these he added a love of beauty and an instinct for religious contemplation. He leaves the chapel in which he was praying as soon as he becomes conscious of the presence of his unknown visitors. They are welcomed, entertained with simple food, and given means for a night's rest in his house. This is a place imbued with an unassuming aesthetic appeal. It is small, 'like a little cage', and is decorated with flowers and greenery; it suited his modest way of life and enabled him to extend happiness to those who needed it. This is, in fact, a point in the action in which it is possible for the reader to reflect upon the ideas so far expressed in Book VI. In this little cage-like house is gathered the excellence of many figures, the royalty of Prince Arthur, the naïvety of the Salvage Man, the beauty of Serena, and the piety of the Hermit. The atmosphere is peaceful: the horses graze upon the green, arms were long ago hung up out of reach and 'all the world's incombraunce' cast aside. For Spenser the change of feeling between this Book and that of Book V with its political struggles is perhaps made most conspicuous in the placid life of the retired knight. He has seen all, learnt all, and has chosen in the end the unbought calmness of a solitary existence.

Solitude is shown to provide the most satisfactory context for the pursuit of virtue. Tristram, the Salvage Man, this retired knight, and later Melibœe, each represents a kind of goodness which belongs only to the undemanding. It is courtesy as it exists in the terms of the Book, and it is reflected in solitary figures. Each lives his own independent life, and each has something to give from this independence to others. Whatever the limitations of his condition, his conduct preserves the quality of courtesy. It is a quality not confined to youth or age, to education or lack of it, to heroism or just plain endurance, but it springs up according to circumstances. Thus, for all his absence of knightly training, Tristram knows how to treat an ill-mannered knight, and for all his lack of any knowledge of human society or even of human speech, the Salvage Man knows how to look after the two human beings who have come to him for protection.

After a night with the Hermit, Prince Arthur decides that his own obligations make it necessary for him to move on. The Salvage Man, surprisingly, indicates a wish to accompany him; the magnificence of the hero of *The Faerie Queene* is instinctively recognised by this unidentified inhabitant of the woods, and this gives some suggestion as to his origins. The two set off together leaving Timias and Serena in the care of the Hermit. This is the occasion when the Hermit's religious knowledge is brought to bear upon the illness which afflicts them. The only cure, he tells them, is to be found internally, by self-discipline, resistance to the temptations caused by physical and emotional desires. The tendency towards sensuous pleasure and the preference for secrecy in carrying out their own personal wishes must not be permitted. This advice is duly accepted. By following the Hermit's principles of asceticism, they succeed in finding their salvation. Here Spenser offers a spiritual standard to which no resemblance will be found elsewhere in the Book. The afflictions of Mirabella are mentioned in this context, but her sufferings are different in cause. Her story will follow later on. The reference to her is one of the seemingly accidental promises for a future account. In due time we shall perceive what is common to the two narratives. Mirabella's errors are not curable by advice, and the methods of their portrayal are dissimilar. Desire for symmetry leads us to set the two stories beside each other, as it must have underlain Spenser's introduction of her. His process of writing is regulated by just such deliberate or chance anticipations.

Arthur and the Salvage Man, having parted from the Hermit, set out to avenge the cruelty of Turpine upon Calepine and Serena. Like all episodes connected with Turpine, there is much that is unpleasing to read. Baseness is his name, and base his nature. Arthur, remembering what he has been told by Calepine, knows that the only means of getting into his castle is to affect the appearance of a wounded knight in search of hospitality. The scheme produces the desired result; the porters, alarmed at the sight of the defiant vigorous man to whom they had refused entrance, flee in search of their master. Turpine returning to expel an undesirable visitor, discovers that he has a dangerous man on his hands, and takes refuge in his wife's room. Cowardice is added to the villainy imputed to him. He lies shaking upon the floor, too frightened to stand up, and Arthur who had granted him his life scornfully moves from his worthless household as soon as the night is over.

The triviality of this story may well discourage any further remark upon it, yet there are two elements which do provoke comment. First, there is the oddity of Arthur's behaviour—that he, the hero of the poem, should obtain his success by a device elsewhere deplored. 'Feigning' is the technique of the wicked or of the weak: it was rebuked in Burbon by Artegall, and Artegall's own conduct in the Radigund episode had to be explained away. Yet now it is assumed that Arthur is right in doing what the situation seemed to him to require. This may be one of the flaws which crop up in the handling of the plots, or it may be the device appropriate to the baseness of a villain who deserves nothing better. Secondly, there is the literary pleasure created by the delineation of Turpine's wife, Blandina. Like Blandamour, she embodies sexual attraction and she has been individually defined. In her is demonstrated a guileful charm. She is a woman whose ability to please is, as Spenser rather strangely says, either a gift of nature or an acquired art. The remark strikes one as strange considering that a similar observation had been made in connection with the difference between the courtesy of Calidore and that of Calepine. But Spenser is not, of course, identifying the charmer with the courteous man. In describing Calidore he leaves no doubt as to the fact that his virtue is positive and internal, while he makes it evident that the virtue of Calepine is equally positive, acquired by effort, 'enforst with pain'. For Blandina, however, there is an ambiguous phrase:

> Whether such grace were given her by kynd,
>   As women wont their guilefull wits to guyde;
>   Or learn'd the art to please, I doe not fynd.

There is often in Spenser a sense of certainty in the treatment of shades of meaning. Here confusion does not occur. The merits of the heroes are stated clearly in open phrasing; the attraction of the more dubious Blandina is never exposed overtly. 'Grave, moral Spenser' noticeably earned these epithets from his certainty. He has committed himself fully to his representation of the goodness of the two heroes; he has committed himself equally fully to the recognition of the ambiguity of Blandina's charm. She has been enlivened in this statement about the source of her attraction. It is scarcely surprising that Arthur succumbs to it and yields to her plea for Turpine.

The rest of Turpine's career continues as might be expected. He bribes two knights, unknown to him, to attack his generous adversary. One, innocent of the real state of affairs is killed, the other (Sir Enias), having learnt the truth from Arthur, returns with a fabricated report of his success. Turpine disguises his satisfaction in a pretence of regret. To Spenser, as to Bunyan, there is close connection between courage and a sense of pity. The death of Arthur is meaningless to the plotter. His appearance of regret is no more than appearance:

> For where's no courage, there's no ruth nor mone.
>
> VI. vii. 18

He then tries to inveigle Sir Enias to carry on the scheme in which he had embroiled him, for Arthur is merely lying asleep. Knightly principles properly prevent the killing of a sleeping man and the falsity of the coward has by then become obtrusive. The Salvage Man arrives in time to rouse the intended victim. The villain meets the fate he deserves. There is little destruction in Book VI; the dénouement is precipitated in the style in which events tend to conclude—without slaughter but with judgment. This is the last sight of Turpine.

In this Canto, too, as in many others, rural imagery is introduced quite apart from the subject of the narrative. Thus Turpine's grooms flee 'like scattered sheep' under the Salvage Man's attack, Blandina exercises her specious attraction by 'smyling smoothly like to a summer's day', and the two honourable agents involved in the plot against Arthur are described in a long simile where they move like a 'cast of Faulcons' attacking

a heron which is more experienced than they prove to be.
Imagery of this kind occurs naturally in the pastoral section but
it is equally evident in places where it is hardly expected to
appear. It slides quietly into the narrative and is inconspicu-
ously but consistently present.

iii

'But turne we now backe to that Ladie free', Spenser observes
to shift his action to the stage in which he had abandoned it
before the Turpine plot began. When it comes, it enables him
to imply contrasts without their having to be stated. Mirabella,
like Blandina, is the opposite of the ideal of courtesy; but where
Blandina possessed too much pleasantness, Mirabella is self-
centred and scornful. This is the old distinction of *The Faerie
Queene*: the Perissa and Elissa opposition. They were minor
figures in Book II; here each is separate and fully developed
into an active member of the design. The portraiture of Mirabella is more tightly set in a Court of Love context. Her attitude
strikes a censorious note:

> What cared she, who sighed for her sore,
> Or who did wayle or watch the wearie night?
> Let them that list their lucklesse lot deplore;
> She was borne free, not bound to any wight,
> And so would ever live, and love her owne delight.
>
> VI. vii. 30

Alliteration, and the rollicking final alexandrine is Spenser's
way of criticising a facile opinion. It is an example of *hubris*, the
pride before the fall that must come. Her languishing admirers
died for grief as she well knew:

> Whylest she, the Ladie of her libertie,
> Did boast her beautie had such soveraine might,
> That with the onely twinckle of her eye,
> She could or save, or spill, whom she would hight:
> What could the Gods doe more, but doe it more aright?
>
> VI. vii. 31

In this casual attitude she was daring the Gods, and one God,
Cupid, placed arrogance where it belonged. Mirabella's verve
was not to survive. Cupid withdrew the bandage from his eyes,

became no longer the blindfold god of the first scene in the House of Busyrane but the torturer of the second where he was able to enjoy the sight of the suffering of Amoret. Similarly, here the penance imposed upon Mirabella is painful. She is to go over the world and resuscitate as many admirers as she had previously destroyed. This is the punishment of the Squire of Dames in reverse, and like him she has found only few to cancel the debt.

Mirabella's penance is described vividly since she is accompanied by personifications of her failure to preserve human relationships. Seated on a 'mangy jade', she is propelled by *Scorne*, a fool, who whips the horse and the rider at the same time; *Disdaine* who drags along her equipage is quite different from the other figures of *Disdaine* in Books III and IV where more 'Courts of Love' figures are placed. He is a Giant and more like the Giant, *Disdayne*, in the Cave of Mammon (II. vii. 41) than any of the personifications elsewhere. He wears no armour but is dressed as were the Irish 'in a jacket quilted richly rare / Upon checklaton'. What makes him even stranger is his turban:

> And on his head a roll of linnen plight,
> Like to the Mores of Malaber, he wore;
> With which his locks, as blacke as pitchy night,
> Were bound about.

> VI. vii. 43

Of the jacket we learn much from *A View of Ireland*:

> ... the quilted leather jacke is olde Englishe for it was the proper wede of the horsemen and ye maye reade in *Chaucer* wheare he describeth: *Sir Thopas* apparell and armour when he wente to fighte againste the Geaunte which Checklaton is that kinde of gilden leather with which they use to imbrother theire Irishe jackes and theare likewise by all that discripcion ye maye see the verye fashion and manner of the Irishe horsemen moste livelye set forthe in his long hose, his Rydinge shoes of Costelye Cordwaine his hacqueton and his habericion with all the rest theareunto belonginge.[1]

[1] *A View of the Present State of Ireland. Variorum* edition, Baltimore, 1949, sections 2177-2185, p. 121. Spenser has fused (or confused) two separate stanzas in Sir Thopas, 19-24 and 149-154.

To the roll of linnen plight there is also a reference in *A View*.[1]
The phrase about the Mores of Malaber appears to derive from a
travel book of Duarte Barbosa, *c.* 1518, which was translated
from Portuguese into Italian and contains numerous allusions
to these figures. All Mohammedans were labelled 'moors' in-
discriminately.[2]

Disdaine's marvellous appearance is made even more the
creation of Spenser's imaginative power by the oddity of his
movement. He is distinguished from other Spenserian giants by
his walk:

> And stalking stately, like a Crane, did stryde
> At every step uppon the tiptoes hie . . .

This peculiarity is part of his pride and also has the effect of
giving him an individuality: the length of the crane's legs and
beak creates an image of an enormous creature which separates
him from other personifications in *The Faerie Queene*. His gilded
attire, his gaze fixed upon his golden feet, his black locks, even
his mighty iron club build him into an unforgettable sight so
that the whole group with the decrepit horse, the weeping
Mirabella, the malevolent little figure of *Scorne*, becomes one
of those memorable pictures with which *The Faerie Queene* is
studded. The inevitable fight which ensues provokes Mirabella
to explain the circumstances in which Arthur found her and to
appeal for the continuation of them as they are: her life depends
upon her acceptance of Cupid's doom and she cannot grant
Arthur's offer of rescue. She has to carry out the penance imposed upon her, and fill her bottle with tears of contrition. Her
intervention at Arthur's attempt to kill *Disdaine* revives the
legend that a sorcerer must be free to undo the spell he has cast
upon his victim. It is reminiscent of the necessity for Britomart
to make Busyrane withdraw the plot he has built round
Amoret so that she can be released from her fate. Here, however,

---

[1] *A View*, sections 2147-2152, p. 120. 'The Leather quilted jacke in jurney-
inge or in Campinge for that it is fittest to be under his shirte for anie
occasion of sodayne service as theare hapen manye to Cover his thinne
breche on horsebacke. The greate linnen rowle which weomen weare to kepe
theare heades warme after Cuttinge theire haire which they use in anye
sicknes.'

[2] See *Variorum*, Spenser, Book VI, p. 226.

it is Mirabella who rejects the escape offered to her because she knows that Cupid's will must be obeyed.

The Mirabella episode is Elizabethan in its content in that it reflects the view of a high-spirited woman who pays small heed to the price paid by her neglected admirers. The court-of-love form provides a structural scheme but the subject matter has its origin in the Elizabethan sonnet. It is the one occasion where the heroine has a chance of expressing her own response to the monotonous plaints of the love-songs. Of course she is heartless and deserves her punishment, but she is also alive, penetrating and determined. Spenser has drawn a *vignette* of a personality of whom we see all too few in Elizabethan poetry. His flair for individual characterisation combined with allegorical personification finds its fulfilment in Mirabella and *Disdaine*. Her introduction brings with it a reminder of the failures of Timias and Serena; her punishment is harder since she is incapable of learning what they had learnt from the Hermit. The anecdotes create a distinction between two kinds of failure and between two kinds of allegory, setting slight weaknesses against strong faults and naturalistic portraiture against allegorical abstractions. What the episodes have in common is tantamount to pointing out the remarkable variety Spenser can achieve in employing his allegorical methods.

The narrative proceeds to the development of the story of Serena. A feeble little creature compared with the energetic Mirabella, she flees from the fight between Timias and *Disdaine* just as she had wandered away from the technical conversation about knightcraft between Calepine and Calidore. Here, however, she occasions one of Spenser's particularly concentrated descriptions of an exciting event. Terror, so strongly defined by him in different stages in *The Faerie Queene*, is given exactness in her suspicion of pursuit:

> ... every foot did tremble, which did tread,
> And every body two, and two she foure did read.

In *A Midsummer Night's Dream* every bush appeared a bear, but in *The Faerie Queene* the sense of loneliness is merely extended and is not explored psychologically. For Serena there is the vast emptiness of the wilderness to face; and her memory of the forest where she was bitten by the Blatant Beast underlines her fright. The kindliness of the Salvage Man is not recalled, and Calepine is blamed for having abandoned her in this distress. What goes on in her mind gathers together the factors which will inspire the power of the episode which is to follow. Exhausted she seeks for rest in the darkness.

Fast asleep, she remains the all too easy object for capture. The cannibals are savage, idolatrous, and horribly conscious of the pleasures of the human feast they will enjoy. Spenser contrives to set out a fierce beastliness in their discussion as to whether their victim should be devoured by degrees or in one huge meal. From the ridiculousness of this argument he can move to the description of the physical beauty of Serena, and to find in the language of *Epithalamion* metaphors worthy of the whiteness of her skin. Her golden hair, her 'alablaster brest', and paps 'which like white silken pillowes were', shine against the crudity of the setting in which she is placed, and arouse erotic desires in the watching barbarians. The priest insists that there must be no pollution of their victim. The author's voice makes the general comment: 'religion held even theeves in measure'. These ferocious characters are shown to be capable of conducting a primitive ritual of sacrifice at an altar made out of turf beside a holy fire. The leisurely preparation occurs at a sinister hour. Total darkness, instead of the glow of Hesperus during Arthur's sleep, covers the scene:

> And now the Eventyde
> His brode black wings had through the heavens wyde
> By this dispred.

The combination of so many aspects of Spenser's art, the wrangling among the cannibals, the description of naked beauty, the careful localisation of the altar, and a characteristic personification of the evening, build up an image which is for him startlingly compact. Suspense hangs over the atmosphere as the cruel knife hovers over the victim and a hideous noise of discordant instruments with the shouts of the crowd direct attention to the situation. Calepine, approaching, can just perceive what is going on when the sound draws him to the grove: the faint light from the dim stars and the pale flames

L

from the fire tell him enough. Serena, rescued, remains silent in her nakedness, and it is only with the daylight that she is recognised. As an isolated event, this episode provides a further brilliant contribution to the human story in Book VI. And like many others, it fades away and is heard of no more.

iv

Book VI is primarily memorable for its pastoral vein. This is nowhere the 'cold pastoral' of Keats but a deeply experienced sense of the activities of the bucolic world and of love among its occupants. The imagery of the early passages in the Book are constantly directed towards the country rather than the city. Tristram and the Salvage Man bring their own rural settings with them. Calepine, left to himself, prefers to be outdoors and to hear the thrush's song, to enjoy natural sights and sounds, just as Serena likes to pick wild flowers and leave the two knights to discuss serious subjects which are outside her interest. There is, of course, in Calepine's scene a bear as surprising as that which devours Antigonus off the coast of Bohemia. And there is also a tiger in the shepherd's world from which Calidore has to rescue Pastorella. The pastoral mode is, it seems, open to extremities of this kind: *A Winter's Tale* and *As You Like It* prove that the Bohemian shore and the forest of Arden are as prone to unfathomable mysteries as is the landscape of *The Faerie Queene*. Calepine was able to move swiftly, unhampered by heavy armour, to rescue a crying baby. He is described as the mighty protector, who had then to solve the problem of taking care of the child, unwrapping its bands to make sure it was uninjured, winding it up again, and carrying it through the wood to find somewhere to house it. One can only recount the event as a fairy tale. In Book VI there was as usual a solution available. A woman, wife of Sir Bruin, crossed his path. She was lamenting her failure to produce a son for her husband whose name introduces a coincidence for the story.[1] The troubles of each were put right. For, as Calepine says,

[1] This is all based on Irish legend. The MacMahons were the sons of a bear and descended from the Fitzursulas. Fabulous stories were told about their exploits.

Oftimes it haps, that sorrows of the mind
Find remedie unsought, which seeking cannot fynd.

The baby was accepted by the woman who 'having over it a litle wept', bore it away to rear it as her own for ever.

All the material in Book VI is accumulated in preparation for its final section when Calidore reappears to take his share in the action. We are reminded of the *Blatant Beast* which he has faithfully pursued everywhere without success. Canto IX opens with an image appropriate to the bucolic setting, that of the ploughman who has abandoned a promising furrow of rich soil and now returns to it. Calidore makes acquaintance with the herdsmen who stoutly deny any sight of the evil creature he is searching for. He now finds himself in the idyllic land which Spenser regards as the centre of the pastoral scene, and obtains his first glimpse of Pastorella. Here begins the thread of love which Calidore feels for this apparent shepherdess, and the growing friendship for her alleged father, Melibœe. They talk about the peacefulness of the shepherd's activity, and Melibœe offers his own philosophy which is grounded upon his rejection of the court-life where he had been a gardener. After ten years, he came to understand that his time there had been empty, and returned to his native home. Lack of ambition, routine which is close to nature, the yearly increase of his flocks and the recreations of hunting and fishing are all that he desires. The lowly occupations of the shepherds had become dearer to him than anything he had experienced previously.[1]

The style Spenser employs to define his outlook is lucid, plain and largely monosyllabic:

It is the mynd that maketh good or ill,

and

For wisdome is most riches VI. ix. 30

---

[1] A hostile interpretation of Melibœe's outlook is set out in Harry Berger Sr. 'A Secret Discipline: *The Faerie Queene*, Book VI'. In his view Melibœe's 'morality' is 'the same kind of excuse for laziness used by the rural pastors of the *Shepheardes Calender*; it is a recreative withdrawal from care', p. 61. This is an interpretation which depends upon assessing the quality of the language used in the context. I read it as a brief, wise attitude and hope my opinion is not among those which have been offered where commentators have 'atrociously glamorised' the character of Melibœe . . ., p. 173, n. 15. *Form and Convention in the Poetry of Edmund Spenser*, ed. William Nelson (New York and London, 1961).

The dialogue illustrates Spenser's power to write reflective verse in the course of an idealised story, as he had already demonstrated in the conversation between Sir Bruin's wife and Calepine.

Calidore all too readily abandons his quest in order to stay within reach of Pastorella. He rapidly dismisses his knightly past as being too much in danger of death and enmity.

> Now surely, syre, I find,
> That all this worlds gay showes, which we admire,
> Be but vaine shadowes to this safe retyre
> Of life, which here in lowlinesse ye lead,
> Fearelesse of foes, or fortunes wrackfull yre . . .

> That even I, which daily doe behold
> The glorie of the great, mongst whom I won,
> And now have prov'd, what happinesse ye hold
> In this small plot of your dominion,
> Now loath great Lordship and ambition;
> And wish the heavens so much had graced mee,
> As graunt me live in like condition;
> Or that my fortunes might transposed bee
> From pitch of higher place, unto this low degree.

VI. ix. 27-28

The fault of Calidore's interpretation of the circumstances in which the shepherds are living is proved by the ensuing events, when the brigands sweep them off to be sold as slaves. Moreover, in his desire to cast aside his undertaking to Gloriana he is failing in his obligation to her. This is not expressed as a decision but only as a hope for an interval of rest. Meliboee is wiser in that he maintains that it is not the heavens who decide what is best for men but the individual himself who must discover what makes him most content, for 'each hath his fortune in his brest'.

In the beginning of Canto x, Spenser comments upon Calidore's evasion from the quest to which he is committed. It is a quest which had been laid upon him and he had been entrapped into a betrayal of it for the sake of love. He is not, perhaps, greatly to be blamed for this since it has led him into a humble, unexploited way of life. Even so Calidore has retreated from the exhaustion of chivalric labours in order to move into a delightful but facile activity. The Faerie Queene demanded something more important from her knights; she outshines not only in beauty but in power all the figures who appear in Spenser's poem. Raleigh's sonnet about the way in which Spenser surpassed Petrarch puts Gloriana strongly in the forefront:

> Oblivion laid him down on Laura's herse.

It is not her beauty but the whole imposition which she has set upon her knights. It may well be, as J. C. Maxwell suggests, that the quest in Book VI is an encumbrance because courtesy is 'not easily allegorised in terms of conflict and best described in terms of exemplifications which display no regular progress'.[1] Nevertheless Book VI does offer a remarkably skilful allegorical construction and even if the quest is too easily neglected there are considerable factors which outweigh this neglect. Extremes of evil are provided in the cannibals and the brigands, extremes of good in the Salvage Man, the Hermit and the Graces. Calidore earns the right to see the Graces by his decision to remain among the shepherds. He abandons his armour and disguises himself in order to win Pastorella's love. Corydon pathetically offers gifts of baby squirrels and sparrows to please her, but she draws no distinction between either wooer and is more charmed by Colin Clout's music.

As Calidore's sentiment for Pastorella progresses there is an interruption in the narrative when he wanders into the woods and comes upon a paradise where Venus meets her lover. This is Mount Acidale, cherished by nymphs and fairies who seat themselves beside the stream running round it. Here Spenser records his strongest emotional commitment, the place where pastoral carries its richest meaning. Calidore sees a hundred maidens dancing to Colin Clout's piping, with the Graces in the centre, and one solitary figure, upon whom Colin Clout's love is directed:

> . . . that faire one,
> That in the midst was placed paravaunt,
> Was she to whom that shepheard pypt alone;
> That made him pipe so merrily, as never none.

---

[1] J. C. Maxwell, 'The Truancy of Calidore', *That Soveraine Light*, ed. William R. Mueller and Don Cameron Allen (Baltimore, 1952), p. 69.

She was, to weete, that jolly Shepheards lasse,
Which piped there unto that merry rout,
That jolly shepheard, which there piped, was
Poore *Colin Clout* (who knowes not *Colin Clout?*)
He pypt apace, whilest they him daunst about.
Pype, jolly shepheard, pype thou now apace
Unto thy love that made thee low to lout:
Thy love is present there with thee in place;
Thy love is there advaunst to be another Grace.

VI. x. 15-16

This is not mere repetition but the weaving of the word 'pype' in and out for the sake of the pattern of the dance. It creates a plangent lilt to intensify the feeling of love. All are dancing in delight on the mount where there is perpetual spring: the echo of their footsteps and of the music can be heard through the woods.

Calidore is granted a vision of the Graces 'which decke the body or adorne the mynde'. They cannot be seen at will but descend independently and belong to an aesthetic world:

Whom by no meanes thou canst recall againe,
For being gone, none can them bring in place,
But whom they of them selves list so to grace.

They represent inspiration, the 'peerelesse poesie' which Spenser had long ago venerated in *The Shepheardes Calender.* In Book VI he set out what had been expanded in the lyrics in the Eclogues. How much the pastoral theme meant to him is united in the vision Calidore witnesses. It meant love, joy, delight and the contentment of perfect creativeness. *Colin Clout* found rapture when the Graces came to dance to his music, and Calidore was enabled both to win Pastorella and also to devote himself to his quest. Courtesy is shown to be not the same virtue as Temperance: Book VI expounds the rhythmical, decorative features of civility, Book II the plain, solid aspect of self-discipline. More than this, Love is always present as the well-head of Courtesy:

For love is lord of truth and loyaltie.

For this reason, Spenser has to apologise to the Queen for having raised a 'country lass' to be the fourth Grace.[1] The

[1] For the celebration of Elizabeth in pastoral poetry see E. C. Wilson, *England's Eliza,* 1939.

natural expectation, created by Spenser in the 'April Eclogue' and in *Colin Clouts Come Home Againe* and by the whole patriotic design of the pastoral, would be to find 'Elisa, Queen of Shepherds all' placed there. Comparative representations are Peele's *The Arraignment of Paris* and Hans Eworth's picture of the three goddesses and Queen Elizabeth in stately attire.[1] But in Spenser's account the figures are naked so that the appearance of Queen Elizabeth was necessarily excluded. A lesser poet would probably have omitted to put any central figure in his scene; Spenser, concerned with normality as the good life, is prepared to exalt it in the simple figure of the shepherd girl, and emphasises his point the more by establishing the climax which readers expect to be different. In effect he contrives to gain both effects by his apology.

Rejoining the shepherds, Calidore goes happily out with them to gather strawberries and is offered his opportunity to save Pastorella's life when a tiger comes to attack her. Corydon's cowardice is exposed but Calidore cuts off the head of the beast of prey and is rewarded by her love. One feature of the pastoral convention is expressed by the power of Fortune over the shepherds. Jealous of the happiness of the two lovers, she urges a group of brigands to come upon their fold and carry them all away to their dark cave on a remote island, illuminated

> with continuall candlelight, which delt
> A doubtfull sense of things, not so well seene, as felt.

There they remain waiting to be sold as slaves whenever merchants arrive to buy them. There arises a violent quarrel between the brigands when Meliboee and his wife are killed. Calidore finding the ruins of the shepherd's dwelling searches for signs of occupation. The rhythm of his movement creates a collective sense of emptiness:

---

[1] By Peele the apple is awarded to Elizabeth to the discomfiture of the competing goddesses. Eworth's picture, 1569, in Hampton Court portrays Elizabeth carrying her orb in lieu of the apple. See Ellis Waterhouse, *Painting in Britain* 1530-1790 (Penguin 1963), p. 17, reproduction, p. 14. See the account of Proserpine in this book, pp. 151-2.

Ne wight he found, to whom he might complaine,
Ne wight he found, of whom he might inquire,
That more increast the anguish of his paine:
He sought the woods, but no man could see there;
He sought the plaines, but could no tydings heare:
The woods did nought but ecchoes vaine rebound;
The playnes all waste and emptie did appeare;
Where wont the shepheards oft their pypes resound,
And feed an hundred flocks, there now not one he found.
                                        VI. xi. 26

The blank landscape is made blanker by the repetitive Spenserian style. Calidore meets Corydon in no condition to tell him the truth about the disaster which had befallen the shepherds. At last he manages to get some sense out of him and persuade him to guide him to the island.

Their journey becomes one of Calidore's ventures: they set out together ('God before')—a phrase which adds weight to the undertaking—and find the thieves trying to look after the sheep, which Corydon recognises as his own. At night they are taken to the island. Calidore, armed though disguised with a smock, enters the cave where he finds Pastorella still alive. The brigands make attacks upon Calidore but he kills all who swarm into the entrance. This is an event in which dreadful slaughter occurs so that the delicacy of the pastoral world is destroyed and what is remembered is the other side of Calidore's activity. Spenser properly returns to the Blatant Beast which has yet to be tackled; he opens the last Canto with his customary image of a ship on the sea 'whose course is often stayd, yet never is astray'.

The story of Pastorella is concluded in Calidore's taking her to a new castle, 'Belgarde', where lives a knight, Bellamour, whom he knows, and his wife Claribel. The narrative is the familiar fairy-tale of the couple who are not allowed to marry but succeed in meeting in the dungeon in which they have been imprisoned, produce a child and send it into the fields to be cared for. Luckily the handmaid has left it where she had seen a shepherd discovering it, and still in the service of the knight identifies the child as Pastorella by her small birth mark. This should be a moving event in the Book, but it does not achieve the impact of a climax. There have been too many similar culminations in Book VI, and we should have preferred to hear more about the Salvage and Sir Tristram, and even Sir Bruin's baby. Still the true climax has yet to be, the destruction of the Blatant Beast.

Here there is much that has been already foreseen. The beast attacks a monastery and a church, and destroys the altar and its images. Its iron teeth and its numerous tongues which imply its extensive range of damage create the need for its removal. The moment when it becomes most impressive is the one when it realises that it cannot succeed against the power of the attacker. It is linked with the Hydra whom Alcides had quelled in his labours and with Cerberus whom he had brought up to earth tied with an iron chain so that it could tell Pluto and the damned about the light of the sun and the doings on earth. The Beast is forced to endure an iron muzzle (like the chain), which prevents it from roaring and slandering the inhabitants of the world. Its final escape is recorded in Spenser's melancholic tone in the hope that it will not attack his own poem. He trusts that no personal allusions will be suspected as they had been in the past. Book VI offers what its author sought to achieve:

> Therefore do you my rimes keep better measure,
> And seek to please, that now is counted wisemens threasure.

It is appropriate that Spenser should conclude his study of Courtesy and Humanity upon the note that establishes all that the whole poem has contained, all in fact that he had shown the art of poetry had been able to create.

Chapter X

BOOK VII. TRUTH: THE FRAGMENT IN THE CANTOS OF MUTABILITIE

THE Mutabilitie Cantos recall to all readers much of what they have encountered throughout *The Faerie Queene*. In them Spenser's delight in his own surroundings, firmly attached to the locality in which he lived, in Arlo-hill beside 'my old father Mole', his preference for anecdotes based upon legends compounded of classical and folk material, his memory of ways of life accepted by human beings during every generation, and above all his desire to explore philosophical truth in terms of direct argument. These recollections are substantiated not merely by identification of detail but also by the consciousness of the presence of an author who is devoted to the nature of what he is describing. This is the Spenser of *The Shepheardes Calender* and of *Complaints*, the poet who has learnt his art from extensive reading in medieval romances, as Rosemond Tuve has illustrated in *Allegorical Imagery*, as well as in classical, Italian and French literature. And he is the poet whose habit of mind has constantly found its most satisfactory outlet in the certainty that 'all that moveth doth in change delight'.

For this reason we can agree that the two Cantos of Mutabilitie are focussed upon the subject of truth. Spenser's poetry everywhere is concerned with ideas which appear unlike each other, are consistently inconsistent, and are forced into accord through the allegorical associations thrust upon them. For him they have become joyful, harmonious objects of contemplation. He makes out of them his own faith as an artist and as a creator. The two Cantos summarise this single conclusion. We therefore accept his final decision. Poetry arises from natural experience, from what is normally part of ordinary daily consciousness, and can be transformed into immense fields of discovery. We look back upon the whole of *The Faerie Queene* as it has been stretched behind us and has become for us a great poem and a great imaginative vision. Like jesting Pilate, the poet has no desire to stay for an answer to the question about the nature of truth.

His way of defining it springs out of the intellectual adventures embodied in the Books here examined, out of 'Illusion', 'Distortion', 'Separation and Solitude', 'Reconciliation and Unity', 'Justice and Politics', 'Humanity and Courtesy'. From them comes the satisfaction of a total agreement about all that the poet can achieve. His style and his context join together so that power and passion combine in the innumerable sections which constitute its entirety.

The Mutabilitie Cantos were published by Matthew Lownes in the folio edition of 1609. The title page states that they 'both for Forme and Matter appeare to be parcell of some following Booke of the Faerie Queene, under the Legend of Constancie'. No reasoned account is given for the acquisition of the manuscript, for the division of the text into Cantos VI, VII and VIII 'unperfite', nor for the name of the subject as Constancie. In effect the peculiarity of their origin remains a mystery.

Inevitably opinions have varied as to the date of composition and to the connection of these special Cantos with the rest of the poem. On the whole they have been recognised as works of genuine creativity which are in many respects an advance on what Spenser had provided elsewhere. Philosophical and mythological features had been treated with outstanding emotional skill in other Books, but it was rare for these elements to be combined with a narrative which gives the impression of belonging to a different category altogether. The topic of what can be regarded as the main action, that based upon Mutabilitie's insistence of her right to rule the universe beyond the asserted dominion of the other gods, is linked with a separate and seemingly irrelevant anecdote in which Faunus witnesses Cynthia bathing in the river, freed from the formal splendours of her appearance as goddess of the moon. The two events seem to follow laws of their own, but are not entirely independent. Of course, the Faunus narrative could be interpreted as an example of comic relief or as an antimasque, and their differences in material and tone can be noted as means of supporting this opinion. Yet we are left with a sense of mistaken reading somewhere. It becomes necessary to return to the first impact, the consciousness of endless change, endless mobility in the constitution of the world. If that impact is neglected, then the slow piling up of the items of which the Cantos are framed carries no weight. Without it the whole becomes distorted.

Each section can easily be analysed separately. The Faunus story is marked by its employment of Spenser's familiar pastoral methods. The forests and lakes, the accuracy of the description of the rivers surrounding Kilcolman, the personifications introduced in the Molanna-Fanchin love tale, the crude reactions from Faunus at the sight of the naked Cynthia, and the use of scornful imagery to ridicule his attitude and reduce it to the level of a trivial disturbance, combine to give the section a typically Spenserian character. It becomes consequently a single episode comparable with passages in Books III and IV where elementary realisations of immediate occasions are recorded, for instance in the Braggadocchio gestures in Satyrane's tournament or in the false interpretation of the Britomart-Amoret relationship. But what is to be said of the authorial voice which interrupts the progress of the story to exalt the beauty of Ireland as the country where the gods are glad to resort for pleasure and repose? The place is recognised as a holy island filled with the charms of peace and loveliness. There nymphs and satyrs abound, there are trees and shadowy woodlands, there the river flows through valleys and spreads widely over the plain before it. Plainly this is a scene which cannot be ignored, and the poet is anxious to make the most of its wealth by holding up the development of his narrative.

The narrative, too, is not in itself a tale without associations with the central plot. The perverse scheme of Faunus to corrupt Molanna and see what he knew to be forbidden brought about the destruction of the perfect landscape enjoyed by the spirits of the rural world. Cynthia abandoned it, it lost its atmosphere of delight and became a haunt of wolves and thieves. Here, indeed, Mutabilitie had conquered. Faunus fulfilled his promise to Molanna and enabled her to marry the river Fanchin, but the prize had to be paid for in the sacrifice of all that holy Ireland had symbolised. Leisure ceased to dwell there; Arlo-hill lacked the splendour it had once possessed. Lament concludes the story just as the narrator had foretold. Spenser had started it with a melancholy prophecy of evil. Mutabilitie's conduct would transform right into wrong, good into bad, and bring death with it. The sadness emerges in the wry summary of all that was to occur, as a 'pittious worke'.

The Faunus anecdote is fitted into the central action which opens with an account of the ambition of the central character. Mutabilitie, the descendant of Saturn, a Titaness, claims her right to replace the domination of Jove and the other gods in the heavens. She begins by invading the realm of Cynthia and causing an unseemly brawl in her throne room. The beauty of the moon's shining palace arouses the Titaness's personal desires. The exquisite iconographical setting of Cynthia's world is described in Spenser's most brilliantly generalised style: the ivory throne, the two steeds, one black, one white, the ten thousand stars which attended her, the thousand crystal pillars which support the hall, present an image of blazing splendour. The effect of this attack upon the moon is experienced upon earth and among the gods. It is within the terms of his mythology that Spenser sees that the messenger, Mercury, has to be despatched by Jove to enquire into the reason for this sudden universal darkness. Mutabilitie's reply to this demand is characterised by several impertinent comments. She tells Mercury that she thinks nothing of 'his Jove' nor of Cynthia either. She has no hesitation in ascending to Jove's palace and facing the majesty of his rebuke. He speaks with the dignity of the chief of the planetary deities but is forced to agree with her that in these circumstances he himself has much to lose and must be partial in his judgment. She maintains that her case must be tried elsewhere:

> But to the highest him, that is behight
> Father of Gods and men by equall might;
> To weet, the God of Nature, I appeale.

A new principle enters at this stage. The introduction of 'Nature' shifts the work into another 'kind'. Reasoning, argument, become prominent but only when they are established upon sensuous foundations which are equally prominent. Nature has to be defined, at once philosophically and physically. The 'highest him', 'the father of gods and men' is also 'great dame *Nature*', unexplained in sex or age:

This great Grandmother of all creatures bred
Great *Nature*, ever young yet full of eld,
Still moving, yet unmoved from her sted;
Unseene of any, yet of all beheld.

Since she is part of the allegory she has to be presented in terms
that are conceptual and physical. It is necessary to portray her
as an idea and a figure capable of taking part in the action.
This Spenser achieves in his own extraordinary fashion. Nature,
he shows, impels the creative principles of the world. Where she
comes things grow voluntarily and automatically; homage is
paid to her instinctively by the trees and flowers which spring
to life and bow to her in adoration. Even old Mole abandons
his wintry guise and adopts the green of the new year. No
imagery is adequate to define her quality; human eyes could
not endure the sight of her leonine appearance; it is only with
the Transfiguration that Spenser finds a suitable analogy to
indicate the character of her being. She is the only figure in
the two Cantos whom Mutabilitie respects. She produces no
restless motion but merely listens, accepts, and draws a different
conclusion.

This technique of personification has been employed in other
Books but in a somewhat different way. There have been
several occasions in which discussions have taken place where
the protagonists have followed the alluring appeal of their
enemies but have demolished their cases by a radical change of
premises. This was what Una achieved in the cave of Despair,
Guyon with Mammon, Artegall with the Giant and with Burbon. Spenser's genius for philosophical debate depends upon
his mastery over the capacity to create illusion; the villains
tend to shift their grounds and make their case appear to be
about something different from the assumptions from which it
started. Hence the really evil figures are those which change
their forms, the Protean creatures such as Archimago, Mammon, Guyle, creatures of physical transformation. Similarly, the
really good characters are those who keep their minds visually
alert and can preserve their own consistency of standard and
carry the argument to the level upon which it properly belongs.
The knights who are heroes may seem simple but do not collapse at the suggestion of the limitations of their perceptions.

They cling to the conviction that ultimately:

> Vertues seat is deepe within the mynd,
> And not in outward shows but inward thoughts defined.

Such formulae are frequently expressed and are familiar enough in the various states of the development of single Books. Episode after episode ends with an awareness of the force of this conviction.

It is in the Cantos of Mutabilitie that Spenser expresses this moral in philosophical terms and combines it with equally powerful sensuous terminology. For Mutabilitie is *not* a villain; she brings all the greatness of the world of the senses to her side, and this is the world upon which Spenser founds his poetic art. All that matters is there. But Nature, while admitting the soundness of her case, qualifies it in pointing out that change is fundamental to stability and that time is a means towards eternity.

The figures whom Mutabilitie employs are at once symbols and creatures possessed of rights of their own, independently of their symbolical meaning. She bases her claim upon the grounds of her legendary origins and upon the historical fact that the gods themselves are changeable too. Here Spenser is occupied with beliefs which have been widely accepted by Elizabethan writers. Time was the great enemy, its power was recorded in the sonnets and in the drama. By Shakespeare we are reminded that 'Time doth transfix the flourish set on youth'; and also that in the organisation of society nothing remains unassailed when degree is ignored by its members (as emphasised by Ulysses in *Troilus and Cressida*). Spenser and Sidney supply the recurring cry of *ubi sunt* when all past glories are remembered. Only poets can preserve the victims of Time:

> For deeds doe die, however noblie done,
> And thoughts of men do as themselves decay.
> But wise words taught by numbers for to runne
> Recorded by the Muses live for aye.
>
> *The Ruines of Time* (400-404)

In the Garden of Adonis the law of destruction is predominant since

All things decay in time, and to their end do draw.

III. vi. 40

Only Adonis survives for he is 'eterne in mutabilitie'. He is often transformed but is made perpetual by succession because he is the father of all forms (III. vi. 47). Here Spenser seems to be getting near to the solution which is finally offered to Mutabilitie by Nature.

In the great scene on Arlo-hill the principles by which man lives in the physical world are set forth in their endlessly temporary shapes. The four elements, the seasons, the months, the hours, night and day, and finally life and death are all portrayed in the pageants.

The progress of all these created examples argues the strength of the case that is being established. Change is the condition of human existence and each illustration provides a detailed presentation of actuality. Spenser suspends the development of the argument by storing up meaning behind every specific image. In the presentation of each month he inserts a streak of the matter of fact to give weight to the underlying idea. Mutabilitie reinforces the consciousness of the physical existence of each month by describing its various activities, its zodiacal emblem, and its appropriate possessions. March, mounted on a ram, bears a spade and box of seeds, April on a bull brings spring plants, May supported by Castor and Pollux scatters the flowers of the period which belong to her, June, a fascinating illustration of Spenser's inventiveness, rides upon a crab which moves backwards like bargemen upon the river (a reference which Bunyan perhaps recalled from a chap-book picture when he pointed out the ancestry of By-ends from 'a Water-man, looking one way and rowing another'), carries a ploughshare for his occupation and brings to mind the summer occupations of the country.

All these pictures are individual versions of conventional scenes, several based upon illuminations of manuscript psalters or Old and New Testament texts. Spenser's interest in this material goes back to *The Shepheardes Calender* where woodcuts provide the signs of the zodiac for each month, and its other aspects are conveyed through the content of the poems. Thus the most distinguished of the lyrics, April, is a spring song listing the flowers peculiar to the beauty of its subject, the faire Eliza, the perfect Shepherdess. The stanzaic form with its subtle rhyme scheme, its varied length of lines, and its syntax of questions and exclamations, creates the exordium for which the lyric is designed. Other parts of *The Shepheardes Calender* are not as closely related to the months to which they are attached, but Spenser frequently uses a brief introduction to the poems where tribute is paid to the month even though he manœuvres the rest of his material into another 'kind' altogether. January is in a wintry setting and concentrates upon the winter in the feeling of disappointed love, February opens with a similar complaint about cold and storms, but proceeds to a narrative of the oak and the briar, March occasions a celebration of the departure of the winter and the beginning of spring even though its main subject is a slight lyric about Cupid disguised as a bird, and so on. Each poem in *The Shepheardes Calender* whatever its main topic never neglects the fact that it is pastoral in form and however varied its style, subject, and characters may be, the aspect of the time of year is not omitted. Even the best of the lyrics—that of August which includes a sestina derived in pattern from Petrarch and that of November, an elegy upon the death of Dido imitated from Marot's funeral ode upon the French Queen, Lois—insist upon the recognition of the moment in time, autumn, in which the event occurred. The context is less important than the quality of the verse but it is so far introduced as a factor in the collection.

That Spenser should have returned to the earliest of his successes and employed their merits to enhance his doctrine of the permanence of sensuous experience can cause no surprise. For in the last resort the elements of the natural world are visionary, temporal manifestations of the world of mind. In the allegorical mode the most intense imaginative experiences be come embodiments of ideas; they exist in another realm of being. The magnificence of Mutabilitie's pageants arises from the acceptance of this doctrine, just as the scenes in Guyon's voyage, in the House of Busyrane, or in Colin Clout's exhibition of the Graces, belong to the fringes of the unknown. Nature assents to all that has been offered but carries Mutabilitie's portrayal to a further stage. The power of change is what it appears to be but it is something else. Nature's final assessment of the components of the physical world divines a more profound truth:

> Yet being rightly wayd
> They are not changed from their first estate;
> But by their change their being doe dilate:
> And turning to themselves at length againe,
> Doe worke their owne perfection so by fate:
> Then over them Change doth not rule and raigne;
> But they raigne over change, and doe their states maintaine.
>
> VII. vii. 58

Mutabilitie is demonstrated to be the servant of creation—its means to completion. Perceptions are abandoned so that their immateriality may be fathomed: they are at once actual and intangible.

To Spenser this belief was the criterion of poetic discipline and the justification of his literary art. The hierarchic order underlying the universe which he had given his ability to describe was known to be exactly this. Hooker summarises it in *Of the Laws of Ecclesiastical Polity*:

> See we not plainly that obedience of creatures unto the law of nature is the stay for the whole world,

and Spenser acted upon it throughout his life. To him, that belief was both the joy and the distress of his function as a poet. Like J. B. Yeats, he was always aware that 'the literature of the senses and the literature of despair go hand in hand'. Allegory was the only mode for so strange and complex an endowment.

INDEX

Abessa, 70-1, 91, 96, 237

Acrasia, and Guyon, 29, 42, 80, 116, 132, 169, 173, 223, 234; and allegory, 64, 172; enchantments of, 128, 134, 142, 180-2; corruption of, 128, 133-5, 171, 185; victims of, 171, 181; and Bower of Bliss, 141-2, 171, 176, 178-80; Garden of, 151

Acrates, 139

Adicia, 283

Adonis, 208-9, 336; Garden of, 151, 174, 202, 207-9, 222, 226-7, 243, 245, 278, 335

Aemylia, 226, 228, 239-40

Agape, 231

Agdistes, 177

Aladine, 308

Albanio, 24

Alciati, Andreas, 65

Aldus, 308

Allegory, and design of poem, 10, 39, 41, 43-5, 48, 51, 57, 225; to emphasise ideas, 29, 120, 337; and multiple meaning, 45-6, 59 89, 94, 109; inconsistencies in, 51, 274-5; recurrent, 58; and Wood of Error, 59-66; in narrative, 66-9, 74, 80, 87; nature of, 75-8; and character, 88-9; of illusion, 91; embodiments, 94; and epyllion, 99, political, 100, 261, 291, 298; techniques of, 101, 128, 269-70; and return to ordinary life, 108; and argument, 113; and Elizabethan psychology, 157; uniting body and soul, 158-9; of general concepts, 162, 195; 221; and human relations,

184, 230; demands of, 189; and rhetoric, 195; pictorial element, 221; of love, 247-8; and myth, 280-1; unifying action, 283, 330; variety of, 320; and courtesy, 325; and Spenser, 338

Alma, 135, 157-8, 166; House of, 40, 48-51, 132-3, 161-2, 245

Alva, 292

Amavia, 76, 128, 131-4, 271

Ambition, 150

Amidas, 270-2, 278

Amoret, redemption of, 20; and Scudamour, 30, 81, 210, 215, 223-4, 226, 229, 236, 241, 243-4, 250; rescue of, 82; and Timias, 188; birth and upbringing, 202, 206-7, 227; suffering in House of Busyrane, 221-3, 318-9; and Britomart, 222-3, 229, 332; behaviour and character, 223-4, 228n, 230, 235-7, 242; chastity, 233-234; as victim of Lust, 237-9.

Amyas, 226, 228, 235-6, 239-40, 247

Anabaptists, 269

Angels, 55, 153-4

Anglicanism, 100, 119

Anima (Alma), 157

Antwerp, 292-3

Archimago, as allegory, 51; disappearance, 55; and dreams, 63; as evil figure, 66, 82, 89, 91, 101, 110, 116, 137-8, 144, 154; scheming, 90; and Una, 99, 102; disguises, 110, 121, 127, 285-6, 334; and Braggadocchio, 137; and Guyon, 137; and idle lake,

339